W9-BUB-727

"A lot of people questioned our sanity when, in the original edition of this book in 1988, we predicted that place names like Dakota and Savannah would become fashionable, that such antique favorites as Felicity and Rose, Stella and Julian would return to vogue. All those names are now among the Top 100."

—Linda RosenKrantz and Pamela Redmond Satran

Beyond Jennifer & Jason, Madison & Montana

What to Name Your Baby Now
(Revised and Updated)

LINDA ROSENKRANTZ

and

PAMELA REDMOND SATRAN

ST. MARTIN'S PAPERBACKS

BEYOND JENNIFER & JASON, MADISON & MONTANA

Copyright © 2004 by Linda Rosenkrantz and Pamela Redmond Satran.

Cover photo © Getty/Ryan McVay.

Library of Congress Catalog Card Number: 2004042753

ISBN: 0-312-94095-5
EAN: 9780312-94095-9

Printed in the United States of America

St. Martin's Griffin trade paperback edition published 2004
St. Martin's Paperbacks edition / September 2006

St. Martin's Paperbacks are published by St. Martin's Press, 175 Fifth Avenue, New York, NY 10010.

10 9 8 7 6 5 4 3 2 1

For our wonderful daughters
Chloe Samantha Finch and
Rory Elizabeth Margaret Satran

Contents

IMAGE   167

Acknowledgments

Once again, our first and foremost thanks go to our peerless editor, Hope Dellon, for her unflagging support and enthusiasm. Special thanks also for their help in putting together this new edition of our book to Kris Kamikawa, Michael Shackleford, Michael Clingman and the Social Security Administration, Bruno Pradels, Rory Satran, Emily Shapiro, Ailsa Gray, and Peggy Orenstein. And finally, of course, loving thanks to our always helpful husbands, Christopher Finch and Dick Satran.

Introduction

In the fifteen years since we began writing about names, the world of baby naming has mushroomed from a sleepy little enterprise, with parents naming their children Jennifer and Jason and wondering whether there might be anything more exciting out there, to an adventurous and intelligent and style-conscious activity in which parents investigate everything from their family trees to names from their ancestors' native lands to atlases and even dictionaries for names that are ever more inventive, individual, and enlightened.

We think we had something to do with that. But it's not a one-way street. From the original publication of *Beyond Jennifer & Jason* in 1988, and through four revisions, our work and the ever-more-creative name choices of parents have influenced each other. We offer new ideas about names, parents adopt them and add twists of their own, and soon we're back reporting on the hottest trends we've heard, which an increasing number of parents pick up on. And next thing we know, we need to write another name book.

If you're a first-time *Beyond Jennifer & Jason, Madison & Montana* baby namer, let us introduce you to how this book works. Our aim here is to help parents figure out how names fit into the real world their children will be entering. We try to provide a yardstick for measuring the effects of an unusual name, a unisex name, or a fashionable name on a child, as well as an easy way to figure out which names are which. All the other name books will tell you that Cameron means "crooked nose" in Scottish Gaelic; we're the only ones who will advise you that while Cameron is moving up on the popularity list for boys, it's quietly being co-opted by the girls—and why that means you should think three times before giving it to your son.

Rather than the conventional dictionary format used by most other name books, ours organizes names by subjective categories—trendy names and saints' names, royal names and feminine names and place names. And we support those categories with text that tells you which trendy names are threatened with overuse, for instance, or why feminine names are beginning to sound stronger in these gender-bending times.

In this new edition, we keep the familiar subjective format in six sections. These are Style, Popularity, Image, Sex, Tradition, and Family.

Style, as always, is completely updated, with all-new categories in the What's Hot section, reflecting our rapidly changing world. We lead off this time with what we're calling the Honest Names: straightforward, down-to-earth choices such as Oscar and Josephine that have a new cachet in these unreliable times. Spiritual Names—from nouveau choices like Pax to Biblical Favorites such as Asher and Delilah—are suddenly red hot too. Nature Names—Fox and Lake and Snow—have made the leap to the Hot section from the wilder climes of What's Cool, where the truly adventurous will still find plenty of unexpected choices, from Murray (for girls), to Mungo (for boys), to Morning (for either).

A lot of people questioned our sanity when, in the original edition of this book in 1988, we predicted that place names like Dakota and Savannah would become fashionable, when we foresaw that former "old lady" names such as Madeleine and Natalie would come back into style, that Americans would adopt Irish names like Riley and Liam, that such antique favorites as Felicity and Rose, Stella and Julian would return to vogue. All those names were in the So Far Out They're In section back then; now they're among the Top 100.

In the Image and Sex sections, we explore the kinds of questions parents in search of a name grapple with themselves. How important is your choice of a name, anyway? Do names really have images and if so, what do they convey? Is there such a thing as a name that's too unusual? In these days of ever-shifting gender identities, what's the best kind of name for a girl, a boy? We turn to hard research, as well as common sense, to come up with these answers.

For our section on Tradition, we delve into the history of names, including all-new chapters on pre-twentieth-century American naming history and on African-American naming traditions. And we go further afield, adding hundreds of new listings of foreign names from Europe, Africa, and Israel. We also offer information and names from the Jewish, Christian, and Muslim religions.

And in the section called Family, we include advice on name wrestling with your spouse and your in-laws, on choosing a family name, on naming siblings and twins, and on living with your ultimate name choice.

All the best parts of the earlier editions, all the elements that make this book different from any other name book, are still here, with the addition of new features. We include the most comprehensive up-to-date listing of celebrity baby names—and then regroup those names to illustrate specific chapters of the book, offering lists of starbabies with ethnic names, for instance, and a list of starbaby girls with boys' names. And we still tell you the whole truth: which names are becoming overexposed, which are becoming too girlish for boys, why you shouldn't spell Brianna "Briyana," no matter how adventurous your sense of style.

You can read this book straight through—the best way, we think—or you can choose a category that interests you and use that as a jumping-off point to the rest of the book, or you can find a name you like in the index and start from there. Whichever method you use, once you've finished you'll have the pleasure of knowing you have made a thoughtful and enlightened choice, whether you choose to move beyond Jennifer and Jason, Madison and Montana or not.

STYLE

W e used to have to explain what we meant by style and names. No more. Now most parents are aware of how style affects names, and have a good idea what kind of style they want their own child's name to reflect.

In this section, we separate the fashionable from the trendy, the names that are coming in from those that are heading out of style. Among the style categories we identify and explore are: What's Hot (names that are in fashion now and why), What's Cool (cutting-edge names for style pioneers), and the Riddle of the Middle (innovative ideas for the increasingly prominent second-name spot).

What's Hot

The world is a very different place today than it was when we undertook the last update of this book in the late 1990s. We've gone from boom times to bust, a nation at peace to one at war, from a country embracing the wider world to one that's become both more xenophobic and patriotic.

What does this have to do with baby naming? Everything. Because our specialty is the changing style of names, we can't help but interpret how global events and popular culture influence name trends.

One category of names to catapult to the Hot category in this edition is the Spiritual Names. While Biblical Names for boys have been hot for some time and continue to be so, names with a more assertively spiritual component—Genesis, for example, and Faith and Pax—are newly fashionable.

Also hot: names we're calling Honest. You can also think of them as Real. Or Simple. Traditional, in a quirky kind of way. Many of these names were last popular a hundred years ago. They're the names of our great-grandparents, solid and reliable as the family tree.

On the other side of the coin are the Kreeatif Names—
many of them modern, even invented, in a wide array of
spellings. These names, often related in sound and feel—
think Hayley and Kaylee and Kylie and Rylea—have become so dominant that, considered as a group rather than
as individual selections, they're more pervasive than all
the Top-10 names rolled into one.

Along with the Kreeatifs are the Two-Syllable Solution names for boys, less traditional and more androgynous, riding up the popularity list and taking over for the
old stalwart names like Bob and Tom.

Foreign names that symbolize parents' ethnic roots or
even just lend an exotic flavor are still hot, too, though as
a group a bit quieter than they were even a few years ago.
We're highlighting individual hotties in this section now
as opposed to wide groups of names. Place names remain hot.

We've got a lot of hot new middle-name ideas in this
category, too, as parents turn to the middle as a place to
get more adventurous—to honor an ancestor or a hero, or
to use an unusual or symbolic name that might be a
stretch as a first name. According to the baby-naming survey we did for parenting.com, only about a third of the
forty thousand parents who answered said they chose a
middle name purely because it sounded good, with over
half using a family name—first or last—in the middle.

Here, the hot name choices today:

Honest Names

These are names with character, an especially appealing
quality in these uncertain times. They're unfussy and
down-to-earth but never boring, strong and soulful just as

you may want your child to be. Last popular a hundred years ago, many of them have slept through recent decades but seem vigorous again.

GIRLS	
ALICE	HOPE
AMELIA	IRIS
ANNA	IVY
AVA	JANE
BEATRICE	JOSEPHINE
BELLE	JOSIE
BILLIE	LAURA
CELIA	LENA
CLAIRE	LILA
CLARA	LILY
CLEMENTINE	LOUISA
CORA	LOUISE
DAISY	LUCY
DIXIE	MABEL
DORA	MAISIE
EDIE	MARGARET
EDITH	MATILDA
ELIZA	MAY
ELLA	MILLIE/MILLY
EVA	NELL
FAITH	NORA
FLORA	OLIVE
FRANCES	PAULINE
GRACE	PEARL
HARRIET	POLLY
HAZEL	ROSE
HELEN	RUBY
HONOR	RUTH

SADIE	TESS
SOPHIE	VIOLET
STELLA	WILLA

BOYS

ABEL	JACK
AMOS	JAKE
ARCHIE	JOE
BARNEY	LEO
CAL	LOUIS
CHARLIE	LUKE
CHESTER	MACK
CLEM	NAT
CLYDE	NATE
ELI	NED
EZRA	OSCAR
FRANK	OWEN
FRED	RAY
GEORGE	TOM
GUS	WALTER
HARRY	WILL
HENRY	ZEKE
HOMER	

Spiritual Names

It's no mystery why names with a spiritual element might hold a new and compelling allure for modern parents. As important as worldly power may be, many of us feel bound to give our children a deeper and more enduring kind of strength. A name that signifies a positive spiritual aspect of life is one way to start. Some of these choices can work for boys as well as girls, though most—especially the classic Virtue Names such as Charity and Patience—tilt toward the feminine:

AMITY	HONOR
ANGEL	HOPE
ANSWER	IMAGINE
ARCADIA	INFINITY
ARIEL	JUSTICE
BLISS	KISMET
CHANCE	LIBERTY
CHARITY	LIGHT
COMFORT	LOVE
DESTINY	MERCY
DISCOVERY	MIRACLE
DIVINITY	MYSTERY
DREAM	PATIENCE
EDEN	PAX
ETERNITY	PEACE
ETHEREAL	PROMISE
EVER	PRUDENCE
EXPERIENCE	REMEMBER
FAITH	SERAFINA/SERAPHINA
FELICITY	SERENITY
FOREVER	SINCERE
FORTUNE	SKY
FUTURE	SPIRIT
GENESIS	TAROT
GRACE	TEMPERANCE
GUARDIAN	TRINITY
GUIDE	TRUE
HARMONY	TRUST
HAVEN	TRUTH
HEAVEN	VERITY

Biblical Boys

The Biblical Boys names have been popular for far longer than we've been writing about names. As each generation of names in this category becomes widely used, parents turn to more unusual choices, with Benjamin and Adam giving way to Nathan and Noah, now leading to Isaiah and Moses, Abraham and Asher. Here, the hot Biblicals for boys:

AARON	GABRIEL
ABEL	GIDEON
ABIAH	HIRAM
ABIEL	ISAAC
ABNER	ISAIAH
ABRAHAM	JABEZ
AMOS	JABIN
ASA	JADON
ASHER	JARED
AZARIAH	JAVAN
BARTHOLOMEW	JEDIDIAH
CAIN	JEREMIAH
CALEB	JOACHIM
CYRUS	JONAH
DARIUS	JOSIAH
ELEAZAR	JUDAH
ELI	KENAN
ELIAS	LEVI
ELIJAH	MALACHI
EMANUEL	MATTHIAS
EPHRAIM	MICAH
ERAN	MOSES
EZEKIEL	NATHANIEL
EZRA	NOAH

OBADIAH	SETH
OMAR	SILAS
PHINEAS	SIMEON
RAPHAEL	SIMON
REUBEN	SOLOMON
RUFUS	TOBIAS
SAMSON	ZACHARIAS
SAMUEL	ZEBEDIAH

Red Tent Names

Anita Diamant's bestselling novel *The Red Tent* raised awareness of biblical women—along with their names. While there are many more male names than female names, period, in the Bible, some of the choices for girls—New Testament as well as *The Red Tent*'s Old Testament names—are suddenly hot. These include:

ADAH	LYDIA
DEBORAH	MARA
DELILAH	MORIAH
DINAH	NOA
DRUSILLA	PRISCILLA
EDEN	SAPPHIRA
ESTHER	SARAI
EVE	SELA
JEMIMA	SUSANNAH
KETURAH	TABITHA
KEZIAH	TALITHA
LEAH	TAMAR

Kreeatif Names

For years now, we've been telling parents not to get overly creative with the spellings of their children's names. We've been explaining that when you insist on spelling Michael "Mykle," you add more confusion than creativity to the mix. Is that pronounced Miklee? people wonder. Or maybe Mike-la? Wait a minute: Is this kid a girl or a boy? Poor little Mykle is condemned to spelling his (or is it her?) name for the rest of his (her?) life. And in the end, whether you spell it Michael or Mykle—or Mikyll or M'Kale—it's still the same name.

Unfortunately, parents didn't listen to us. They didn't listen to us in a major way. Not only did they insist on varying the spellings of many of the most popular names, but they're constantly adding new and more "kreeatif" variations.

Well, if you can't beat 'em . . .

No, no, no. We haven't crossed over to the dark side. We are still not advocating that you get too adventurous with the spelling of your child's name. But we offer here a look at the range of spellings we've seen for some popular names.

And we have to admit these names, every last variation of them, are hot. Too hot? That depends on your viewpoint. You should be aware that, because the national popularity list counts each spelling of a name *separately*, it's really easy for parents to get the wrong idea about how widely used these names are.

Caleigh, for instance, doesn't appear at all on the Social Security Top 1,000, which would make any sensible parent think it was a fairly unusual name. But add the count for Callie, Kayleigh, Kailey, and Kaylee, and you've got nearly eight thousand baby girls given that name in a single year, putting it among the thirty-five most popular names. And then add in the similar Kylie, Kylee, Kyleigh, Kayla, and Kyla, and you've got a Number One name.

It's important to note how closely related many of these names are. You can almost play a kind of connect-the-dots game with them, linking Kyle to Kyla to Kylie to Kayley to Kayla to Kaylon to Jalen to Bralen to Baylee to Rylee to Skyla and back to Kyle. You can think of it as MegaName, with literally hundreds of thousands of children receiving some variation each year.

Many of these names are fluid in terms of gender, and sometimes spelling makes the difference. Riley seems boyish while Rylea girlish, for instance; Peyton could be a boy's name while Paighton seems feminine. Rather than separating the names by gender, we've constructed one master roster—and make no claim to include a comprehensive list of spellings. The changes can, and do, go on and on and on.

With the most traditional spelling first, and variations following, the hot names with kreeatif spellings include:

AARON *Aahron, Aaran, Aaren, Aarin, Aarron, Aaryn, Aeron, Aren, Ahren*

ABIGAIL *Abagail, Abigayle, Abbagail, Abbegayle, Abbygale*

AIDAN *Aiden, Aidin, Aydan, Aden, Adin, Ayden, Aydin*

AISHA *Aishah, Aesha, Aiesha, Ayeesha, Ayisha, Iesha, Ieesha*

ALYSSA *Alissa, Alisa, Elissa, Alisza, Allissa, Ilissa, Illissa, Ilyssa, Elysa*

ASHLEY *Ashlee, Ashleigh, Ashly, Ashlie, Ashlei, Asheley*

ASIA *Aisia, Asiah, Asya, Aysia, Aja, Aijsia*

AUSTIN *Austen, Auston, Austyn, Osten*

BAILEY *Baylee, Baileigh, Bailley, Baylie, Bayly*

BRADEN *Braeden, Braydin, Brayden, Bradan, Bradin*

BRIANA *Brianna, Breana, Breanna, Breeana, Breeanna, Bri'ana, Bryanna*

BROOKLYN *Brooklin, Brookelyn, Brookelynn, Brooklynne*

BRYLEN *Brylyn, Brilyn, Brylin, Brilynn, Brylynne*

CAIN *Cane, Kane, Kain, Kaine, Kayne, Caine*

CAITLIN *Kaitlyn, Katelynn, Katelyn, Kaitlynne, Kaitlin, Katlyn, Caitlyn, Kaetlyn*

CAMERON *Camryn, Kamryn, Kameron, Cameran, Camerin, Cameren, Camron*

CARSON *Carsyn, Karson, Karsyn, Carrson*

CASEY *Kasey, K.C., Kaci, Kaycee, Kacy, Kacey, Kayci*

CHELSEA *Chelsee, Chelsey, Chelcy*

CHEYENNE *Cheyanne, Chyanne, Sheyenne, Sheyen, Shyan, Scheyann*

CHIARA *Kiara, Keiara, Kieara, Kyara, Keara, Kearra, Kiarra, Chiarra*

DAMIAN *Damien, Daemian, Daemyan, Damean, Daymian*

DESTINY *Destini, Destinee, Destyni, Destanie, Destanee*

DEVON *Devin, Devan, Devyn, Devinne, Devann, Deven, Deaven*

ERIC *Erik, Eriq, Erique, Erick, Erric, Eryc, Eryk, Errick*

HAYDEN *Haden, Hadon, Haydn, Haydon*

HAYLEY *Haley, Hailey, Hailee, Hailley, Haylee, Haylie, Hayleigh*

ISABEL *Isabelle, Isabell, Isobel, Izabel, Izabelle*

JACQUELINE *Jacklyn, Jaclyn, Jackalyn, Jacquelyn, Jacquillin, Jacquelynne*

JADA *Jayda, Jaida, Jadah*

JADON *Jaden, Jadin, Jaeden, Jaidon, Jaydon, Jayden, Jadyn*

JALEN *Jaylen, Jalin, Jalon, Jaylin, Jaylon*

JASMINE *Jasmyn, Jasmin, Jazmin, Jazmine, Jasman, Jazman, Jazzmyn, Jazzmine*

JONATHAN *Johnathan, Johnathon, Jonathon, Jonothan*

JORDAN *Jorden, Jordin, Jordon, Jordyn, Jordynne, Jordanne*

KAYLEE *Cailey, Cayley, Caillie, Caylee, Caylie, Kayleigh, Kaylea, Kaelee*

KAYLON *Kaylin, Caelan, Kalin, Kaylynn, Kaelyn, Kaelan, Kaelynne, Kaelin, Kalyn*

KELSEY *Kelsy, Kelcey, Kelci, Kellsey, Kelsea, Kelcie, Kelcy*

KIANA *Keanna, Kianna, Kionna, Quiana, Quianna, Keiana*

KYLIE *Kylee, Kyleigh, Kylea, Kiley, Keilly*

KYRA *Kira, Keira, Kiera, Kierra, Kera, Keera, Kyrah*

MACKENZIE *McKenzie, Macenzie, McKenzi, Mackensi, Mackenzee, Mackenzy, Mykenzie*

MADELEINE *Madeline, Madelyn, Madaline, Madalyn, Madelynn, Madlyn*

MADISON *Madisen, Madissen, Maddison, Madesyn, Madisyn, Madysen, Madyson*

MASON *Maison, Maesyn, Mayson*

MEGAN *Meagan, Maegan, Meaghan, Megen, Meggan, Megyn, Meghann*

MICHAELA *Mikaela, Mikayla, McKayla, Makayla, Makaila, Mychaela, Micheala*

RILEY *Reilly, Rylea, Ryleigh, Rylee, Rilie, Rylie, Ryley, Reilley*

SCARLETT *Scarlet, Scarlette, Scarlotte, Skarlette*

SCHUYLER *Schuylar, Skylar, Skyler, Skila, Skyla, Skylor*

SIERRA *Cierra, Siarah, Sierrah, Siera, Cierrah, Cyera*

STEPHANIE *Stefanie, Steffany, Stefani, Stefannie, Stefanny, Stefanee, Stephney*

SYDNEY *Cydney, Sydni, Sydnee, Sydnie, Sidni, Sidnee, Cydni*

ZACHARY *Zachery, Zacharie, Zaccary, Zacary, Zaccari, Zacharey, Zachry*

ZOE *Zoey, Zoie, Zoee, Zooey*

The Two-Syllable Solution

One of the hottest new genres of boys' names has a surname-name feel, a distinctly masculine flavor, and contains, invariably, two syllables. These choices seem to be an alternative to both the traditional male names—William, Henry, and brothers—as well as to newer names that may feel a tad girlish. A few of these names are also included on the Kreeatif list because they appear with so many spelling varieties, but most of the following are usually spelled the conventional way.

AIDAN	BRODY
ASHTON	BRYANT
AUSTIN	CALEB
BAILEY	CAMDEN
BRADEN	CARSON
BRADLEY	CARTER
BRADY	CASEY
BRANDON	CHANDLER
BRENDAN	CLAYTON
BRENNAN	CLIFTON

CODY	JALEN
COLBY	JAREN
COLEMAN	JARRETT
COLIN	JONAS
COLTON	JORDAN
CONAN	JUSTIN
CONNOR	KADEN
COOPER	KEEGAN
CORBIN	KEENAN
COREY	KENYON
CORMAC	KIERAN
DALTON	KYLER
DAMON	LANDON
DAWSON	LENNON
DECLAN	LIAM
DEREK	LOGAN
DEVIN	LUCAS
DUNCAN	MASON
DUSTIN	MAXWELL
DYLAN	NATHAN
EAMON	NOLAN
EMMETT	OWEN
ETHAN	PARKER
EVAN	PEYTON
GARRETT	PRESTON
GAVIN	QUENTIN
GRADY	QUINTON
GRIFFIN	REDMOND
HARLEY	RILEY
HAYDEN	ROAN/ROWAN
HOLDEN	ROMAN
HUDSON	RONAN
HUNTER	RORY
JADEN	RYDER
JAGGER	RYLAN

SAWYER	TREVOR
SKYLER	TRISTAN
SPENCER	TRUMAN
TANNER	TUCKER
TAYLOR	TYLER
TOBY	TYSON
TRAVIS	WALKER
TRENTON	WYATT

The One-Syllable Solution

Same song, different rhythm. These hot one-syllable names for boys are the shorter brothers to the two-syllable choices. Warning: None would feel out of place on a soap opera.

Brock	Keen
Brooks	Lane
Cade	Pierce
Clay	Quinn
Cole	Reed
Colt	Reese
Dane	Reeve
Drew	Shaw
Finn	Shea
Flynn	Slade
Gage	Steel
Heath	Storm
Jett	Tate
Kai	Wade
Kane	Zane

The Brits & the Celts

For those parents with a more cultured sensibility, in search of a name that combines the traditional with the exotic, we offer these names from the British Isles: English favorites less well-used here, along with Scottish and Welsh and Irish imports.

GIRLS

AILSA	FENELLA
AISLING (*ASH-ling*)	FINOLA
ALTHEA	FIONA
AMABEL	GEMMA
ANNABEL	GEORGINA/
ANTHEA	GEORGIANA
ANWEN	GILLIAN
ARABELLA	GRANIA
BEATRIX	GREER
BRIDGET	GWYNETH
BRONWYN	HENRIETTA
BRYONY	HERMIONE
CAMILLA	HYACINTH
CARYS	IMOGEN
CECILY	IONA
CLARISSA	IVY
CLEMENTINE	JESSAMINE
CRESSIDA	JESSAMY
DAPHNE	JOCASTA
DEIRDRE	KERENZA
DULCIE	LETTICE
ELSPETH	LIVIA
EMMELINE	MAEVE
EUGENIE	MARIGOLD

MIRABELLE	POPPY
MIRANDA	PORTIA
MOIRA	POSY
MYFANWY	PRUDENCE
NERISSA	RHIANNON
NESSA	*(Ree-AHN-nun)*
NICOLA	RHONWYN
OONA/UNA	ROISIN *(ROH-sheen)*
OPHELIA	ROSEMARY
OTTOLINE	SAFFRON
PANDORA	SIDONIE/SIDONY
PANSY	SIOBHAN
PERSIS	*(Shi-VAUN)*
PETULA	TAMSIN
PETUNIA	TANSY
PHILIPPA	UNITY
PIPPA	

BOYS

ADRIAN	CRISPIN
ALEC	DAMIAN
ALISTAIR/ALASTAIR	DECLAN
AMBROSE	DERMOT
AMYAS	DESMOND
ANGUS	DUNCAN
ARCHIE	EAMON
ARTHUR	EGAN
AUBERON/OBERON	EWAN
AUBREY	FELIX
BENEDICT	FERGUS
CALLUM	FINLAY
CLEMENT	FINNEGAN
COLM	FINNIAN
CORMAC	FLYNN

GARETH	MALCOLM
GAVIN	PADRAIG
GRAHAM/GRAEME	PIERS
GULLIVER	QUENTIN
GUY	REDMOND
HAMISH	REX
HUGH	RHYS
HUGO	ROHAN/ROWAN
INIGO	ROLAND
IVAR	RONAN
IVO	RUPERT
IVOR	SEAMUS
JARVIS	SEBASTIAN
KEIR	TARQUIN
LACHLAN	TIERNAN
LAIRD	TORQUIL
LORCAN	TREVOR
MALACHY	TRISTAN

The Italianates

The British have had a long love affair with Italy, with a special fondness for Italianate girls' names. Many proper young ladies in England have distinctly Latin first names paired with their upper-crust last one. While some of these choices are not exactly Italian—Fleur or India or Saskia, for example—they have a stylishly exotic flavor that qualifies them to be in this company. Here are some of the favorites, definitely hot in the U.S., too:

Alessandra	Lola
Allegra	Lucia
Anabella	Luciana
Anaïs	Ludovica
Anastasia	Marina
Angelica	Nadia
Antonia	Natalya
Arabella	Natasha
Bianca	Octavia
Camilla	Oriana
Carlotta	Palma
Cleo	Paloma
Consuelo	Pandora
Cosima	Patrizia
Davina	Phyllida
Elena	Raffaela
Estella	Ramona
Flavia	Reine
Fleur	Renata
Francesca	Romy
Gabriella	Sabine
Gemma	Sabrina
Georgiana	Saskia
India	Serena
Letitia	Tatiana
Liliana	Venetia
Livia	

Place Names

In the mid-eighties we met a young girl named London.
What an original name! we thought. How charming, how

distinctive. Then we met a woman named Holland. Heard of a baby Indiana. Encountered a young Asia, a little Siena.

> **But No Iberia**
>
> *A Latin twist on the place name game: Renan Almendarez Coello, host of southern California's top-ranked Spanish-language morning radio show, and his wife named their three daughters Irlanda, Italia, and Francia.*

By the time Melanie Griffith and Melissa Gilbert gave birth, in the same year, to their baby Dakotas (one male, one female), what had seemed an offbeat style a short time before had mushroomed into a full-blown trend. Place Names, drawn not from name books but from maps and often signifying a locale important to the child's parents, became one of the premier name fashions combining originality and personal meaning.

Today, Madison is among the Top Ten girls' names, and Austin is near the head of the boys' popularity lists. Savannah and Sierra make the girls' Top 100, while Dakota, Dallas, and Devon rank among the most stylish boys' names. Those few Place Names that haven't been over-touristed are those far off the beaten name track: Ireland, chosen by Kim Basinger and Alec Baldwin for their daughter, was a delightful surprise; Lauryn Hill's Zion is an original choice, combining place with the Bible; truly eccentric choices such as Sicily or Peru retain their vibrancy. A place with real significance to you or your family can always make an appropriate choice, whether it's an established option such as Georgia or one you've turned into a name—Wisconsin, say, or Reno or Thames.

One note: As with many names that start out unisex, Place Names are drifting further and further into all-girl territory. We don't even include a boys' list any longer, because many of the formerly male choices—Dakota, Devon—are now nearly as often used for girls. As with most unisex names, if you choose one for your son, be aware that there's a strong possibility it will float further toward the female camp in years to come.

GIRLS

ABILENE	GUERNSEY
AFRICA	HAIFA
ARABIA	HAVANA
ASIA	HIMALAYA
ASPEN	HOLLAND
ASSISI	IBERIA
ATLANTA	INDIA
AUSTRIA	INDIANA
AVALON	IRELAND
BOLIVIA	ITALIA
CAIRO	ITHACA
CALEDONIA	JAMAICA
CALIFORNIA	JAVA
CAROLINA	JUNEAU
CATALINA	KENYA
CHINA	LOUISIANA
COLOMBIA	LOURDES
EDEN	MAJORCA
EGYPT	MALTA
ELBA	MIAMI
FLORENCE	MILAN
FLORIDA	ODESSA
FRANCE	OLYMPIA
GENEVA	PANAMA
GENOA	PERSIA
GEORGIA	QUINTANA ROO
GLASGOW	ROMA

SAHARA	SONOMA
SAMARA	SONORA
SAMARIA	TRINIDAD
SAMOA	VALENCIA
SAVANNAH	VENETIA
SICILY	VENICE
SIENA	VERONA
SIERRA	VIENNA

UNISEX

ALBANY	MACON
AMERICA	MONTANA
AUSTIN	MOROCCO
BOSTON	NAIROBI
BRAZIL	NEVADA
BROOKLYN	PACIFIC
CAMDEN	PARIS
CUBA	PERU
DAKOTA	PHILADELPHIA
DALLAS	PHOENIX
DENVER	RIO
DEVON	SCOTLAND
DUBLIN	SENEGAL
EVEREST	SWEDEN
GALWAY	TANGIER
HARLEM	TRENTON
HOUSTON	TROY
HUDSON	TULSA
INDIO	VAIL
ISRAEL	YORK
JERSEY	ZAIRE
LONDON	

Nature Names

Word Names are a huge new area of exploration for parents in search of unusual choices, and perhaps the most familiar—and hottest—category of these are Nature Names. This is where Word Names really started, with older flower and gem names (Rose, Pearl), moving through hippie names such as River and Cloud, up to more modern choices such as Lake and Indigo.

While many of the wilder Nature Names remain in the What's Cool category, these have catapulted to Hot status:

ACADIA	FERN
ANGELICA	FIELD
AQUA	FINCH
ASH	FLEUR
AUTUMN	FLINT
AZURE	FLOWER
BAY	FOREST
BEACH/BEECH	FOX
BIRCH	FROST
BLUE	GREEN
BRIAR	INDIGO
CALICO	IVORY
CAMELLIA	IVY
CANYON	JADE
CASSIA	JUNIPER
CAYENNE	LAKE
CLOUD	LAUREL
CLOVER	LEAF
DAISY	LILAC
DRAKE	MAHOGANY
EBONY	MEADOW
ECHO	MYRTLE

NORTH	SLATE
OAK	SNOW
OCEAN	STAR
RAIN	STONE
RAINBOW	STORM
RED	SUMMER
RIVER	TEAL
SAFFRON	TOPAZ
SAGE	WEST
SKY	WILLOW

Riddle of the Middle

Middle names have suddenly become a new hot spot in the naming process, taking on a greater presence and significance than they've had since Peggy Sue got married. And why? Perhaps it's because so many more young women in the spotlight are using all three of their names—the Sarah Michelle Gellar/Evan Rachel Wood/Jennifer Love Hewitt syndrome—or maybe it's because parents are realizing that this is an arena where they can be more creative than they can with their child's main name.

No longer do baby namers want to settle for ho-hum middle names that do nothing but euphonically bridge the all-important first and last names. Rather, middle names represent an opportunity to provide a spot for a favorite choice—say Felix or Frederica—that seems to cross the line into the overly eccentric when used as a first name. It can also be a safe slot for a name you really don't like that much but feel a certain obligation to include. This scenario doesn't arise as often these days as it once did, that of having to pay homage to Great-aunt Hortensia and thus pave a direct path to the family fortune. That kind of thinking, we hope, went out with screwball comedies and fifties sitcom plots, but there are still times when you do want to honor a beloved relative or friend whose name you like but don't love, and the middle position is the perfect place to put it.

Middle naming is also a good way to honor a special hero or heroine, someone you particularly admire in the arts, history, politics, or spiritual life, or whose values you would like your child to emulate. One musical couple we know gave their son the middle name of Amadeus, after

> ### Meaningful Monograms
>
> *A study conducted by researchers from the University of California at San Diego says that people with initials such as ACE or GOD are likely to live longer than those whose initials spell out words like APE, DUD, RAT, or PIG. People with good monograms, such as JOY or WOW, lived 4.48 years longer than a control group of people with neutral or ambiguous monograms. Those with negative initials, such as BUM or UGH, died an average of 2.8 years earlier.*
>
> —*AUSTIN AMERICAN-STATESMAN*

Mozart, and of course the child grew up with a keen interest in the composer. Another gave their daughter the middle name Eleanor, honoring Mrs. Roosevelt, and a third used Ray, after jazzman Charles. And, because many parents feel that anything goes with a middle name, some choose a place name with significance for them—or even a word, such as Truth.

Last names are often first names these days, and they're even more often middle names. The long-held tradition of using the mother's maiden surname for a middle name is alive and thriving. Some parents are taking this practice a step further and considering other ancestral surnames as middle names, such as those of both maternal and paternal grandmothers, that might otherwise be lost to history.

Another trendlet we've spotted is giving girls a boy's middle name, as in Jennifer Jason Leigh. Some possibilities noted: Duncan, Gary, Elliot, Michael. This is another way in which celebrities from the Spielbergs to the Beattys have been trendsetters, bestowing on their daughters such middle names as Max, Ray, Glenn, George, Allyn, Ira, Dean, and Lewis.

Finding an interesting middle name can also be a nice way of accommodating all members of the family. For one thing, it can give both parents a chance to have equal input on the issue of what to name their baby. One mother we know, for example, wanted to honor her Irish heritage by naming her son Liam, while her husband opted to give the child the middle name Henry (which she didn't particularly like), after his father. It can even be a way for older siblings to get in on the baby-naming act.

With middle names, just about anything goes. You may prefer traditional first names, for instance, yet honor your child's place of conception by using a place name in the middle. Or you can use one of the new word names as a middle name: One mom we know gave her son the middle name Red, for her favorite color. And multiple middle names, à la royalty, are fine too, say, to pay homage to both grandmothers, at once.

Hero Middle Names

One alternative to using a family name in the middle is using the spot to honor a hero—political, historical, sports, artistic. Appropriate hero surnames work for both boys and girls (though some sound better for one sex than

the other); and range far beyond the choices here. But
these will give you a good start:

ALCOTT	KENNEDY
BALZAC	KUROSAWA
BERGMAN	LENNON
BOGART	LINCOLN
CHANEL	LODGE
CHAPLIN	LOEWY
CHURCHILL	MacARTHUR
EARHART	MANDELA
EMERSON	MARQUEZ
FITZGERALD	MCCARTNEY
GANDHI	MISHIMA
GARCIA	MONROE
GARVEY	MORRISON
GATES	MOZART
GAUGUIN	OAKLEY
GEHRIG	O'CASEY
GIACOMETTI	O'CONNOR
GIBSON	O'HARA
GILLESPIE	OLIVIER
GORKY	ORWELL
GUEVARA	PENN
HALE	PICABIA
HALSEY	POE
HAMMETT	POWELL
HARPER	RALEIGH
HART	RUNYON
HAZLITT	TENNYSON
HENDRIX	THOREAU
HERRERA	TWAIN
HUNTER	WEBSTER
JAGGER	WHARTON
KEATON	

One-Syllable Middle Names

There are a couple of guidelines in the midname game. The first is to think of a balance of syllables. Kyle Jefferson Reed makes a stronger impression than Kyle Paul Reed, whereas Samantha Jane Kennedy is more rhythmic than, say, a mouthful such as Samantha Brittany Kennedy. The other is the old caveat about being careful what damage a certain middle initial can do to your child's monogram. So no Peter Ian Greenbergs, please, and no Ashley Sarah Sloans—or your child will never forgive you.

The only other absolute rule is not to fall into using one of the last generation's Designated Middle Names—Ann or Marie, Lee or Jon—just because you can't think of anything better. If you still like the idea of a short, connective, one-syllable middle name, look for one that moves far away from the last generation's ubiquitous Sues and Lynns. Following is a list of ideas primarily for girls, though several can work for boys, too:

BAY	BRITT
BECK	BROOKE
BELLE	BROWN
BESS	BRYN
BLAINE	CASS
BLAIR	CEIL
BLAKE	CHAN
BLANCHE	CHASE
BLUE	CLAIR/CLAIRE/CLARE
BLYTHE	CLAUDE
BOYD	COLE
BREE/BRIE	CRAIG
BRETT	DALE

DEAN	LAURE
DELL	LIV
DOE	LORNE
DOONE	LUZ
DREE	LYLE
DREW	MAE/MAY
EVE	MAEVE
FAITH	MAI
FAY	MAIRE
FLANN	MAUDE
FLEUR	MAX
GEORGE	MERLE
GLENN	MOSS
GRACE	NEIL/NEAL
GRAY	NELL
GREEN	PAIGE
GREER	PAUL
GWYNNE	PEARL
HART	PRU
HOPE	QUINN
JADE	RAE/RAY
JAMES	RAINE
JAY	REECE/REESE
JUAN	ROONE
JUDE	ROSE
KAI	ROY
KANE	RUE
KATE	RUTH
KENT	SAGE
KERR	SCOTT
KYLE	SEAN
LAKE	SETH
LANE	SHAW
LANG	SHAY/SHEA
LARK	SKYE

SLOAN/SLOANE	TYNE
SPENCE	WREN
TATE	WYNNE
TEAL	XAN/ZAN
TESS	YALE/YAEL
TROY	ZANE

A Garden of Roses

Rose continues to be *the* middle name for girls these days, as evidenced by this rose garden of starbabies. (The Stallones liked it so much they used it three times.)

Aidan **Rose**	*Faith Daniels*
Amber **Rose**	*Simon Le Bon*
Catherine **Rose**	*Cheryl Hines*
Claudia **Rose**	*Michelle Pfeiffer*
Emerson **Rose**	*Teri Hatcher*
Esther **Rose**	*Ewan McGregor*
Hayley **Rose**	*Jeff Bridges*
India **Rose**	*Heather Thomas*
Julie **Rose**	*Eric Clapton*
Kelsey **Rose**	*Gabrielle Carteris*
Lucky **Rose**	*Cedric the Entertainer*
Sarah **Rose**	*Marlee Matlin*
Scarlet **Rose**	*Jennifer Flavin & Sylvester Stallone*
Sistine **Rose**	*Jennifer Flavin & Sylvester Stallone*
Sophia **Rose**	*Jennifer Flavin & Sylvester Stallone*
Stephanie **Rose**	*Jon Bon Jovi*
Vivienne **Rose**	*Rosie O'Donnell*

Starbaby Middle Names

Here are some of the inventive middle names celebrities have used for their offspring:

ASAR	*Wesley Snipes*
AUTRY	*Willie Nelson*
BAY	*Lucy Lawless*
BLEU	*Kelly Preston & John Travolta*
BLUE	*Maria Bello; Rosanna Arquette*
BOO	*Jamie Oliver*
BRAE	*Mary Lou Retton*
BUSINA	*Dave Matthews*
CHI	*Melanie Brown*
CHIVAN	*Angelina Jolie*
CY	*Elle MacPherson*
DIAMONTE	*Kobe Bryant*
DUMAINE	*Soon-Yi & Woody Allen*
FOX	*Mariel Hemingway*
GRAY	*Lisa Rinna & Harry Hamlin*
GREV	*Phil Collins*
GUGGI	*Bono*
HAVEN	*Dylan Walsh*
HENDRIX	*Donnie Wahlberg*
HONEY	*Jamie Oliver*
INSPEKTOR	*Jason Lee*
JAGGER	*Pamela Anderson & Tommy Lee*
JIGME	*Carey Lowell & Richard Gere*
KESHVAR	*Geena Davis*
KY	*Toni Braxton*
LACOSTA	*Tanya Tucker*
LaRUE	*Demi Moore & Bruce Willis*
LOSEL	*Adam Yauch*
LOVING	*Rick Derringer*

MAINE	*Garth Brooks*
MARU	*Gillian Anderson*
MASAKO	*Wayne Brady*
MAYI	*David Byrne*
MIAMI	*Nastassja Kinski & Quincy Jones*
MIRO	*Lucy Lawless*
MOBY	*David Brenner*
MOOREA	*Lou Diamond Phillips*
PATRICUS	*Bono*
PAULIN	*Will Ferrell*
PINE	*Simon Le Bon*
RAINN	*Vanilla Ice*
RAYNE	*David Boreanaz*
REIGN	*Jada Pinkett & Will Smith*
ROMILLY	*Emma Thompson*
SAHARA	*Simon Le Bon*
SCHAE	*Debbie Dunning*
SCIENCE	*Shannyn Sossamon*
SIRIUS	*Erykah Badu*
STREET	*Elisabeth Shue*
SUSHIL	*Sarah McLaughlin*
TRIXIEBELLE	*Bob Geldof*
TRU	*Josie Bisette & Rob Estes*
WEST	*Téa Leoni & David Duchovny*
WILDHORSE	*John Mellencamp*
YASIN	*Sandra Bernhard*
ZAHRA	*Iman & David Bowie; Eddie Murphy*
ZHIVAGO	*Nia Long*

What's Cool

How far out do you have to go to get to a truly cutting-edge name these days? Pretty far, with many categories, from old-fashioned names to place names, surname names to exotic names, making the leap to Hot and becoming fit for widespread consumption.

The newest names are those from little-explored frontiers. There are the ancient names revived for use after long periods of lying dormant, including mythological names from cultures around the world. There are boys' names for girls, not the androgynous names such as Taylor and Dylan that have become standard feminine fare, but real masculine standards: James, Gregory, Zachary.

And then there are the farthest-out names of all, the word names that pick up where place names and virtue names leave off. Can you really name your baby Pike and Pace, Christmas and (perfect for a writer) Story? You can and, increasingly into the future, you will.

If cool choices like Gulliver and Hugo, Sawyer and Primrose are still not quite cool enough for you, you might dare to venture here.

Word Names

With the explosion of unconventional names over the past few years, the parent in search of something really different may feel there is no ground left unexplored. That's not entirely true: The world of word names, names that for the most part have never been names at all, is set to open its boundaries.

At first glance, most of these names seem bizarre, too far out to be considered at all. And for many people, they will be. But bear in mind that this category does not come as completely out of the blue as it may initially seem. Think of it as a continuation of the place names, an adjunct to invented names and spellings, a step beyond names like Sunshine and Freedom first heard in the sixties.

Popular culture has been preparing us for the advent of word names. A few notable celebrities have chosen them for their children: Toni Braxton's Denim; Ving Rhames's Freedom; director Robert Rodriguez's three boys Rebel, Race, and Rocket; Christie Brinkley's Sailor; Forest Whitaker's True; Jason Lee's Pilot; Sylvester Stallone's Sistine and Sage. In one memorable episode, *Seinfeld*'s George declared that if he had a child, boy or girl, he would name it Seven. And singer Erykah Badu *did* in fact name her son Seven. Then there are the celebrities who bear word names, from Judge Reinhold to the singer Seal. In traditional literature, we have Huckleberry Finn and Scarlett O'Hara. And soap opera characters, always on the cutting edge, have names like Star and Steel, Stone and Storm.

Perhaps best of all, the word names introduce hundreds of new name possibilities into the lexicon, opening up a universe of options to parents in search of a name that's highly unusual and yet embodies personal meaning. Not every word—not even very many words—qualify as name possibilities. We offer the following lists with a caveat, urging you to think long and hard of possible peer repercussions before you make your final choice.

Wilder Nature Names

Familiar nature names such as Bay and Meadow have flown up to the Hot group, but wilder choices remain for the adventurous.

ACACIA	CHAMOMILE
ACANTHUS	CINNAMON
AIR	CITRON
AMARYLLIS	COBALT
AMBROSIA	COLUMBINE
ANEMONE	COMET
ANGORA	CORONA
ARBOR	CRIMSON
ARCADIA	DAHLIA
AUBURN	DIAMOND
AZALEA	ELM
BLAZE	FAUNA
BRANCH	FENNEL
BROWN	FLAME
BURR	FORSYTHIA
CALYX	FREESIA
CARAWAY	GALAXY
CARNELIAN	GARDENIA
CASCADE	GLADE
CASHMERE	GRANITE
CATALPA	GRAVITY
CEDAR	GROVE

HARBOR	PRIMROSE
HYACINTH	QUARRY
JONQUIL	RUE
LANTANA	RUSH
LARK	SEQUOIA
LAVENDER	SHADE
LIANA	SILVER
MAGNOLIA	SORREL
MERCURY	SPRUCE
METEOR	TAMARIND
MICA	TARRAGON
MIMOSA	THUNDER
ORCHID	TIMBER
PEONY	VERBENA
PIKE	WOLF
PINE	ZINNIA
PRAIRIE	

Day Names

The first Africans in North America often bore day names—names that signified the day of the week on which they were born. Through the years, the African day-naming custom was Anglicized and expanded to include months, seasons, holidays. While African-Americans, postslavery, left their old day names behind, some of the names that connect to times of the year have lived on. April, May, June, and Dawn, of course, have long been well-used girls' names. More recently, August, Summer, and Autumn have come to the fore. Season Hubley and Spring Byington were actresses of some note. And who can forget Tuesday Weld or Wednesday Addams? Day names worth considering now include:

AFTERNOON	MARCH
ARIES	MONDAY
AUGUST	MORNING
AUTUMN	NOON
CALENDAR	NOVEMBER
CHRISTMAS	OCTOBER
DECEMBER	SCORPIO
EARLY	SEASON
EASTER	SEPTEMBER
GEMINI	SUNDAY
JANUARY	WINTER
LIGHT	

Postvirtue Names

The Puritans paved the way with virtue names, giving us Hope and Charity, Faith and Honor, as well as several other selections that have been all but lost to time: Justice, Reverence, Purity. Now, it's time for a new complement of virtue names, word names that set forth the values and ideals of our time. Some of these—Simplicity and Trust, for example—relate directly to the classic Puritan virtue names, while many others vary in syntax and viewpoint. But they all evidence some ineffable human quality or feeling. At least two of the names here, Remember and Experience, were used by early New England settlers. As with the virtue names, these are most appropriate for girls, though some—such as True, the name of actor Forest Whitaker's son—can work as well for boys.

ADMIRE	AMIABLE
AFFINITY	BENEVOLENT
ALLIANCE	BLITHE

CLARITY	GENEROUS
DECLARE	GENTLE
DEMOCRACY	GLIMMER
DIPLOMACY	ILLUMINATION
DIVERSITY	INSPIRATION
ECCENTRICITY	INTEGRITY
ELOQUENT	LEGEND
ENDEAVOR	LIVELY
ENERGY	MEMORY
ENTERPRISE	MUSE
ESSENTIAL	PHILOSOPHY
ETERNAL	PLEASANT
ETHICAL	POWER
EXCELLENCE	PROSPER
FASCINATION	RHYTHM
FAVORITE (*but be*	RULE
careful with	SERENDIPITY
this one)	SIMPLICITY
FORWARD	SINCERITY
FREE	SOCIETY
FREEDOM	SPIRIT
FRIEND	STRATEGY
GALLANT	TENDER

Profession Names

When Christie Brinkley named her third child Sailor, she set the course for a new brand of baby names, those that relate to an activity or profession: Scout, the name of Demi Moore and Bruce Willis's second daughter and the nickname of the young heroine of *To Kill a Mockingbird*, falls in this category, too. Occupational names include:

ARCHER	JUDGE
BREWER	NAVIGATOR
COOK	PAINTER
DANCER	PILOT
DEACON	RACER
EXPLORER	RANCHER
FARMER	RANGER
FIELDER	SAILOR
FLETCHER	SCOUT
GARDENER	TEACHER
GLAZIER	TRAVELER

Word Names

The most adventurous of the adventurous word names are those that can't be fit into any familiar categories. These words become name-worthy by virtue of euphony or symbolism, or both. Words that make the grade have to do more than be easy on the ear. Atrocity and Captivity, for instance, Salary and Shallow, are attractive-sounding words, but not fit for a child's name. Nor can the meaning be too simple: a name like Sweet, Pretty, or Sugar, for ex-

---

As for their daughter's nautical name, {Christie} Brinkley explains: "Peter's family dates back to Captain Cook, who discovered the Big Island of Hawaii. It's also where we found out we were pregnant, so we called her Captain Cook during the pregnancy. That evolved into Sailor."

—JIM JEROME,
LADIES' HOME JOURNAL

ample, might belittle a child. And one like Splendid or Extraordinary could set too high a bar. A lot of words get eliminated by these rules. Those that remain are, admittedly, wild and woolly, but undeniably interesting.

ABACUS	FABLE
ALCHEMY	GLASS
ANALOGY	HALCYON
ANCHOR	HISTORY
ANSWER	HOLIDAY
ANTIQUITY	HORIZON
ARIA	LYRIC
ARMOR	MUSIC
ARROW	OPERA
AVALANCHE	PACE
AXIOM	PALACE
BLADE	PYRAMID
BOUNDARY	QUINTESSENCE
BRIDGE	SAFARI
CADENCE	SCIENCE
CAMEO	SERENE
CAMERA	SEVEN
CANOE	SONNET
CANTATA	STANZA
CASTLE	STERLING
DANCE	STORY
ELEVEN	TAFFETA
ENGLISH	THEATER
EVERY	

Word Name Imports

And why stop at words in our own language? Additional inspiration can be found in the dictionaries of other countries as well, and we offer a small sampling for starters:

Aerien	French
Alea	Italian
Alouette	French
Amapola	Spanish
Ange	French
Aquila	Italian
Baia	Italian
Bichette	French
Cadeau	French
Calia	Italian
Charra	Spanish
Cruz	Spanish
Faro	Italian
Galaxia	Spanish
Janvier	French
Lienzo	Spanish
Lumiere	French
Maggio	Italian
Matiz	Spanish
Mirabelle	French
Neige	French
Ombra	Italian
Quinta	Spanish
Soleil	French
Tiza	Spanish

Valletta	**Italian**
Vrai	**French**
Zana	**Italian**

Endangered Species

In the ever-escalating search for distinctive names, forward to entirely new names and outward toward more exotic names aren't the only directions in which to go. You can also move backward, in search of those ancient names now teetering on the edge of oblivion.

There's an attic full of names waiting to be rediscovered. Some of the girls' names are long-neglected variations on male names: Augusta and Cornelia, Henrietta and Josepha. Many of the boys' names have biblical—Ezekiel, Phineas, Silas—or Greco-Roman—Thaddeus, Cyril—roots. And then there is an entire subcategory of long-dormant mythological names: Ulysses, for instance, or Minerva, the Roman goddess of wisdom and invention, the arts and martial strength. Less familiar names from myths of other cultures, from Irish to Hindu, also qualify for revival.

What all these names have in common is a quaint, quirky quality. Musty? Maybe. But if you gravitate toward names that combine the historic with the eccentric, these choices are perfect for you.

The parent who wants an unusual name can rest assured that these won't be heard in every playground and on every nursery-school roll. Hardly any children in the United States are given these names anymore. In a recent complete list of names used for babies born in the state of Maine, for example, there was only one boy named Bartholomew and one girl called Evangeline.

GIRLS

ADA	ISIDORA
AGATHA	JACINDA
AGNES	JOSEPHA
AMABEL	LAVINIA
ARAMINTA	LEONORA
AUGUSTA	LETITIA
CANDIDA	LOTTIE
CHRISTABEL	LUCRETIA
CLARISSA	MATILDA
CLAUDIA	MYRTLE
CORDELIA	OCTAVIA
CORNELIA	OPHELIA
DESDEMONA	PEARL
DRUSILLA	PHILOMENA
EDWINA	PORTIA
ELEONORA	ROWENA
ELVIRA	THALIA
ERNESTINE	THEODORA
ESMÉ	THEODOSIA
EUDORA	THOMASINA
EULALIA	URSULA
EVANGELINE	VIOLA
GENEVIEVE	WILHELMINA
GUINEVERE	ZENOBIA
IMOGENE	ZULEIKA

BOYS

ABSALOM	AXEL
ALONZO	BALTHAZAR
ARCHIBALD	BARNABAS
ARTEMAS	BARTHOLOMEW
AUGUSTINE	CASPAR

CECIL	LEOPOLD
CEDRIC	LINUS
CLEMENT	LLEWELYN
CLIVE	LUCIUS
CONRAD	MUNGO
CORNELIUS	NICODEMUS
CYRIL	OBADIAH
CYRUS	OCTAVIUS
DEXTER	PERCIVAL
DIGBY	PERCY
EBENEZER	PEREGRINE
ELMO	PHILO
ERASMUS	PHINEAS
EUSTACE	QUINCY
EVANDER	RODERICK
FERDINAND	ROLLO
GILES	ROSCOE
GODFREY	RUFUS
HECTOR	SEPTIMUS
HIRAM	THADDEUS
HORATIO	TITUS
HUMPHREY	ULYSSES
ISHMAEL	URIAH
LEANDER	VIRGIL
LEMUEL	WALDO

Mythological Names

GIRLS

ANANN	Irish
ANCASTA	British
ANDROMEDA	Greek
ANNIKI	Finnish

ANNONA	Roman
APHRODITE	Greek
ARANI	Indian
ARIADNE	Greek
ARTEMIS	Greek
ASTARTE	Phoenician
ASTRA	Greek
ATALANTA	Greek
ATHENA	Greek
AURORA	Greek
BELINDA	Babylonian
BRANWEN	Welsh
BRIGHID (*Breed*)	Irish
CALLIOPE	Greek
CALYPSO	Greek
CASSANDRA	Greek
CASSIOPEIA	Greek
CERELIA	Roman
CERES	Greek
CHANDA	Indian
CHLORIS	Greek
CLIO	Greek
CLIONA	Irish
CYBELE	Greek
CYNTHIA	Roman
DAMARA	British
DAMONA	Celtic
DANA/DANU	Irish
DAPHNE	Greek
DEIRDRE	Celtic
DELIA	Greek
DEMETER	Greek
DIANA	Roman
ECHO	Greek
ELARA	Greek

ELECTRA	Greek
EURYDICE	Greek
FAUNA	Roman
FLORA	Roman
FORTUNA	Roman
FREYA	Norse
GAIA/GAEA	Greek
GALATEA	Greek
GODIVA	British
GWENDYDD (*GWED-eth*)	Welsh
HERMIONE	Greek
HESTIA	Greek
INGRID	Norse
IRENE	Greek
IRIS	Greek
ISIS	Greek
JANA	Roman
JOCASTA	Greek
JUNO	Roman
KALI	Hindu
KALINDI	Hindu
KALMA	Finnish
KARA	Norse
LEDA	Greek
LUNA	Roman
MAIA	Greek
MINERVA	Roman
MORRIGAN	Irish
NANNA	Teutonic
NIX/NIXIE	Teutonic
NORNA	Norse
OLWYN	Welsh
PALLAS	Greek
PANDORA	Greek
PAX	Roman

PHAEDRA	Greek
RANA/RANIA	Norse
RHEA	Greek
RHIANNON	Welsh
SELENE	Greek
SULLA (*Silla*)	Celtic
SURYA	Indian
TAMESIS	British
TAMRA	Indian
TARA	Indian
TERRA	Roman
THALIA	Greek
VENUS	Roman

BOYS

ACHILLES	Greek
ADONI	Phoenician
ADONIS (*though he'd better be great-looking*)	Greek
AENGUS (*Angus*)	Irish
AJAX	Greek
ANGUS	Celtic
ANTAEUS	Greek
APOLLO	Greek
ARAWN (*Roan*)	Welsh
ARES	Greek
ARION	Greek
ATLAS	Greek
BALIN	British
BORVO	Celtic
BRAN	Welsh
CADMUS	Greek
DAEDALUS	Greek
DAMON	Greek

DIARMUID (*Dermud*)	Irish
DONAR	Teutonic
DONN	Irish
DYLAN	Welsh
ELIUN	Phoenician
ENDYMION	Greek
FERGUS	Irish
FIONN	Irish
GARETH	Britain
GUNNAR	Norse
HELIOS	Greek
HERMES	Greek
ICARUS	Greek
JANUS	Roman
JUPITER	Roman
KRONOS	Greek
LEANDER	Greek
LOKI	Scandinavian
MARS	Roman
MERCURY	Roman
NAKKI	Finnish
NEPTUNE	Roman
ODIN	Norse
ORION	Greek & Roman
ORPHEUS	Greek
OSIRIS	Egyptian
PARIS	Greek
RA	Egyptian
REMUS	Roman
SALEM	Phoenician
SILVANUS	Roman
THOR	Norse
ULYSSES	Greek
VULCAN	Roman
ZEUS	Greek

A Girl Named Boy

With Taylor near the top of the girls' popularity lists, and such unisex choices as Madison, Morgan, Jordan, Bailey, and Mackenzie firmly among the most widely used names for girls, where's the next frontier for parents who would like masculine names for their daughters but want to move beyond the choices we've been hearing most often? Firmly in male territory, with Andrew and Graham, Jeremy and Thomas, names we've long thought of as exclusively male.

Hollywood has helped forge the path into this new area. There are the actresses with male names: Drew Barrymore, Glenn Close, Daryl Hannah, Sean Young. And then there is the increasing number of celebrities who've given their daughters boys' names, from Diane Keaton's Dexter Dean to Spike Lee's Satchel Lewis, from Steven Spielberg and Kate Capshaw's Destry Allyn to Sting's Eliot.

Giving boys' names to girls is less of an innovation than you might initially think. In Olde England, girls were commonly called Alexander, Aubrey, Basil, Douglas, Edmund, Eustace, Gilbert, Giles, James, Nicholas,

---

Women Will Be Men

Q: Why do so many of your female characters have men's names?

A: When I was growing up, my parents knew George Gershwin's sister. Her name was Frankie, which struck me as being extremely glamorous. Now, I just love men's names—they give characters a flip, jazz-age feeling.

—*LOS ANGELES MAGAZINE,*
JUDITH KRANTZ

Philip, Reynold, and Simon. And we've long been paving the modern-day road into this androgynous land, via such sixties boyish nickname names as Jody and Jamie and Ricki and, later, Victorian gentlemen's favorites such as Ashley and Lindsay and Courtney.

But these days, once a name crosses the line from masculine to feminine, it's unusual for it ever to travel back again. As more and more previously all-boy names are claimed by girls, we worry that boys will have fewer decidedly masculine choices left.

This may be bad news for boys, but it's good news for girls, giving them more and more interesting options. And many boys' names acquire new life when used for girls. Stalwarts like James and Neil, Gary and Seth seem melodic and jaunty and stylish again when applied to a female. Here are some of the best new choices for girls:

AARON	CARMINE
ABBOTT	CARSON
AIDAN	CARTER
ANDREW	CECIL
ARLO	CHAZZ
AUBERON	CHEVY
AUGUST	CLAUDE
AUSTIN	CLAY
AVERY	CLOVIS
BAILEY	CODY
BARNABY	COLE
BARRY	COLIN
BECKETT	CONNOR
BRADLEY	CORNELL
BRADY	CULLEN
BRENNAN	CURTIS
BRONSON	DALLAS
BRUCE	DAMIAN

DANE	GRIFFITH
DARIUS	HARLEY
DARREN	HUNTER
DARRYL	IAN
DEAN	IRA
DEREK	IVO
DEWEY	JAKE
DEXTER	JAMES
DOMINIC	JARED
DONOVAN	JASON
DUANE	JAY
DUNCAN	JEREMY
DUSTIN	JONAH
DYLAN	JUBAL
EBEN	JUDE
ELI	JULIAN
ELIAS	KEITH
ELIOT	KENT
ELISHA	KENYON
ELLERY	KIERAN
EMERSON	KILLIAN
EMERY	KIMBALL
EMMANUEL	KIRBY
FABIAN	KYLE
FARRELL	LAURENCE
FINN	LEANDER
FLORIAN	LEO
FLYNN	LEWIS
GARETH	LIONEL
GARY	LOWELL
GEORGE	LUCIAN
GIDEON	LYLE
GLENN	MASON
GRAHAM	MAX
GREGORY	MICHAEL

MORLEY	SEAN
MURRAY	SETH
NEIL	SEYMOUR
NICHOLAS	SIMON
NOLAN	SPENCER
NORRIS	STUART
ORLANDO	THEO
PATRICK	THOMAS
PERRY	TIERNEY
PETER	TIMOTHY
PHILIP	TOBIAS
QUENTIN	TRAVIS
QUINCY	TRISTAN
RAFAEL	TROY
RALEIGH	TYSON
REED	VAUGHN
REESE	WENDELL
ROY	WYATT
RYAN	WYLIE
SAWYER	ZACHARY
SCOTT	

The Exotics

Names from around the world are one way for adventurous parents to combine fresh choices with tradition, to find names with personal meaning that also have an unusual feel. You can choose a name that reflects your ethnic roots or one that's from a country you love, or simply pick a name that appeals to your taste for the exotic. For even more choices, check the extensive lists in the Tradition section. These are some of the most style-worthy selections:

GIRLS

ADRIANA	ELODIE
AIDA	ESMÉ
ALIZA	ESMERELDA
AMANDINE	EULALIA
AMELIE	FABIENNE
ANGELIQUE	FERNANDA
ANOUK	GAELLE
ANYA	GIOIA
ARABELLA	GIOVANNA
ARMEL	GRAZIELLA
ASTRID	HERMIONE
AURELIA	ILIANA
AXELLE	INGRID
AZIZA	ISALINE
BASIA	JUNO
BATHSHEBA	KATYA
CALISTA	KENZA
CANDIDA	LAETITIA
CARINA	LILIA/LILYA
CARMEN	LILIANA
CHANTAL	LINNEA
CHIARA	LOURDES
CLEA	LUCIENNE
CONCHITA	LUDOVINE
DAGNY	MANON
DANICA	MARIAMNE
DARIA	MARIELLA
DEANDRA	MARINE
DELTA	MARISOL
DEMETRIA	MERCEDES
DIANTHA	MIGNON
DOMINIQUE	MIRABELLE

NICOLETTE	SASHA
NOELLE	SIGNE
ODILE	SIMONE
OTTILIE	SOLANGE
PAOLINA	SOLEDAD
PIA	TALLULAH
PILAR	TAMARA
PRIMA	TATIANA
RAINE	THALIA
RAQUEL	VALENTINA
SABRINE	VIOLETTA
SALOMÉ	VIVEKA
SANNE	VIVIANA

BOYS

ALDO	BORIS
ALEJANDRO	BRAM
ALEXEI	BRUNO
ALONZO	CARLO
AMADEO	CLAUDIO
ANATOLE	CORENTIN
ARAM	COSMO
ARLO	DAAN
ARMEL	DANTE
ARNO	DIEGO
AUGUST	DIETER
AURELIEN	DMITRI
AXEL	EMILIO
BALTHAZAR	ENZO
BARNABUS	ETIENNE
BASTIEN	FABIAN
BENNO	FEDERICO
BJORN	FLORENT
BLAISE	GREGOR

GUIDO	ORLANDO
GUNTER	OTTO
IVOR	PABLO
JOAQUIN	PAOLO
KNUT	PEDRO
KRISTOF	PHILIPPE
LARS	PIERS
LEONARDO	RAOUL/RAUL
LORCAN	RAPHAEL
LORENZO	ROCCO
LUC	ROMAIN
LUCIEN	ROMAN
MARCO	RUTGER
MAREK	SOREN
MARIUS	STEFAN
MATHIS	TANGUY
MATTEO	TARQUIN
MIGUEL	THEO
NELS	THOR
NIALL	WILLEM
NICO	YANN
OLAF	

Exotic Surname Names

After more than two decades in the limelight, many of the Waspy surname names—Cooper, Morgan et al.—are beginning to pale. What's cooler are exotic last-names-as-firsts, whether you find them on your family tree or adopt one that's pleasing to the ear. The universe of these exotic surname names is much wider than what can be included in these pages (check the phone book), but here's a sampling:

BAIO	JENSON
BARBEAU	KENNEDY
BOONE	KIERNAN
BRANIGAN	LENNOX
BRONTË	LENO
CABRERA	LIOTTA
CALHOUN	LORCA
CALLAHAN	LOWRY
CALLOWAY	LURIE
CAMPBELL	MADIGAN
CARUSO	MAGUIRE
CHAN	MCALLISTER
CLAUDEL	MCCABE
CONNOLLY	MOLINA
CORTEZ	MONTOYA
CROSBY	MORRISON
CRUZ	MURPHY
CUEVA	NASH
DEMPSEY	NAVARRO
DEVEREUX	NILSSON
DIAZ	O'BRIEN
DONAHUE	O'HARA
DUARTE	O'KEEFE
DUFFY	ONO
FALLON	OROZCO
FARRELL	ORTIZ
FITZGERALD	PAXTON
FLORES	PHELAN
FUENTES	QUAID
GALLAGHER	QUINTERO
GARCIA	RAFFERTY
GUTHRIE	REMINGTON
HANSEN	ROMERO
HAYES	ROONEY
JARREAU	SAWYER

63

SHERIDAN   WHELAN
SLATER   WILLOUGHBY
TAM   ZAHN
TANDY   ZECCA
TIERNEY   ZOLA
VEGA

Fashion Limbo

There is a whole generation of names that is decidedly not in, but may not be out forever. Rarely chosen by contemporary name-givers, these names are suspended in a state of stylistic limbo, a great proportion of them consigned there because they were overused for and by our own parents. Chances are, in fact, that you'll find your own name on this list as well as those of your mom and dad.

Some of them, in the cyclic pattern of these things, will inevitably be rediscovered by our own children when it comes time to name their babies. And, no doubt, we will be more than a little disconcerted by the idea of having grandchildren named Phyllis or Donald or Arlene or Gary, just as our parents are dismayed at this generation's little Sams, Maxes, and Natalies.

But others of these names will not fare so well (or so badly, depending on your point of view), and will eventually pass on to a future edition of the So Far Out They'll Probably Always Be Out list.

GIRLS

ADELE	JANET
ANITA	JANICE
ANNETTE	JEAN
ARLENE	JEANETTE
BARBARA	JOAN
BERNICE	JOANNE
BETSY	JODY
BETTY	JOY
BEVERLY	JOYCE
BONNIE	JUDY
BRENDA	JUNE
CANDY	KAREN
CAROL	KELLY
CARRIE	KIM
CHARLENE	LARAINE/LORRAINE
CHERYL/SHERYL	LAVERNE
CINDY	LEONA
CONNIE	LINDA
DARLENE	LISA
DENISE	LOIS
DIANE	LORETTA
DOLORES	LUCILLE
DONNA	LYNN
DOREEN	MANDY
DOROTHY	MARCIA/MARSHA
EILEEN	MARCY
ELAINE	MARGERY/MARJORIE
ESTELLE	MARIAN
FRANCINE	MARIANNE
GAIL	MARILYN
GLORIA	MARLENE
HEIDI	MARYLOU
HELENE	MAUREEN

MAXINE	ROBERTA
MINDY	ROCHELLE
MONA	RONA
MURIEL	ROSALIE
MYRA	ROSEANNE
NADINE	SANDRA/SONDRA
NANCY	SHARI
NANETTE	SHARON
NOREEN	SHEILA
NORMA	SHELLEY
PAM	STACEY
PATSY	SUZANNE
PATTY	SYLVIA
PAULA	TERESA
PEGGY	TRACEY
PENNY	TRUDY
PHYLLIS	VIVIAN
RENEE	WENDY
RHODA	WILMA
RHONDA	YVONNE
RITA	ZELDA

BOYS

ALAN	DONALD
BARRY	DUANE/DWAYNE
BRUCE	DWIGHT
CARL	ERNEST
CARY	EUGENE
CLARK	GARTH
CLIFFORD	GARY
DARREN	GERALD
DARRYL	GERARD
DEAN	GILBERT
DENNIS	GLENN

HAROLD	RANDOLPH
HARRIS	ROGER
HOWARD	ROLAND
IRA	RONALD
IRWIN	ROY
IVAN	SIDNEY
JAY	STANLEY
JEROME	STUART/STEWART
JOEL	TERRY
KENNETH	TODD
LANCE	VAUGHN
LARRY	VERNON
LEE	VICTOR
LEONARD	VINCENT
LUTHER	WALLACE
MARSHALL	WARREN
NEIL	WAYNE
NORMAN	WENDELL

So Far Out They'll Probably Always Be Out

When you talk about baby names, there are two words that are very risky to use: always and never. After all, in the first edition of this book, we stated firmly that two names that would never come back were Raymond and Murray. Well, since then, two hip media stars—Jack Nicholson and Lisa Kudrow—have used them for their sons, and others have resurrected such long-slumbering selections as Clara and Ella and Lorraine and Renee and Zelda and Wolfgang, just as Elijah and Isaiah and Abigail are making their way up the popularity charts, and we have a nonmouse movie star named Minnie. Nevertheless, although it is with some trepidation, we submit the

> ### The Eugene Syndrome
> *"I call it the Eugene Syndrome," {Jim} Carrey says, "because my middle name is Eugene. I always figured my parents named me that to keep me humble. You can never get too cool with a name like Eugene."*
>
> *—LOS ANGELES TIMES*

following list of names we're pretty sure are so far out they'll never come back as baby names. Just don't remind us of what we said when Hortense and Herman make it to the top of the list in the year 2020.

GIRLS

BERTHA	HORTENSE
BEULAH	IRMA
DORIS	MILDRED
ENID	MYRNA
ETHEL	SELMA
EUNICE	SHIRLEY
GERTRUDE	THELMA
GLADYS	VELMA
HILDA	VERDA
HILDEGARD	WANDA

BOYS

ADOLPH	HUBERT
ALVIN	HYMAN
ARNOLD	IRVING
BERNARD	JULIUS
BERTRAM	LESTER
BURTON	MARVIN
CLARENCE	MAURICE
EARL	MELVIN
EDGAR	MERVYN
ELMER	MILTON
FRANKLIN	MORTIMER
HERBERT	MORTON
HERMAN	MYRON

OSBERT   SHERMAN
OSWALD   WILBUR
SEYMOUR   WILFRED
SHELDON

POPULARITY

S tyle may in many ways be personal, but it's never isolated: A name's fashion status can only be determined in relation to what everybody else is doing. Here, we look at what the rest of the country—and the rest of the world—is doing about names. You'll find lists of the most popular names in the United States and in several other countries as well. You'll see what the rich and famous, who often influence our own tastes and ideas, are naming their children. And you'll get an insight into how famous names, real and fictional, current and historic, are influencing naming trends.

Prospective parents are increasingly concerned—you might even say obsessed—with issues of popularity.

Some, particularly those with names like Jennifer and Jessica, who suffered the fate of sharing their name with four others in their class when they were growing up, will go to any lengths to avoid similarly common names for their kids. Others take the reverse approach, based on the theory that having a popular and accepted name will make their child feel popular and accepted as well, in synch with the tastes of the times. These days, hardly anyone seems to be neutral. To help deal with this issue, a valuable tool was provided a few years ago, when Michael Shackleford of the Social Security Administration began to issue an annual list of the 1,000 most popular names given to American babies. From that point on, anyone wondering just how widespread Madison or Mason was could consult the Social Security Web site and ascertain the precise standing of each name.

The one caveat stipulated on the site is that different spellings of similar names are not combined, so that, for example, Kaitlin, Kaitlyn, Katelyn, Katelynn, etc., all have separate listings. Since we feel that this completely skews the results, we have undertaken in our list below to treat as one those variations that are essentially the same name, giving a much more realistic picture. This means that, for instance, Kaitlyn, instead of being number 32, as it is on the official ratings, leaps up to take its rightful place as number 7, and Hailey and her sisters jump from 34 to 2. Other names similarly affected because of their multispellings are Brianna, Jasmine, Mackenzie, Kaylee, Madeline, Makayla, Kylie, Riley, Jaden, and Skylar.

Looking at the current list, and comparing it to that of a few years ago, we see certain consistencies, as well as some marked new trends. Emily has been the top girls' name since 1996, and Jacob has held first place since 1999. Emma has catapulted to number three, but the real news here is that, for the first time, the biggest and most surprising differences were to be found on the boys' list, which in the past has been relatively conservative and constant. Sure, prominent spots are still held by the likes of Michael, Matthew, Christopher, Joseph, Andrew, and Daniel. But a massive sea change has taken place in attitudes toward naming boys, as parents have suddenly become much more daring and creative in their choices than ever before. How else to explain the fact that Caden (and Kaden, Cayden, and Kayden) leaped from number 460 on the Social Security list in 1998 to number 59 in 2003, and in the same period, Brayden climbed from 285 to 71 and Jaden rose from 352 to 37, following their more conventional cousin Aidan, who moved from 200 all the way up to 23? Other boys' names moving on up? Ethan, Caleb, Elijah, Mason, and Jackson are following an upward course, while those that have started to slip include Brandon, Tyler, Austin, Kyle, Cody, Dakota, and Tanner: Looks like the baby-cowboy contingent is beginning to ride off into the sunset.

For girls, the epidemic of invented names and trying-to-be-unique spellings (see Kreeatif Names, p. 15) has reached fever pitch, so that the various forms of Kylie have moved from 117 to 31, Skylar, up from 195 to 94, and, most astonishing of all, the ambisexual Jaden, up 770 places from 841 to 71. Two other big success stories among female baby names, both with media boosts, are Aaliyah, which, following the success and tragic death of the single-named singer, went from a low-key 233 to just outside the Top 50, and Trinity, whose big-screen exposure in the *Matrix* movies helped propel it from number 555 five years ago to number 69. As a balance, more traditional names also saw increasing popularity, in particular Sophia, Ava, Isabel and Isabella, Chloe and Zoe, Grace and Faith, Ella and Gabriella, and Mia and Maya (names do often rise in pairs). Falling down, if not off, the Top 100 were nineties' favorites Tiffany, Kelly, Kelsey and Chelsea, Mariah and Miranda.

For the most part, these trends are national, but the parents in some states seem to have minds of their own when it comes to baby naming, so that while Emily and Jacob ruled, they were not number one across the map. On the boys' side, for example, William, in eleventh place nationwide, was the very top choice in five southern states—Alabama, Mississippi, Georgia, South Carolina, and Tennessee. Other boys' names to reach the premier position in at least one state were Daniel, Michael, Matthew, Joshua, Ethan, Anthony, and José, with such surprise breakthroughs into the Top 5 as Caleb in Oklahoma, Samuel and Andrew in Minnesota, Mason and Carter in South Dakota, Gabriel and Isaiah in New Mexico, and also Hunter in Montana, West Virginia, and Wyoming. For the girls, Emily and Emma won almost equal numbers of states' top spots, but they did have some competition, with Madison beating them out in several states, Hannah number one in Alaska, and Alexis in New Mexico. Other isolated examples to make it into the Top 5 included Ashley,

Alyssa, Samantha, Sarah, Abigail, Isabella, Olivia, Mia, Taylor, Kayla, and Grace. Puerto Rico's interesting lineup: Alondra, Paola, Gabriela, Adriana, and Genesis, while Colorado, one of the few states to break names down into ethnic groups, lists the Top 10 African-American names for girls as Jasmine, Taylor, Trinity, Jayla, and Sydney; and for boys, Isaiah, Elijah, Michael, Joshua, and Anthony. In New York City, Jason was identified as the first choice for Asian boys. The State Department of Pennsylvania took a different tack and offered some of the uniquely named babies in its state, including Flame, Fancy, Juniper, Journey, Santa, Mystery, Check, Technique, Church, Pity, Rowdy, Robot, and Deny—none of which is likely to end up on next year's top-of-the-pops list.

A minor trend that has begun to surface on the lower ranks of popularity lists is the growing tendency for naming babies after cars, perfumes, and other commercial products. As outlined in a recent study of baby naming by the psychology department at Bellevue University in Nebraska, there are hundreds of children now coming into the world with such luxury brand names as Armani (both boys and girls), Lexus, Porsche, and Chanel—a trend that we fear could easily get out of hand.

Another point to note when considering the whole topic of popularity is the fact that even the most popular choices are not really as prevalent as they were a hundred years ago when there was a much smaller name pool. In the first decade of the twentieth century, 63 percent of girls and 66 percent of boys received one of the Top 100 names. By contrast, in the last decade of the century, the 1990s, as more and more names were being imported and invented, the dominance of the Top 100 was down to 43 percent, meaning that there are fewer Emilys and Jacobs today than there were—in proportion to the population—Johns and Marys in 1904.

Here, the Top 100 names for girls and the Top 100 names for boys in 2003. Note that the most commonly used spelling variations are given in italics.

THE TOP 100 GIRLS' NAMES

1. EMILY, *Emilee, Emely, etc.*
2. HAILEY, *Haley, Hayley, etc.*
3. EMMA
4. MADISON, *Madisyn, Madyson, etc.*
5. HANNAH, *Hanna, Hana*
6. BRIANNA, *Breanna, Briana, etc.*
7. KAITLYN, *Katelyn, Caitlin, etc.*
8. SARAH, *Sara*
9. ABIGAIL, *Abbigail, Abigayle, etc.*
10. ASHLEY, *Ashleigh, Ashlee, etc.*
11. OLIVIA
12. ALEXIS, *Alexus, Alexys*
13. ALYSSA, *Alissa, Alisa, etc.*
14. ELIZABETH, *Elisabeth*
15. ISABELLA, *Izabella*
16. SAMANTHA
17. KATHERINE, *Catherine, Kathryn, etc.*
18. SOPHIA, *Sofia*
19. GRACE
20. KAYLA, *Kaila, Cayla, etc.*
21. ANNA, *Ana*
22. LAUREN, *Lauryn, Loren*
23. JASMINE, *Jasmin, Jazmine, etc.*
24. MAKAYLA, *Mikayla, Michaela, etc.*
25. MADELINE, *Madelyn, Madeleine, etc.*
26. TAYLOR, *Tayler*
27. NATALIE, *Nataly, Nathalie, etc.*
28. JESSICA
29. SYDNEY, *Sidney, Sydni*
30. MEGAN, *Meghan, Meagan*
31. KYLIE, *Kylee, Kiley, etc.*
32. MACKENZIE, *Mckenzie, Makenzie*

33. CHLOE
34. VICTORIA
35. ALLISON, *Alison, Allyson*
36. KAYLEE, *Kailey, Kaylie, etc.*
37. RACHEL, *Rachael*
38. SAVANNAH, *Savanna, Savanah, etc.*
39. DESTINY, *Destinee, Destiney, etc.*
40. JENNIFER, *Jenifer*
41. MORGAN
42. GABRIELLA, *Gabriela*
43. JORDAN, *Jordyn*
44. RILEY, *Rylee, Rylie, etc.*
45. MAYA, *Mya, Maia, etc.*
46. JULIA
47. MIA, *Miah*
48. ISABEL, *Isabelle, Isabell*
49. ZOE, *Zoey, Zoie*
50. REBECCA, *Rebekah, Rebecah*
51. NICOLE, *Nichole*
52. ALEXANDRA
53. MARIA
54. AVA
55. BROOKE, *Brook*
56. STEPHANIE, *Stephany*
57. LILY, *Lilly, Lillie*
58. ELLA
59. PAIGE
60. SIERRA, *Cierra, Ciera*
61. FAITH
62. JADA, *Jayda, Jaida, etc.*
63. AMANDA
64. AALIYAH, *Aliyah, Aliya*
65. JENNA
66. JACQUELINE, *Jaqueline, Jacquelyn, etc.*
67. CAROLINE, *Carolyn*
68. ANDREA
69. TRINITY
70. CHRISTINA, *Kristina, Cristina*
71. JADEN, *Jayden, Jadyn, etc.*
72. MARY
73. LESLIE, *Lesly, Lesley*
74. MICHELLE
75. KIMBERLY
76. ADRIANA, *Adrianna*
77. LEAH, *Lia, Lea*
78. ALEXA
79. BAILEY, *Baylee, Bailee*
80. VANESSA, *Vanesa*
81. GABRIELLE

82. LILLIAN, *Lilian*
83. ARIANNA, *Aryanna, Aryana*
84. MARISSA, *Marisa*
85. ERICA, *Erika, Ericka*
86. AMBER
87. MELANIE, *Melany*
88. LINDSEY, *Lindsay, Lyndsey*
89. AUTUMN
90. CLAIRE, *Clare*
91. AUDREY
92. ERIN
93. DANIELLE
94. SKYLAR, *Skyler, Skyla*
95. AVERY
96. COURTNEY, *Kourtney*
97. SHELBY
98. MELISSA
99. JADE
100. MOLLY

THE TOP 100 BOYS' NAMES

1. JACOB, *Jakob, Jakobe*
2. MICHAEL, *Micheal*
3. MATTHEW, *Mathew*
4. JOSHUA
5. NICHOLAS, *Nicolas, Nickolas*
6. CHRISTOPHER, *Kristopher, Cristopher*
7. ANDREW
8. ETHAN, *Ethen*
9. JOSEPH
10. DANIEL
11. ANTHONY
12. WILLIAM
13. RYAN
14. JONATHAN, *Johnathon, Jonathon*
15. DAVID
16. TYLER, *Tylor*
17. ALEXANDER, *Alexzander*
18. DYLAN, *Dillon, Dillan*
19. JOHN, *Jon*
20. CHRISTIAN, *Cristian, Kristian*
21. ZACHARY, *Zackary, Zackery*
22. JAMES
23. AIDAN, *Aiden, Aden*
24. BRANDON, *Branden*
25. CALEB, *Kaleb*

Make Way for José

Move over, John. Make way for José, which has become the most popular baby boy's name in California and Texas. For much of the last two centuries, experts say, immigrants chose so-called "American" names as a way of assimilating into their new lives. Not so long ago, José would probably have been Joseph . . . but no longer. "This gives us a window on society of how much things have changed," said Edward Callary, professor of English at Northern Illinois University and editor of the American Name Society's journal. "Thirty years ago, most people would not have given their child an ethnic name. A lot of folks tried to blend in and fold into American society as quickly as they could."

But even in the choice of José, some Latino parents say they are bowing to American sensibilities. It is widely recognized and easy to pronounce. "Imagine the problems I would have to pass my name on to my son," said Gildardo Vasquez.

—MEGAN GARVEY AND PATRICK J. MCDONNELL,
LOS ANGELES TIMES

26. SAMUEL
27. BRIAN, *Bryan*
28. BENJAMIN
29. JUSTIN, *Justyn*
30. NATHAN, *Nathen*
31. JOSE
32. LOGAN
33. CONNOR, *Conner, Conor*
34. GABRIEL
35. ERIC, *Erik, Erick*
36. KEVIN
37. JAYDEN, *Jaden, Jaiden, etc.*
38. AUSTIN, *Austen*
39. NOAH
40. ROBERT
41. CAMERON, *Kameron, Camron*
42. THOMAS

43. JASON, *Jayson*
44. ELIJAH
45. SEAN, *Shawn, Shaun*
46. JACKSON, *Jaxon, Jaxson*
47. HUNTER
48. ANGEL
49. EVAN
50. JACK
51. GAVIN, *Gaven, Gavyn, etc.*
52. STEVEN, *Stephen, Stephan, etc.*
53. LUKE
54. ISAAC, *Isaak*
55. KYLE
56. LUIS
57. DEVIN, *Devon*
58. JUAN
59. CADEN, *Kaden, Cayden*
60. MASON
61. COLIN, *Collin*
62. CHARLES
63. ADAM
64. NATHANIEL, *Nathanael, Nathanial*
65. DOMINIC, *Dominick, Dominik*
66. ALEX
67. LUCAS, *Lukas*
68. CARLOS
69. IAN
70. ADRIAN, *Adrien*

71. BRAYDEN, *Braden, Braydon*
72. JESUS
73. COLE
74. CODY, *Kody*
75. JULIAN, *Julien*
76. DIEGO
77. TIMOTHY
78. TRISTAN, *Tristen, Triston, etc.*
79. HAYDEN, *Haden*
80. BLAKE
81. JESSE, *Jessie*
82. SETH
83. CARSON, *Karson*
84. XAVIER
85. RICHARD
86. JALEN, *Jaylen, Jaylon*
87. CHASE
88. SEBASTIAN
89. JEREMIAH
90. PATRICK
91. ANTONIO
92. RILEY, *Rylee, Reilly*
93. ALEJANDRO
94. JAKE
95. LANDON
96. TREVOR
97. GARRETT, *Garett, Garret*
98. JEREMY
99. DEREK, *Derrick, Derick*
100. COLBY, *Kolby*

But I've Always Loved Emily

Oh, no! Ever since the days when you were playing house and cutting out paper dolls, you've planned to name your first daughter Emily. But now that the time has almost arrived, you find that thousands of other mothers got there first and Emily is currently the most popular girl's name in the country. What to do?

Well, you've got two options. You can stick with your lifelong love and risk the perils of popularity described above. Or you can look for a worthy substitute, a name that relates to your first choice in either style or sound or ethnicity. To help you in the process, here is a list of possible substitutes, all at least a shade more creative and crisp than the original.

GIRLS

Instead of:

ALEXANDRA	ARABELLA, ALBANY, ANASTASIA
ALYSSA	ALEXA, ALICE, ALICIA
AMANDA	AMABEL, AMITY
ASHLEY	AVERY, ASTRID
BAILEY	BELLAMY, BAY
BRIANNA	BREE, ARIANA, BRYONY, BIANCA
BRITTANY	BRONTË, PARIS
CHELSEA	CELESTE, LONDON
COURTNEY	KENNEDY, CORDELIA
DANIELLE	LUCIENNE, DANICA, DELILAH
EMILY	EMMELINE, EMELIA, ELLERY
EMMA	GEMMA, ELIZA, JANE
HALEY	HELENA, HARLEY, HAZEL
HANNAH	DINAH, ANYA, LEAH
JASMINE	LILAC, JAMAICA, YASMIN

JENNIFER ..... GENEVIEVE, GEMMA, JENICA
JESSICA .... JESSA, JESSAMINE, JERSEY
JORDAN ...... GEORGIA, JUSTINE, GEORGE
KAITLYN ...... BRONWYN, KATYA
KAYLA .... LAYLA, KAY, KAIA
KELSEY ...... GELSEY, KALINDI
KIMBERLY ..... KIRBY, KIMBALL
KRISTIN ..... INGRID, BRITTA, CHRISTIANE
LAUREN ...... LAUREL, LAURENCE, NORA
MADISON ..... MAISIE, INDIANA, MADALENA
MEGAN .... REGAN, MARGARET, MARINE
MELISSA ...... LARISSA, MELANTHA, MELISANDE
NICOLE .... NICO, NICOLA
SAMANTHA .... SUSANNAH, SAMARA, SAWYER
SARAH .... SAHAR, SERENA, SALLY
SHELBY .... TRILBY, SICILY
TAYLOR ...... THALIA, THEA, TALIA

BOYS

AARON .... ABEL, ABNER, ASA
ALEX .... ALEC, LEX, ASHER
ALEXANDER ... CONSTANTINE, ALASDAIR
AUSTIN .... AUGUST, HOUSTON
BRANDON ..... BRAM, BRANIGAN
CAMERON ..... ANGUS, MALCOLM, CAMPBELL
CHRISTOPHER .. CRISPIN, CHRISTO, KRISTOF
CODY .... RIDER, CROSBY
CONNOR ...... QUINN, CALLUM
COOPER ...... KENYON, SLATER
DUSTIN .... DUNCAN, DUFF
DYLAN .... FINN, KILLIAN, DEXTER
JACOB .... JAMES, JETHRO, JONAH
JAKE .... JOE, MOE
JORDAN ...... GEORGE, OWEN, GORDON

```
JOSHUA . . . . . . . JOSIAH, ISAIAH
JUSTIN  . . . . . . . JULIAN, JASPER
KYLE . . . . . . . . KAI, KANE
LOGAN  . . . . . . . HOGAN, LORCAN
MATTHEW  . . . . MATTHIAS, MATHIS, MATTEO
MAX . . . . . . . . . MAC, GUS
RYAN  . . . . . . . . CORMAC, RILEY, O'BRIEN
SEAN . . . . . . . . . SEAMUS, SHAW
TREVOR  . . . . . . GRAHAM, ADRIAN, COLIN
TYLER . . . . . . . . TOBIAS, CYRUS
ZACHARY  . . . . . ZEBEDEE, ZANE, BARNABY
```

Regional Flavor

Over the years, certain names have taken on regional accents, often as much from literature and movies as from real life. What, for example, could Scarlett be but a Southern belle, and Rhett but her male counterpart? Prudence and Priscilla have a distinctly New England aura, and it's hard not to picture Dallas riding the range. So although this may smack of stereotyping and, in an era when national media influences have blurred geographical differences, little Scarlett Prudence may at this moment be playing in her Boise backyard, we still offer these lists for parents seeking a name with a zonal feel.

Southern Belles & Beaus

GIRLS

ABRA	ARABELLA
ACACIA	ATLANTA
ALTHEA	AURELIA

AURORA	GEORGIA
BELLE	HALLIE
BETHANY	HARPER
BETHIA	HYACINTH
BEULAH	IVY
BLOSSOM	JASMINE
CALISTA	JEMIMA
CALLA	JEZEBEL
CAMELIA	LACEY
CAMILLA	LAVINIA
CATALINA	LETITIA
CHLOE	LOUELLA
CLARISSA	LUCINDA
CLEMENTINE	MAGNOLIA
CORDELIA	MARIAH
CORINNE	MELANTHA
DAISY	MELISANDE
DELIA	MIRABELLE
DELILAH	MIRANDA
DELTA	ODELIA
DESIRÉE	PEYTON
DIANTHA	RUBY
DINAH	SABRINA
DIXIE	SAVANNAH
DULCY	SCARLETT
EMMALINE	SELENA
ESMÉ	SUSANNAH
EUDORA	TALLULAH
EVANGELINE	TANSY
FALLON	VIOLET
FLORIDA	VIRGINIA

BOYS

ABBOTT	JACKSON
ABSALOM	JARED
ALONZO	JASPER
ASA	JEFFERSON
ASHLEY	JETHRO
BARNABY	JUDAH
BENEDICT	KENYON
BLAKE	KIMBALL
BRETT	LOGAN
BURL	MACON
CAMERON	MOSES
CHAUNCEY	MOSS
CLAY	QUENTIN
DARCY	REED
DAVIS	RHETT
DEVEREUX	RUFUS
DEX	SAWYER
DORIAN	SCHUYLER
GARETH	TANNER
GUY	THADDEUS
HARPER	TRAVIS
HYATT	VIRGIL
JABEZ	YANCY

Western Cowboys

AUSTIN	CHEYENNE
BEAU	CLINT
BEN	CLYDE
BRADY	CODY
BUCK	DALLAS
CASSIDY	DALTON

GANDY	LUKE
JACK	MATT
JAKE	SAM
JEB	SIERRA
JED	WYATT
JESSE	ZEB

New England Names

GIRLS

ABIGAIL	MARTHA
AGATHA	MATILDA
AMITY	MAUDE
CLARA	PATIENCE
EDWINA	PRISCILLA
ELIZA	PRUDENCE
EMILY	PRUNELLA
FAITH	UNITY
GRACE	VERITY
HONOR	WINIFRED
HOPE	ZENOBIA
KETURAH	

BOYS

AMBROSE	DUDLEY
ARCHIBALD	EBENEZER
AUGUSTUS	ELIHU
BARTHOLOMEW	EMORY
CALEB	EVERETT
CALVIN	EZRA
CHESTER	FRANCIS
CLIFFORD	HIRAM
CORNELIUS	HOMER
DEXTER	HUGH

ICHABOD	NOAH
ISAIAH	OGDEN
ISHMAEL	PRESCOTT
JEREMIAH	QUINCY
JONAH	SPENCER
JOSIAH	TITUS
LELAND	TOBIAS
LEMUEL	WINSLOW
LOWELL	WINSTON
NATHANIEL	ZACHARIAS

What the Rest of the World Is Doing

It is interesting to look at the top names in other countries, both to see international trends and to find more region-specific favorites that might match your own ethnic roots. Certain names are enjoying enormous popularity in many different parts of the world: Chloe, for example, is number one in England and Scotland and high on the lists in Canada, Ireland, Australia, France, and Belgium. Also multinational are Hannah/Hana and Anna/Ana, Megan, Sophia/Sofia, Sarah/Sara (the last is big in Germany and Spain), and Emma (number one in Sweden), while male classics such as Thomas, Jack, James, Daniel, and Joshua maintain a strong international presence. Among the names that are megapopular in some countries but would make unusual and appealing selections here would be Emy (Quebec), Manon and Oceane (France), Fleur (the Netherlands), Violeta, Pilar, Amalia, and Catalina (Spain), Linnea (Sweden), Viivi (Finland), Alla (Russia), Riko (Japan), Collum (England), Lachlan (Australia), and Vadim (Russia).

Canada

The most recent popularity list from our next-door neighbor includes two U.S. geographical imports—Madison and Brooklyn:

GIRLS	BOYS
1. EMILY	ETHAN
2. EMMA	JOSHUA
3. MADISON	MATTHEW
4. SARAH	JACOB
5. HANNAH	RYAN
6. SYDNEY	LOGAN
7. MEGAN	NICHOLAS
8. ASHLEY	TYLER
9. TAYLOR	DYLAN
10. PAIGE	CONNOR
11. SAMANTHA	DANIEL
12. OLIVIA	ALEXANDER
13. JESSICA	ZACHARY
14. HAILEY	WILLIAM
15. GRACE	KYLE
16. MACKENZIE	LIAM
17. KAITLYN	NOAH
18. ABIGAIL	NATHAN
19. ISABELLA	BENJAMIN
20. JENNA	COLE
21. CHLOE	BRANDON
22. ALYSSA	AUSTIN
23. LAUREN	MICHAEL
24. JULIA	AIDAN
25. BROOKLYN	JUSTIN

In addition, the Canadian roster included babies named Autumn, Summer, Spring, Winter, and Wynter. The province of Alberta produced one or more children called Rocky, Rockey, Echo, Sky, Star, Meadow, River, Timber, Sunny, Sunshine, Storm, Stormy, and Cool.

The province of Quebec has two separate lists for their French- and English-speaking populations. Top 10 for each are:

(FRENCH)

GIRLS	BOYS
1. MEGANE	WILLIAM
2. LAURIE	JEREMIE
3. CAMILLE	SAMUEL
4. ARIANE	GABRIEL
5. SARAH	XAVIER
6. NOEMIE	OLIVIER
7. GABRIELLE	ANTHONY
8. EMY	MATHIS
9. AUDREY	ZACHARIE
10. MAUDE	FELIX

(ENGLISH)

GIRLS	BOYS
1. SARAH	DANIEL
2. EMILY	NICHOLAS
3. EMMA	JOSHUA
4. MADISON	DAVID
5. JULIA	MATTHEW
6. SOPHIA	MICHAEL

	GIRLS	BOYS
7.	BRIANNA	TYLER
8.	JESSICA	LUCAS
9.	MEGAN	MOHAMMAD
10.	MARIA	BRANDON

Moving across the ocean to other English-speaking countries:

England & Wales

	GIRLS	BOYS
1.	CHLOE (*sixth year in a row*)	JACK (*eighth year in a row*)
2.	EMILY	JOSHUA
3.	JESSICA	THOMAS
4.	ELLIE	JAMES
5.	SOPHIE	DANIEL
6.	MEGAN	BENJAMIN
7.	CHARLOTTE	WILLIAM
8.	LUCY	SAMUEL
9.	HANNAH	JOSEPH
10.	OLIVIA	OLIVER
11.	LAUREN	HARRY
12.	KATIE	MATTHEW
13.	AMY	LUKE
14.	MOLLY	LEWIS
15.	HOLLY	GEORGE
16.	ELLA	COLLUM
17.	BETHANY	ADAM
18.	REBECCA	ETHAN
19.	GRACE	ALEXANDER
20.	MIA	RYAN
21.	GEORGIA	BEN

22. ABIGAIL	MOHAMMED
23. CAITLIN	LIAM
24. LEA	JAKE
25. AMELIA	NATHAN

One recent development in the British Top 100 is the marked increase in the use of short forms as full given names, including Ellie, Katie, Millie, Rosie, Libby, Evie, and Charlie for girls and Charlie (again), Jamie, Alfie, Ben, Joe, Archie, Sam, Billy, Josh, and Tom for boys. Some other names that have scaled the heights of name popularity in England but have not yet made it in this country are: Georgia and Georgina, Amelia, Alice, Phoebe, Daisy, Maisie, Freya, Niamh, Harriet, Imogen, Eve, Louise, and Poppy; and Callum, Toby, Kai, Kian, Oscar, Finlay, Ewan, Ellis, and Kieron.

Scotland

In neighboring Scotland, these names took the Top 25 places:

GIRLS	BOYS
1. CHLOE	JACK
2. SOPHIE	LEWIS
3. EMMA	CAMERON
4. AMY	RYAN
5. ERIN	JAMES
6. ELLIE	JAMIE
7. RACHEL	LIAM
8. LAUREN	MATTHEW
9. MEGAN	ROSS
10. HANNAH	CALLUM

11.	REBECCA	DYLAN
12.	EMILY	KYLE
13.	CAITLIN	BEN
14.	LUCY	CONNOR
15.	HOLLY	ADAM
16.	KATIE	DANIEL
17.	NICOLE	ANDREW
18.	SARAH	SCOTT
19.	ABBIE	KIERAN
20.	MORGAN	NATHAN
21.	ANNA	AIDAN
22.	NIAMH	MICHAEL
23.	SHANNON	JOSHUA
24.	EILIDH	THOMAS
25.	ZOE	DAVID

Ireland

Eight traditional Gaelic names are found among the Irish Top 25:

GIRLS		BOYS
1.	SARAH	JACK
2.	AOIFE	SEAN
3.	CIARA	ADAM
4.	EMMA	CONOR
5.	CHLOE	JAMES
6.	AMY	DANIEL
7.	KATIE	CIAN
8.	NIAMH	MICHAEL
9.	SOPHIE	DAVID
10.	LAUREN	LUKE
11.	MEGAN	DYLAN

GIRLS	BOYS
12. HANNAH	AARON
13. RACHEL	PATRICK
14. REBECCA	RYAN
15. LEAH	JOHN
16. LAURA	EOIN
17. JESSICA	MATTHEW
18. KATE	THOMAS
19. EMILY	BEN
20. CAOIMHE	JOSHUA
21. ANNA	SHANE
22. SHAUNA	MARK
23. ELLEN	JAMIE
24. NICOLE	DARRAGH
25. ROISIN	OISIN

In Northern Ireland, the list is very similar, except that Chloe is the top name for girls, and some of the Gaelic names, such as Cian and Aiofe, do not appear in the Top 25.

Australia

Australia and New Zealand show fewer regional differences than might be expected:

GIRLS	BOYS
1. EMILY	LACHLAN
2. OLIVIA	JACK
3. ELLA	JOSHUA
4. GEORGIA	THOMAS
5. CHLOE	SAMUEL
6. SOPHIE	BENJAMIN
7. JESSICA	LIAM
8. EMMA	ETHAN

	GIRLS	BOYS
9.	ISABELLA	WILLIAM
10.	CHARLOTTE	MATTHEW
11.	SARAH	LUKE
12.	HANNAH	JAMES
13.	GRACE	MITCHELL
14.	ZOE	NICHOLAS
15.	AMY	DANIEL
16.	RUBY	JORDAN
17.	LUCY	HARRISON
18.	MIA	RYAN
19.	CAITLIN	ALEXANDER
20.	HAYLEY	MAX

New Zealand

	GIRLS	BOYS
1.	JESSICA	JOSHUA
2.	OLIVIA	JACK
3.	HANNAH	SAMUEL
4.	EMMA	BENJAMIN
5.	SOPHIE	ETHAN
6.	GRACE	JAMES
7.	SARAH	LIAM
8.	ELLA	THOMAS
9.	GEORGIA	JACOB
10.	EMILY	DANIEL

Crossing over to the continent of Europe, we find much more distinctive national differences:

Germany

GIRLS	BOYS
1. MARIE	ALEXANDER
2. SOPHIE	MAXIMILIAN
3. MARIA	PAUL
4. ANNA	LEON
5. LAURA	LUKAS
6. LEA	JAN
7. KATHARINA	NIKLAS
8. SARAH	TIM
9. JULIA	DANIEL
10. LENA	JONAS

France

The Top 10 names for *jeunes filles* and *petits garçons* are:

GIRLS	BOYS
1. LEA	THEO
2. CHLOE	HUGO
3. EMMA	LUCAS
4. CAMILLE	THOMAS
5. MANON	QUENTIN

Also popular for French baby girls: Sarah, Oceane, Margaux, Mathilde, Emma, Marie, Julie and Laura; for boys: Alexandre, Alexis, Nicolas, Antoine, Maxime, Valentin and Clement.

The Netherlands

In Holland, the most popular names are for the most part short and straightforward. The distinctive girl's name Sanne has been number one for several years.

	GIRLS	BOYS
1.	SANNE	THOMAS/TOMAS
2.	LISA/LIZA	DAAN
3.	ANNE	RICK/RIK
4.	FLEUR	TIM
5.	ANNA	LUUK/LUC/LUKE
6.	IRIS	LARS
7.	BRITT	MAX
8.	JULIA	TOM/THOM
9.	SARAH/SARA	LUCAS/LUKAS
10.	SOPHIE/SOFIE	NIELS/NILS

Belgium

	GIRLS	BOYS
1.	LAURA	THOMAS
2.	MARIE	MAXIME
3.	EMMA	LUCAS
4.	SARAH	NICOLAS
5.	JULIE	ROBBE
6.	MANON	NOAH
7.	CHARLOTTE	LOUIS
8.	AMBER	NATHAN
9.	LISA	ARTHUR
10.	CAMILLE	SIMON

Italy

A strong percentage of top Italian names are venerable classics—the equivalents of John and Mary.

GIRLS	BOYS
1. MARIA	GIUSEPPE
2. ANNA	GIOVANNI
3. GIUSEPPINA	ANTONIO
4. ROSA	MARIO
5. ANGELA	LUIGI
6. GIOVANNA	FRANCESCO
7. TERESA	ANGELO
8. LUCIA	VINCENZO
9. CARMELA	PIETRO
10. CATERINA	SALVATORE
11. FRANCESCA	CARLO
12. ANNA MARIA	FRANCO
13. ANTONIETTA	DOMENICO
14. CARLA	BRUNO
15. ELENA	PAOLO
16. CONCETTA	MICHELE
17. RITA	GIORGIO
18. MARGHERITA	ALDO
19. FRANCA	SERGIO
20. PAOLA	LUCIANO

Spain

Here, as in many other countries, boy babies tend to be given traditional names, while parents are more creative when it comes to girls:

GIRLS	BOYS
1. ANNA	ALEJANDRO
2. ISABEL	JORGE
3. NADIA	JUAN
4. PILAR	JOSE
5. NURIA	PEDRO
6. ELENA	CARLOS
7. SARA	MIGUEL
8. AMALIA	JAVIER

Norway

Norway, like France and Germany, has strict laws governing first names—for the most part, only established personal names on an official list can be used.

GIRLS	BOYS
1. IDA	MARTIN
2. THEA	SANDER
3. JULIE	JONAS
4. NORA	MATHIAS
5. EMMA	ANDREAS

Sweden

GIRLS	BOYS
1. EMMA	OSCAR
2. ELIN	ERIK
3. JULIA	FILIP
4. HANNA	EMIL

5. LINNEA	ALEXANDER
6. IDA	WILLIAM
7. WILMA	ANTON
8. MATILDA	LUCAS
9. MOA	VIKTOR
10. AMANDA	SIMON

Finland

Many Finnish names are filled with more vowels than we are accustomed to, giving them an energetic air:

GIRLS	BOYS
1. SARA	EETU
2. VIIVI	JUKO
3. EMMA	NIKO
4. ANNI	JERE
5. NEA	VEETI

Other Finnish favorites are, for girls: Veera, Iida, Roosa, Nea, Noora, Oona, and Aino; for boys: Ville, Juho, Joona, Leevi, Joonas, and Arttu.

Croatia

GIRLS	BOYS
1. SARA	LUKA
2. LUCIJA (*Loo-SEE-yah*)	IVAN
3. HANA	MARKO

4. KLARA   JAN
5. ANA   FILIP

Russia

Since no official popularity list for Russian names is available, here are some top current names, not given in order:

GIRLS	BOYS
ALEXANDRA/SASHA/SHURA	ALEXANDR/SASHA
ALLA	ALEXEY/ALEXEI
ANNA/ANJA	ANATOLY
IRINA/IRA	ANDREY
KSENIA	BORIS
LARISA/LARA	DMITRY
LJUDMILA/MILA	GENNADY/GENA
LUDOVINE/LUDOVICA	IGOR
NATALIA/NATASHA	KONSTANTIN
SVETLANA	LEONID
TATIANA/TANJA	MAXIM
VALENTINA	MIKHAIL/MISHA
VERA	NIKOLAY
VIKTORIA/VIKA	OLEG
YEKATERINA/EKATERINA/	PAVEL
KATJA	ROMAN
YELENA/LENA	SERGEY/SERGEI
YULIA/YULJA	VADIM
	VALERY
	VIKTOR
	VLADIMIR
	YURY

Good-bye, Dick; Good-bye, Jane

First-time parents, unaware of today's wild baby-naming trends, often ask, "Where do you guys get this stuff?" No, we don't make it up. We track class lists and birth announcements, on the statistically grounded theory that more adventurous names favored by fashion-forward big-city parents tend to make their way over the years to the population at large. Here, a list of the names of children at two hip nursery schools, one in Tribeca and one in L.A., which evidence many of the naming trends detailed in our What's Hot and What's Cool sections. And there's nary a Dick or Jane in sight.

GIRLS

ADE	MAXINE
ANAIS	PERSEPHONE
DAHLIA	QUILLER
ELLA	RAVEN
JULIA	SONIA
LILY	THAIS
MAIA	UMA
MARISA	ZOE
MASHA	

BOYS

BREAKER	NAZARETH
CYRIL	NOLAN
DEXTER	OWEN
GRAHAM	RAY
JASPER	SAMSON
MILES	SAWYER
NATE	THEODORE

Whether we care to admit it or not, we're all influenced to some degree by what celebrities do and say, how they wear their hair, and choose their clothes, and decorate their homes. We're also extremely interested in what they name their babies, partly because they've set so many trends in this area, but also because with names, the playing field is leveled—we don't need money or talent or beauty or fame to choose star-quality names for our own children—just star-quality taste and cool.

Stars have been blazing fresh trails for several years now, beginning when, almost simultaneously, Melanie Griffith and Don Johnson had a daughter they named Dakota and Melissa Gilbert had a son she also named Dakota. The confluence of these choices started two important naming trends, opening up a whole new territory of unisex names, and putting Western place names on the map. Other high-profile celebrities followed suit, calling their kids Montana, Sierra, and Cheyenne, and before long some of these newly coined names were among the most popular in America.

Stretching the limits even further were the names of

William and Harry rocketed in popularity among Times *readers naming their babies immediately after the death of Diana, Princess of Wales. At the same time, Charles dipped dramatically. As the nation mourned the Princess, new parents appear to have paid their own tribute by naming their children after her sons. The name William appeared twice as often in the September birth columns as it did in any other month; Harry's appearances were up a third that month, while Charles went into temporary decline . . . Diana's Christian name is, however, nowhere near as popular as the Princess was herself and the name appeared only once in the birth columns—back in the spring.*

—HELEN RUMEBELOW,
BRITAIN

the three Demi Moore—Bruce Willis girls. First came Rumer Glenn, inspired by the Anglo-Indian novelist Rumer Godden. She was followed by Scout LaRue, whose first name harks back to the nickname of the tomboy character in *To Kill a Mockingbird.* And finally, they were joined by the saucy Tallulah Belle.

But surely the most publicized and eagerly awaited celebrity baby-name decision was that buzzing around Madonna's little girl. For months, there were discussions in newspaper and magazine columns, on television and radio shows, until finally the pundits declared that a name had been chosen. And the name was—Lola. It seemed like a perfect choice, a name that oozes sex and determination, one that suited Madonna herself. Whatever Lola wants, Lola gets. But then, at the last minute, it was announced that Mama Madonna didn't want the name Lola for her child at all, choosing instead a dark horse of a name that was less flashy, more unusual, but in the end even more appropriate for her offspring. Madonna's daughter would be called Lourdes, the name of the French town where the original Madonna is said to have appeared to Saint Bernadette. And her nickname is—Lola.

But even though we're not all rushing to name our own babies Lourdes or Scout or Rebop (as Todd Rundgren did), the trend among celebrities toward ever-more-outrageous baby names reflects and influences our own increasing penchant for distinctive names and also inspires us mere mortals to stretch the baby-naming boundaries further and further beyond Madison and Montana. They've pointed the way toward a new world of place names (Kim Basinger and Alec Baldwin's Ireland, for example), characters from literature (Gary Oldman's Gulliver), boys' names for girls (Kelsey Grammer's Mason), word names (Christie Brinkley's daughter Sailor), formerly fusty names (Jude Law's Iris), and in many other novel directions as well.

To help make sense of how starbaby names dovetail with the major naming trends today, we divide this list into categories you'll recognize from the Style section. We've restricted our list to relatively recently born children of well-known celebrities. Middle names appear when they were accessible. And again we admit that we do realize that none of these children arrived without two parents, and offer our apologies to those lesser-known parents who might not have received billing here.

The Three R's

Robert Rodriguez, director of the *Spy Kids* movies and *Once upon a Time in Mexico,* named his three sons Racer, Rebel, and Rocket. In a more delicate vein, actress Poppy Montgomery—her full name is Poppy Petal Ema Elizabeth Devereaux Donahue—is one of five sisters, all of whom have floral names: Rosie Thorn, Daisy Yellow, Marigold Sun, and Lily Belle. The sole son in the family is called Jethro Tull.

Hotties

Here are the trendiest starbaby names of the moment and the celebrity parents who picked them:

AUGUST.................. *Garth Brooks, Lena Olin, Jeanne Tripplehorn*

AVA .... *Gil Bellows, Heather Locklear & Richie Sambora, John McEnroe, Aidan Quinn, Reese Witherspoon & Ryan Philippe, Peri Gilpin*

CHARLES .... *Russell Crowe, Julia Louis Dreyfuss & Brad Hall, Jodie Foster, Cynthia Nixon, Chris O'Donnell, (Dixie Chick) Emily Robison*

CHARLOTTE............. *Amy Brenneman, Harry Connick Jr., Sigourney Weaver*

DAISY .... *Lucy Lawless, Jamie (Naked Chef) Oliver, Markie Post*

DASHIELL .... *Harry Anderson, Cate Blanchett, Alice Cooper, Lisa Rinna & Harry Hamlin*

DYLAN .... *Pamela Anderson & Tommy Lee, Tracy Austin, Pierce Brosnan, Joan Cusack, Kenneth "Babyface" Edmons,*

Catherine Zeta Jones & Michael Douglas, Stephanie Seymour, Robin Wright & Sean Penn

ELIJAH .... *Bono, Wynonna Judd, James Spader, Tiffany, Donnie Wahlberg*

ELLA .... *Annette Bening & Warren Beatty, Eric Clapton, Kelly Preston & John Travolta, Gary Sinese, Ben Stiller, Mark Wahlberg*

ESMÉ .... *Anthony Edwards, Samantha Morton, Tracy Pollan & Michael J. Fox, Meshach Taylor*

GRACE .... *Lance Armstrong, Faith Hill, Wynonna Judd, Dave Matthews, Rupert Murdoch, Lou Diamond Phillips, Christy Turlington & Ed Burns*

HANNAH .... *Jilly Mack & Tom Selleck, Elizabeth Perkins, Helen Slater, Kristin Scott Thomas, Vendela*

HENRY .... *Julia Louis Dreyfuss & Brad Hall, Dennis Hopper, Amanda Pays & Corbin Bernsen, Steve Zahn*

HOMER .... *Anne Heche, Carey Lowell & Richard Gere, Bill Murray*

ISABELLA .... *Nicole Kidman & Tom Cruise, Lorenzo Lamas, Lori Laughlin, Jane Leeves, Andrew Lloyd Webber, Chelsea Noble & Kirk Cameron, Lou Diamond Phillips*

JACK .... *Ellen Barkin & Gabriel Byrne, Christie Brinkley, Matt Lauer, Virginia Madsen & Antonio Sabato Jr., Chelsea Noble & Kirk Cameron, Vanessa Paradis & Johnny Depp, Luke Perry, Bill Pullman, Meg Ryan & Dennis Quaid, Susan Sarandon & Tim Robbins, Joanne Whalley & Val Kilmer, Mare Winningham*

JACKSON .... *Maria Bello, Susanna Hoffs, Spike Lee, (Dixie Chick) Natalie Maines & Adrian Pasdar, Katey Sagal, Patti Smith*

JADEN .... *David Boreanaz, Steffi Graf & Andre Agassi, Jada Pinkett & Will Smith, Cheryl Tiegs, (JADON: Christian Slater)*

JAMES .... *Kirk Cameron & Chelsea Noble, Colin Farrell, Sarah Jessica Parker & Matthew Broderick, Liz Phair, Annie Potts*

JULIAN .... *Robert De Niro, Lisa Kudrow, Jessica Sklar & Jerry Seinfeld*

LILY .... *Kate Beckinsale, Lisa Hartman & Clint Black, Kathy Ireland, Greg Kinnear, Amy Madigan & Ed Harris, Chris O'Donnell, Vanessa Paradis & Johnny Depp, Meredith Viera*

LOLA .... *Jennie Garth, Annie Lennox, Kate Moss, Kelly Ripa & Mark Consuelos, Chris Rock*

MASON .... *Josie Bisette & Rob Estes, Cuba Gooding Jr., Kelsey Grammer, Laura San Giacomo*

MILES .... *Lionel Richie, Susan Sarandon & Tim Robbins, Elisabeth Shue*

OLIVIA................... *Beverly D'Angelo & Al Pacino, Lori Loughlin, Julianne Moore, Denzel Washington*

OWEN .... *Phoebe Cates & Kevin Kline, Ricki Lake, Christopher Reeve, Noah Wyle*

PARIS .... *Pierce Brosnan, Michael Jackson, Blair Underwood*

SADIE .... *Joan Allen, Michael Ontkean, Elvira (Cassandra Peterson)*

SCOUT .... *Tai Babilonia, Tom Berenger, Demi Moore & Bruce Willis*

SOPHIA .... *Rebecca De Mornay & Patrick O'Neal, Jennifer Flavin & Sylvester Stallone, Talisa Soto & Benjamin Bratt*

SPENCER................ *Debbe Dunning, Cuba Gooding Jr., Cynthia McFadden & James Hoge, Gena Lee Nolin*

STELLA................... *Donna Dixon & Dan Ackroyd, Jennifer Grey, Melanie Griffith & Antonio Banderas, Dave Matthews, Elisabeth Shue, Molly Shannon, Dylan Walsh*

ZOE .... *Rosanna Arquette, Woody Harrelson, Melina Kanakaredes (ZOEY: Leah Thompson)*

Honest Names

ANNA .... *Chelsea Noble & Kirk Cameron*

ANNA LISE.............. *Lee Ann Womack*

ANNIE .... *Jamie Lee Curtis*

ANNIE MAUDE......... *Glenn Close*

BEATRICE .... *Emma Samms*

BEATRICE MILLY..... *Heather Mills & Paul McCartney*

BELLE .... *Donna Dixon & Dan Ackroyd*
   KINGSTON

BILLIE .... *Carrie Fisher*
   CATHERINE

BILLY .... *Helena Bonham Carter & Tim Burton*

CHESTER .... *Rita Wilson & Tom Hanks*

CLAIRE .... *Albert Brooks*
   ELIZABETH

CLARA .... *Ewan McGregor*
   MATHILDE

CLYDE .... *Catherine Keener & Dermot Mulroney*

DAISY (*see Hotties*)

ELLA (*see Hotties*)

FAITH ANN............. *Rick Schroder*

GENE...................... *Liam Gallagher*

GEORGE.................. *Kristin Scott Thomas*

GRACE (*see Hotties*)

HARRY JOSEPH .... *David Letterman*

HARRY SPENCER..... *Richard Dreyfuss*

HENRY (*see Hotties*)

HOMER (*see Hotties*)

HONOR .... *Tilda Swinton*

HOPE .... *Brad Garrett*

IRIS......................... *Sadie Frost & Jude Law*

JACK (*see Hotties*)

JAKE (*twin*) .... *Niki Taylor*

JOE......................... *Christine Lahti, Kate Winslet & Sam Mendes*

JOSEPHINE.............. *James Cameron & Linda Hamilton, Vera Wang*

KATE .... *Joan Lunden*
   ELIZABETH

LILY (*see Hotties*)

LOUIS .... *Bill Pullman*
LOUISA .... *Meryl Streep*
   JACOBSON
LUCY .... *Mimi Rogers*
LUKE .... *Lance Armstrong*
LUKE WILLIAM .... *Rick Schroder*
MABLE .... *Tracey Ullman*
MASON (*see Hotties*)
MATHILDA .... *Molly Ringwald*
MATILDA .... *Elizabeth Perkins*
MAX AARON .... *Joan Lunden*
MAY THEODORA ..... *Madeleine Stowe & Brian Benben*
MILLIE .... *Amy Grant*
OSCAR .... *Hugh Jackman*
OWEN (*see Hotties*)
PHOEBE ADELLE ..... *Melinda & Bill Gates*
ROSE .... *Rene Russo*
RUBY .... *Matthew Modine, Suzanne Vega*
SADIE (*see Hotties*)
SOPHIE (*see Hotties*)
STELLA (*see Hotties*)
TIM .... *Marion Jones*

Biblical

AARON .... *Robert De Niro*
BENJAMIN .... *Annette Bening & Warren Beatty*
CALEB .... *Julianne Moore*
DARIUS JOHN .... *Christiane Amanpour*
DELILAH BELLE ..... *Lisa Rinna & Harry Hamlin*
ELIAS .... *Vincent D'Onofrio*
ELIJAH (*see Hotties*)
ESTHER ROSE .... *Ewan McGregor*
EVE .... *Bono*

EZEKIEL .... *Beau Bridges*

EZRA SAMUEL .... *Paul Reiser*

GABRIEL .... *Jason Alexander*

GABRIEL KANE .... *Isabelle Adjani & Daniel Day-Lewis*

GABRIEL .... *Jerry Hall & Mick Jagger*
    LUKE BEAUREGARD

GIDEON .... *Mandy Patinkin*

HANNAH (*see Hotties*)

ISAAC HARRIS .... *Annie Potts*

ISAIAH .... *Allen Iverson*

JACOB ELI .... *Albert Brooks*

JACOB HURLEY .... *Jon Bon Jovi*

JACOB .... *James Caan*
    NICHOLAS

JADON ZACH .... *Christian Slater*

JARED .... *Paula Zahn*
    BRANDON

JONATHAN .... *Paulina Porizkova & Rik Ocasek*

JUDAH MIRO .... *Lucy Lawless*

LEVI .... *Dave "The Edge" Evans*

LUKE WILLIAM .... *Rick Schroder*

LYDIA .... *Bill Paxton*

NOAH .... *Jason Alexander*

NOAH ALEXIS .... *Kim Alexis*

NOAH LINDSEY .... *Billy Ray Cyrus*
    (*girl*)

NOAH MERCER .... *Scott Weiland*

RAPHAEL .... *Juliette Binoche*

SALOME .... *Alex Kingston*
    VIOLETTEA

SAMUEL .... *Sally Field*

SARA KATE .... *Harry Connick Jr.*

SARAH JUDE .... *Kiefer Sutherland*

SARAH .... *Andie MacDowell*
    MARGARET

SARAH ROSE .... *Marlee Matlin*
SELAH LOUISE .... *Lauryn Hill & Rohan Marley*
SIMEON .... *Wynton Marsalis*
ZION .... *Lauryn Hill & Rohan Marley*

Kreeatif & Unusual

ALCHAMY .... *Lance Hendriksen*
ALIZEH .... *Geena Davis*
   KESHVAR
AMAI ZACHARY ...... *Marlon Wayans*
ANAIS .... *Noel Gallagher*
APPLE BLYTHE .... *Gwyneth Paltrow & Chris Martin*
   ALISON
AQUINNAH .... *Tracy Pollan & Michael J. Fox*
   KATHLEEN
ARIE .... *Jody Whatley*
ARPAD FLYNN .... *Elle Macpherson*
ATTICUS .... *Isabella Hoffman & Daniel Baldwin*
AUDIO SCIENCE ...... *Shannyn Sossamon*
AURELIUS .... *Elle Macpherson*
   CY ANDREA
BANJO PATRICK ...... *Rachel Griffiths*
BAYLEE THOMAS .... *(Backstreet Boy) Brian Littrell*
BLUE ANGEL .... *Dave "The Edge" Evans*
BOMEN .... *Matthew Modine*
BRAEDON .... *Kevin Sorbo*
   COOPER
BRAISON .... *Billy Ray Cyrus*
   CHANCE
BRAWLEY KING ...... *Nick Nolte*
BRIA LIANNA .... *Eddie Murphy*
CAMBRIE .... *Rick Schroder*

CANNON	*Larry King*
EDWARD	
CASHEL BLAKE	*Rebecca Miller & Daniel Day-Lewis*
CHELSY	*Scott Bakula*
CHORDE	*Snoop Doggy Dog (Calvin Broadas)*
CRISTIAN	*Marc Anthony*
CRUMPET	*Lisa Vidal*
DANILEE	*Chuck Norris*
KELLEY	
DEACON	*Reese Witherspoon & Ryan Philippe*
DECLYN	*Cyndi Lauper*
WALLACE	
DENI MONTANA	*Woody Harrelson*
DENIM COLE	*Toni Braxton*
DESTRY ALLYN	*Kate Capshaw & Steven Spielberg*
DIEZEL KY	*Toni Braxton*
DREE LOUISE	*Mariel Hemingway*
EJA	*Shania Twain*
FIFI TRIXIEBELLE	*Bob Geldof*
FREEDOM (*boy*)	*Ving Rhames*
FUSCHIA	*Sting*
KATHERINE (*called Kate*)	
GAIA ROMILLY	*Emma Thompson*
GALEN GRIER	*Dennis Hopper*
GULLIVER	*Gary Oldman*
FLYNN	
HAILE JADE	*Eminem*
SCOTT	
HEAVEN	*Lil' Mo*
HUD	*John Mellencamp*
IMANI	*Jasmine Guy*
JAKOB WILLIAM	*Roseanne Cash*
JELANI ASAR	*Wesley Snipes*
(*boy*)	

JERMAJESTY	*Jermaine Jackson*
JETT	*George Lucas, Kelly Preston & John Travolta*
JUSTICE	*Steven Seagal*
KAI	*Jennifer Connelly*
KARSEN	*Ray Liotta*
KEARA	*Kristi Yamaguchi*
KEEN	*Mark Ruffalo*
KRISTOPHER STEVEN	*Jane Seymour*
KYD MILLER	*Téa Leoni & David Duchovny*
LAYNE	*Lars (Metallica) Ulrich*
LIBERTY	*Jean & Casey Kasem*
LOEWY	*John Malkovich*
LULU	*Edie Brickell & Paul Simon*
MAESA	*Bill Pullman*
MAGNUS PAULIN	*Will Ferrell*
MAILE MASAKO	*Wayne Brady*
MALU VALENTINE	*David Byrne*
MANZIE TIO	*Soon-Yi & Woody Allen*
MASSAI ZHIVAGO	*Nia Long*
MIKAELA KATHARINA	*Deborah Norville*
NAJEE (*boy*)	*LL Cool J*
NALA	*Keenan Ivory Wayans*
NEVIS (*girl*)	*Nelly Furtado*
PILOT INSPEKTOR	*Jason Lee*
PRINCE MICHAEL JACKSON JR.	*Michael Jackson*
RACER MAXIMILLIANO	*Robert Rodriguez*
RAUI LYNDON	*Kelli Williams*
REBEL ANTONIO	*Robert Rodriguez*

REBOP .... *Todd Rundgren*

RENNON .... *Griffin O'Neal*

ROCKET .... *Robert Rodriguez*
    VALENTIN

ROMEO .... *Victoria "Posh Spice" Adams & David Beckham*

ROMEO JON .... *Jon Bon Jovi*

RUMER GLENN .... *Demi Moore & Bruce Willis*

SAILOR LEE .... *Christie Brinkley*

SAREME JANE .... *Kelli Williams*

SATCHEL LEWIS...... *Spike Lee*
   (girl)

SCOUT (*see Hotties*)

SELAH LOUISE .... *Lauryn Hill & Rohan Marley*

SEVEN SIRIUS .... *Erykah Badu*
   (boy)

SHAQIR RASHON ..... *Shaquille O'Neal*

SHAYLA RAE........... *Mary Lou Retton*

SHAYNE AUDRA...... *Eddie Murphy*

SINDRI .... *Björk*

SISTINE ROSE.......... *Jennifer Flavin & Sylvester Stallone*

SKYLA BRAE .... *Mary Lou Retton*

SKYLAR .... *Sheena Easton*

SKYLAR GRACE....... *Joely Fisher*

SONNET NOEL .... *Forest Whitaker*

SOSIE RUTH .... *Kyra Sedgwick & Kevin Bacon*

SPECK .... *John Mellencamp*
   WILDHORSE

SY'RAI .... *Brandy*

TAINA...................... *Jimmy Smits*

TAJ (*boy*)................ *Steven Tyler*

TARIAN.................... *Travis Tritt*
   NATHANIEL

TENZIN LOSEL .... *Adam (Beastie Boy) Yauch*
   (girl)

TRINITY	*Dennis Rodman*
TRUE (*boy*)	*Forest Whitaker*
WHIZDOM	*Jayson Williams*
XEN	*Tisha Campbell Martin*
ZOLA IVY	*Eddie Murphy*

The Two-Syllable Solution

AUSTIN	*Sela Ward*
AUSTIN BRYCE	*Paula Zahn*
AUSTIN LEONARD	*Tommy Lee Jones*
BAILEY	*Anthony Edwards*
BAILEY VINCENT	*Tracey Gold*
BRANDON	*Pamela Anderson & Tommy Lee*
BRANDON JOSEPH	*Marlee Matlin*
BRANDON SCOTT	*Tracy Austin*
CALEB	*Julianne Moore*
CODY ALAN	*Robin Williams*
CONNOR	*Ruth Pointer*
CONNOR ANTONY	*Nicole Kidman & Tom Cruise*
COOPER	*Tim Matheson, Bill Murray*
DECKER NILSSON	*Nikki Sixx*
DYLAN (*see Hotties*)	
EVAN JOSEPH	*Jenny McCarthy*
GARRETT	*Bo Jackson*
GRADY THOMAS	*Harry Smith*
GRIFFIN ARTHUR	*Brendan Frasier*
HOLDEN	*Dennis Miller*

HOLDEN .... *Rick Schroder*
   RICHARD

HUNTER (*twin*) .... *Niki Taylor*

JADEN (*see Hotties*)

JARED .... *Paula Zahn*
   BRANDON

JORDAN .... *Pia Zadora*
   MAXWELL

JUSTIN .... *Andie MacDowell*

LIAM .... *Calista Flockhart*

LIAM .... *Rachel Hunter & Rod Stewart*
   MCALLISTER

LUCAS .... *Andy Dick*

LUCAS AUTRY .... *Willie Nelson*

MARLON .... *Dennis Miller*

MARSTON .... *Hugh Hefner*

MASON (*see Hotties*)

MAXWELL .... *Andrew Dice Clay*

OWEN (*see Hotties*)

PARKER JAREN .... *Rosie O'Donnell*

RILEY .... *David Lynch, Mare Winningham*

RYDER LEE .... *John Leguizamo*

RYDER RUSSELL ..... *Kate Hudson & Chris Robinson*

TYLER DANIEL .... *Marlee Matlin*

The One-Syllable Solution

CHANCE .... *Paul Hogan*

CHANCE .... *Larry King*
   ARMSTRONG

CLYDE .... *Catherine Keener & Dermot Mulroney*

FLYNN .... *Elle Macpherson*

JETT .... *George Lucas, Kelly Preston & John Travolta*

KAI .... *Jennifer Connelly*

KEEN .... *Mark Ruffalo*

KYLE .... *Deborah Norville*

LEV .... *Candace Cameron*

MILES (*see Hotties*)

MYLES .... *Sherilyn Fenn & Toulouse Holliday*
   MAXIMILLIAN

MYLES .... *Eddie Murphy*
   MITCHELL

SAGE....................... *Tracey Gold*

SLADE LUCAS .... *David Brenner*
   MOBY

TY .... *Wayne Gretzky*

VANCE .... *Chynna Phillips & William Baldwin*
   ALEXANDER

XEN .... *Tisha Campbell Martin*

The Brits & the Celts

ADRIAN .... *Edie Brickell & Paul Simon*
   EDWARD

AIDAN .... *Scott Hamilton*

ANGUS MOORE .... *Amanda Pays & Corbin Bernsen*

BRIDGET .... *Anthony LaPaglia*

BRIGIDINE .... *Sinead O'Connor*

CARYS ZETA .... *Catherine Zeta Jones & Michael Douglas*

CICELY YASIN .... *Sandra Bernhard*

DAMIAN.................. *Elizabeth Hurley*
   CHARLES

DONOVAN .... *Charisma Carpenter*
   CHARLES

FINLAY .... *Amanda Pays & Corbin Bernsen*

FINLEY .... *Sadie Frost*

FINLEY FAITH .... *Angie Harmon & Jason Sehorn*
  (*girl*)
FINN WILLIAM .... *Jane Leeves*
FINNIGAN .... *Eric McCormack*
  HOLDEN
GULLIVER .... *Gary Oldman*
  FLYNN
HUGO JAMES .... *Amy Carter*
JILLIAN .... *Vanessa Williams*
MAEVE .... *Kathryn Erbe & Terry Kinney*
MALCOLM............... *Denzel Washington*
PADDY .... *Mare Winningham*
ROAN JOSEPH .... *Sharon Stone*
ROISIN .... *Sinead O'Connor*
RONAN .... *Rebecca Miller & Daniel Day-Lewis*
ROWAN FRANCIS..... *Brooke Shields*
  (*girl*)
SAFFRON .... *Simon Le Bon*
  SAHARA
SAOIRSE ROISIN ...... *Courtney Kennedy & Paul Hill*
SEBASTIAN .... *James Spader*
SHANE.................... *Sinead O'Connor*
TREVOR .... *Wayne Gretzky*
TRISTAN .... *Travis Tritt*
TRISTAN RIVER .... *Natasha Henstridge*

The Italianates & Other Imports

ADRIANA .... *Fred (Limp Bizkit) Durst*
ALAIA..................... *Stephen Baldwin*
ALESSANDRA .... *Andy Garcia*
ALINA..................... *Dave Foley*
ALVARO .... *Lorenzo Lamas*

AMANDINE .... *John Malkovich*

AMEDEO .... *John Turturro*

ANABELLA .... *Sela Ward*

ANDRES .... *Andy Garcia*
   ANTONIO

ANNELIESE.............. *Kelly LeBrock & Steven Seagal*

ANTON .... *Beverly D'Angelo & Al Pacino*

ARPAD FLYNN .... *Elle Macpherson*

ATIANA CECILIA ..... *Oscar de la Hoya*

BIANCA .... *Jean-Claude Van Damme*

BRUNO .... *Nigella Lawson*

COLETTE .... *Dylan McDermott*

COSIMA................... *Nigella Lawson*

CROIX .... *Cedric the Entertainer*
   ALEXANDER

DANTE..................... *Chazz Palminteri*
   LORENZO

ELIANA SOPHIA ...... *Ryan Haddon, Christian Slater*

ELOISA .... *Penelope Ann Miller*

ENZO...................... *Patricia Arquette*

ETIENNE .... *Sheryl Lee Ralph*

FRANCESCA .... *Erik Estrada*
   NATALIA

FRANCESCA .... *Frances Fisher & Clint Eastwood*
   RUTH

GIACOMO .... *Sting*
   LUKE SUMMER

GRETA .... *David Caruso*

GRETA SIMONE .... *Phoebe Cates & Kevin Kline*

ISABELLA (*see Hotties*)

JOAQUIN................. *Kelly Ripa & Mark Consuelos, Jimmy Smits*

KARINA ELENI........ *Melina Kanakaredes*

KATIA .... *Denzel Washington*

KATYA .... *Hunter Tylo*

LENI .... *Heidi Klum*

LOURDES .... *Madonna*
MARIA
LUCA (*boy*) .... *Colin Firth*
LUCA BELA............. *Jennie Garth*
(*girl*)
LUCIA...................... *Giovanni Ribisi*
MALU .... *David Byrne*
VALENTINE
MARCO .... *Jill Hennessy*
MARINA .... *Matt LeBlanc*
MATEO.................... *Colin Firth*
MERCEDES .... *Joanne Whalley & Val Kilmer*
NAYIB..................... *Gloria Estefan*
NEVE...................... *Conan O'Brien*
NIKOLAI .... *Barry Bonds Jr.*
PALOMA .... *Emilio Estevez*
PAULINA MARY ...... *Wayne Gretzky*
JEAN
PEDRO .... *Frances McDormand & Joel Coen*
PRIMA..................... *Connie Selleca & John Tesh*
SELLECHIA
RAPHAEL................ *Juliette Binoche*
RENE-CHARLES ...... *Celine Dion*
ROCCO JOHN........... *Madonna & Guy Ritchie*
ROMAN ROBERT...... *Cate Blanchette*
ROMAN WALKER..... *Debra Messing*
ROMY .... *Matt Lauer*
ROMY MARION........ *Ellen Barkin & Gabriel Byrne*
SASCHA .... *Jessica Sklar & Jerry Seinfeld*
SASHA .... *Vanessa Williams & Rick Fox*
GABRIELLA
SINDRI (*boy*)........... *Björk*
SOFIA...................... *Lionel Richie*
SOFIA GRACE .... *Felicity Huffman & William H. Macy*
STELLAN .... *Jennifer Connelly & Paul Bettany*

TATIANA .... *Caroline Kennedy & Ed Schlossberg*
   CECILIA
VALENTINA .... *Lolita Davidovich & Ron Shelton*
WILLEM WOLF .... *Billy Idol*
WOLFGANG .... *Valerie Bertinelli & Eddie Van Halen*

Place Names

ALEXANDRIA .... *Iman & David Bowie*
   ZAHRA
ASSISSI .... *Jade Jagger*
ATLANTA .... *Amanda De Cadenet & John Taylor*
AUSTIN .... *Sela Ward*
AUSTIN BRYCE .... *Paula Zahn*
AUSTIN .... *Tommy Lee Jones*
   LEONARD
BROOKLYN .... *Victoria "Posh Spice" Adams & David*
   JOSEPH .... *Beckham*
CAIRO .... *Beverly Peele*
CALEDONIA .... *Shawn Colvin*
   JEAN-MARIE
CHELSEA .... *Rosie O'Donnell*
   BELLE
DAKOTA (*girl*) .... *Melanie Griffith & Don Johnson*
DAKOTA ALAN .... *Chuck Norris*
   (*boy*)
DAKOTA MAYI .... *Melissa Gilbert*
   (*boy*)
DALLAS (*boy*) .... *Fred Durst*
GEORGIA .... *Hope Davis*
GEORGIA MAY .... *Jerry Hall & Mick Jagger*
GEORGIA .... *Harry Connick Jr.*
   TATOM

INDIA ANN .... *Sarah MacLachlan*
   SUSHIL
INDIA .... *Marianne Williamson*
   EMMELINE
INDIA ROSE............. *Heather Thomas*
INDIO .... *Deborah Falconer & Robert Downey Jr.*
IRELAND .... *Kim Basinger & Alec Baldwin*
   ELIESSE
ITALIA .... *LL Cool J*
KENYA JULIA .... *Nastassja Kinski & Quincy Jones*
   MIAMI
LONDON .... *Slash (Saul Hudson)*
   EMILIO
LOURDES .... *Madonna*
   MARIA
MEMPHIS EVE .... *Bono*
MONTANA .... *Judd Hirsch*
   EVE
PARIS (*see Hotties*)
PHOENIX CHI.......... *Melanie "Scary Spice" Brown*
RIO KELLY .... *Sean Young*
   (*boy*)
SAVANNAH .... *Jimmy Buffett*
   JANE
SHILOH (*girl*) .... *Tom Berenger*
SIERRA ALEXIS .... *James Worthy*
SONORA .... *Kelly McGillis*
   ASHLEY
ZION .... *Lauryn Hill & Rohan Marley*

Nature Names

AMBER ROSE........... *Simon Le Bon*
DAISY (*see Hotties*)
IRIS......................... *Sadie Frost & Jude Law*
IVY-VICTORIA......... *Sheryl Lee Ralph*
JADE........................ *Daryl Strawberry*
JASMINE .... *Michael Jordan*
JASMINE PAGE .... *Martin Lawrence*
LILY (*see Hotties*)
OCEAN.................... *Forest Whitaker*
   ALEXANDER
PEACHES................. *Bob Geldof*
POPPY HONEY .... *Jamie (Naked Chef) Oliver*
RAINBOW .... *Ving Rhames*
   (*girl*)
ROSE....................... *Rene Russo*
RUBY .... *Matthew Modine, Suzanne Vega*
SAFFRON .... *Simon Le Bon*
   SAHARA
SAGE (*boy*) .... *Tracey Gold*
SAGE ARIEL .... *Lance Hendriksen*
   (*girl*)
STORM (*girl*)........... *Nikki Sixx*
SUMMER .... *Dr. Dre*
WILLOW .... *Gabrielle Anwar*
WILLOW .... *Jada Pinkett & Will Smith*
   CAMILLE REIGN
ZEPHYR.................. *Karla De Vito & Robby Benson*

In addition there are a few other starbaby-syndrome categories, some of them representing new trends, others that have been around for a while. In most cases, names mentioned previously have been omitted.

Boys' Names for Girls

AIDAN ROSE .... *Faith Daniels*

AUGUST ANNA .... *Garth Brooks*

BAILEY JEAN .... *Melissa Etheridge*

DESTRY ALLYN .... *Kate Capshaw & Steven Spielberg*

DEXTER DEAN .... *Diane Keaton*

DOMINIK .... *Andy Garcia*

ELIOT PAULINE ...... *Sting*

ELLIOTT .... *George Stephanopoulos*
    ANASTASIA

EMERSON ROSE .... *Teri Hatcher*

FINLEY FAITH .... *Angie Harmon & Jason Sehorn*

JAMESON LEON ...... *Chynna Phillips & William Baldwin*

JAMISON BESS .... *James Belushi*

JORDAN .... *Leeza Gibbons*
    ALEXANDRA

LANGLEY FOX .... *Mariel Hemingway*

MASON OLIVIA .... *Kelsey Grammer*

MORGAN .... *Clint Eastwood*

NOAH LINDSEY .... *Billy Ray Cyrus*

REILLY MARIE .... *Roma Downey*

REMINGTON .... *Tracy Nelson & Billy Moses*
    ELIZABETH

RILEY PAIGE .... *Howie Mandel*

ROWAN .... *Brooke Shields*
    FRANCIS

SAM .... *Denise Richards & Charlie Sheen*

SATCHEL .... *Spike Lee*
    LEWIS

SCHUYLER .... *Tracy Pollan & Michael J. Fox*
    FRANCES

SPENCER SHAE .... *Debbe Dunning*

TYSON .... *Nenah Cherry*

WYLIE QUINN .... *Richard Dean Anderson*
    ANNAROSE

Last Names First

ATHERTON .... *Don Johnson*
    GRACE

AUDEN .... *Amber Valletta*

BECKETT .... *Melissa Etheridge & Julie Cypher*

CASSIDY ERIN .... *Kathie Lee & Frank Gifford*

DELANEY .... *Martina McBride*

HARLOW JANE........ *Patricia Arquette*

HOPPER JACK.......... *Robin Wright & Sean Penn*

JEFFERSON .... *Tony Randall*
    SALVANI

KEEGAN (*girl*) .... *Maureen O'Boyle*

KELSEY .... *Kelly McGillis*

KELSEY ROSE.......... *Gabrielle Carteris*

KENDALL .... *Bruce Jenner*
    NICOLE

LENNON .... *Patsy Kenset & Liam Gallagher*
    FRANCIS

LINCOLN .... *Bill Murray*

MADDOX................. *Angelina Jolie*
    CHIVAN

MASON (*see Hotties*)

MATALIN .... *Mary Matalin & James Carville*
    MARY

MCCANNA............... *Gary Sinise*

MCKENNA............... *Mary Lou Retton*

MINGUS .... *Helena Christensen*
    LUCIEN

PRESLEY .... *Cindy Crawford*

PRESLEY .... *Tanya Tucker*
   TANITA (*girl*)
QUINN .... *Sean Young*
RAFFERTY .... *Sadie Frost & Jude Law*
REILLY .... *Roma Downey*
REMINGTON .... *Tracy Nelson & Billy Moses*
   ELIZABETH
RILEY .... *David Lynch, Mare Winningham*
RIPLEY (*girl*) .... *Thandie Newton*
SAWYER.................. *Kate Capshaw & Steven Spielberg*
TRUMAN................. *Rita Wilson & Tom Hanks*
   THEODORE
TULLY .... *Deirdre Hall*
WALKER .... *Adrienne Barbeau*
   STEVEN
WESTON .... *Nicolas Cage*

Nickname Names

ALLIE .... *Garth Brooks*
   COLLEEN
BILLY RAY .... *Helena Bonham Carter & Tim Burton*
BOBBI .... *Whitney Houston & Bobby Brown*
   KRISTINA
BUCK...................... *Roseanne*
DEX .... *Dana Carvey*
DUKE...................... *Diane Keaton*
DUKE...................... *Justine Bateman*
   KENNETH
DUSTY RAINN .... *Vanilla Ice*
FRANKIE-JEAN .... *Donna D'Errico & Nikki Sixx*
FUDDY.................... *Damon Wayans*
GENE...................... *Liam Gallagher*

GRACIE .... *Faith Hill & Tim McGraw*
  KATHERINE
JAZ ELLE .... *Steffi Graf & Andre Agassi*
JOE .... *Christine Lahti, Kate Winslet & Sam Mendes*
KIT .... *Jodie Foster*
LEV .... *Candace Cameron*
LIV HELEN .... *Julianne Moore*
LUCKY ROSE .... *Cedric the Entertainer*
MAGGIE .... *Faith Hill*
  ELIZABETH
MAGGIE MARIE .... *Pat Sajak*
MEG .... *Andy Dick*
PADDY .... *Mare Winningham*
RAINIE .... *Andie MacDowell*
RUDY .... *Sadie Frost & Jude Law*
SAM .... *Patricia Heaton, Emily Mortimer*
SAM MICHAEL .... *Tracy Pollan & Michael J. Fox*
THEO .... *Kate Capshaw & Steven Spielberg, Cheryl Tiegs*
TY ....*Wayne Gretzky*
TY CHRISTIAN .... *Pam Dawber & Mark Harmon*

Traditionals

And then there are those celebrities who have chosen names that have been perennials, or others that were more popular in earlier times:

ALEXANDER .... *Lauren Holly*
  JOSE
AMELIA GRAY .... *Lisa Rinna & Harry Hamlin*
AUDREY .... *Faith Hill & Tim McGraw*
  CAROLINE
BENJAMIN .... *Annette Bening & Warren Beatty*
CAROLINE .... *Katie Couric*

CASPAR................... *Claudia Schiffer*
   MATTHEW
CATHERINE .... *Crystal Gayle*
   CLAIRE
CATHERINE .... *Cathy Moriarity*
   PATRICIA
CATHERINE .... *Cheryl Hines*
   ROSE
CECILIA .... *Vera Wang*
CHARLES (*see Hotties*)
CHARLOTTE (*see Hotties*)
CHRISTIAN.............. *Sean "P. Diddy" Combs*
   CASEY
CHRISTIAN.............. *Pete Sampras*
   CHARLES
CHRISTINA.............. *Maria Shriver & Arnold Schwarzenegger*
   MARIA AURELIA
CHRISTOPHER......... *Chris O'Donnell*
   EUGENE JR.
CHRISTOPHER......... *Maria Shriver & Arnold Schwarzenegger*
   SARGENT SHRIVER
DANIEL JACK.......... *Natasha Richardson & Liam Neeson*
DAVID...................... *J. K. Rowling*
   GORDON
ELEANOR................ *Diane Lane & Christopher Lambert*
ELINOR.................... *Katie Couric*
ELOISE..................... *Penelope Ann Miller*
EMILY GRACE .... *Alex Trebeck*
EMILY MARIE.......... *Gloria Estefan, Wayne Gretzsky*
EMMA .... *Mary Matalin & James Carville,*
                             Eric Roberts
FREDRIC .... *Don Imus*
   WYATT
GRACE (*see Hotties*)
IDA SIGRID............... *Dolph Lungren*

ISABEL IRA .... *Annette Bening & Warren Beatty*
   ASHLEY
ISABELLE................ *Lance Armstrong, Chelsea Noble & Kirk*
                             Cameron
ISABELLE JANE....... *Marlee Matlin*
ISADORA .... *Björk & Matthew Barney*
JAMES (*see Hotties*)
JASPER.................... *Don Johnson*
JASPER.................... *Wynton Marsalis*
   ARMSTRONG
JOHN ALBERT......... *Tracey Ullman*
   VICTOR
JOHN DAVID .... *Denzel Washington*
JOHN STACY .... *Jane Seymour*
JOHN OWEN .... *Rob Lowe*
JOSEPH .... *Kristin Scott-Thomas*
JULIA .... *Vendela*
   ANNETTE
JULIA JONES........... *Shawn Cassidy*
JULIA .... *Tony Randall*
   LAURETTE
JULIAN (*see Hotties*)
JULIE ROSE............. *Eric Clapton*
JULIUS.................... *Lucy Lawless*
   ROBERT BAY
KATHARINE .... *Maria Shriver & Arnold Schwarzenegger*
   EUNICE
LEILA GEORGE .... *Greta Scacchi & Vincent D'Onoforio*
LEILA RUTH .... *Deborah Roberts & Al Roker*
LILA .... *Kate Moss*
LILA SIMONE .... *Chris Rock*
LILLIAN.................. *Baz Luhrmann*
   AMANDA
LORRAINE .... *Jack Nicholson*
LUCIAN .... *Steve Bucsemi*

MADELAINE............ *Jon Favreau*

MADELAINE............ *Téa Leoni & David Duchovny*
   WEST

MADELINE.............. *Lea Thompson*

MARY LOUISA......... *Jane Kaczmarek & Bradley Whitford*

MATTHEW .... *Rob Lowe*
   EDWARD

MATTHEW .... *Eddie Money*
   JULIAN

MICHAEL .... *Natasha Richardson & Liam Neeson*
   RICHARD ANTONIO

NICHOLAS .... *Vanna White*

NICHOLAS .... *Deborah Roberts & Al Roker*
   ALBERT

NICHOLAS .... *Phil Collins*
   GREV AUSTIN

NICHOLAS .... *Marilu Henner*
   MORGAN

OLIVER .... *Martin Short*

OLIVIA (*see Hotties*)

RAYMOND............... *Jack Nicholson*

SAMUEL.................. *Sally Field*

THOMAS .... *Dana Carvey*

VERONICA .... *Rebecca De Mornay & Patrick O'Neal*

VICTORIA................ *Tommy Lee Jones, Lorenzo Lamas*

WILLIAM .... *Mary-Louise Parker & Billy Crudup*

WILLIAM .... *Adrienne Barbeau*
   DALTON

XAVIER .... *Tilda Swinton*

XAVIER .... *Donnie Wahlberg*
   ALEXANDER

ZACHARY .... *Cheryl Tiegs & Tony Peck*

ZACHARY .... *Elizabeth Varga*
   RAPHAEL

ZELDA.................... *Robin Williams*

And a few other high-profile celeb choices of note:

KAYA JORDAN	*Cindy Crawford*
KEARA KIYOMI	*Kristi Yamaguchi*
MAYA GRACE	*Garrison Keillor*
MAYA RAY	*Uma Thurman & Ethan Hawke*
MIA	*Kate Winslet*
MILO JACOB	*Camryn Manheim*
MILO SEBASTIAN	*Ricki Lake*
PIPER	*Melissa Sue Anderson, Brian De Palma*
PIPER MARU	*Gillian Anderson*
TALLULAH BELLE	*Demi Moore & Bruce Willis*
TALLULAH PINE	*Simon Le Bon*
TOBY COLE (girl)	*Emme*

TV Reception

If a new name crops up, seemingly out of nowhere, all across the country, chances are it can be found in the pages of *TV Guide* or—even more likely—*Soap Opera Digest*. Sometimes there's a bit of a gap, the time it takes for impressionable young viewers to reach child-bearing age, but surprisingly often, the impact is almost spontaneous.

This is a pattern that dates back to the very beginnings of television. It first became noticeable when the phenomenally popular westerns of the 1950s and 1960s reintroduced a genre of names that hadn't been heard in this country for almost a century—grizzled old great-grandpa names like Joshua, Jason, Jeremy, and Jesse. Practically before you could say Ponderosa, those very names had taken on enough muscle and magic to start replacing old stalwarts like Robert and Richard on baby name popularity lists.

That was also the era of cute-kid TV names, often in the form of unisex nicknames. There were boy Kellys and girl Kellys, boy Jodys and girl Jodies, reflecting and affecting the newborns in real life. A more glamorous element entered in the *Charlie's Angels* seventies, an age of Sabrinas and Kimberlys and Tiffanys and other dainty three-syllable names. When *Dynasty* exploded onto the small screen in 1981, it created a mini–baby-naming boom all its own. Blakes of both sexes appeared in ever-increasing numbers on birth announcements and, in its various spellings, Krystle/Krystal/Crystal vaulted onto popularity charts. As for Alexis Carrington, she was at least partly responsible for a still rampant epidemic of Alexi—not only Alexises and Alexes but Alexas, Alexanders, Alexandras, Alexandrias, and Lexies. *Dynasty*'s creators also played with the idea of surname and male names for girls—Fallon, Kirby, and others—which would explode in the nineties.

But for decades it has been the daytime dramas that have been most in the vanguard of baby-naming trends. The classic case is the name Kayla. When the character of Kayla Brady was introduced on *Days of Our Lives* in 1982, the name was barely mentioned in any of the standard baby-naming manuals. But within a few years, Kayla began an unprecedented leap up the lists, still registering in the top fifteen a decade and a half later. Soaps also anticipated the trend of using place names for people—there were Egypts and Indias, Sierras and Friscos back when the current parents of little Dakotas and Dallases were still in junior high.

This timeline displays the key TV character names, and the shows they appeared in, over the past four decades, with the most trendsetting set in boldface.

1955	*Cheyenne*	CHEYENNE
	Gunsmoke	**MATT**
1956	*Maverick*	BART
		BRET
		BEAU
1957	*Bachelor Father*	KELLY (*f*)
	The Real McCoys	LUKE
1958	*Wanted: Dead or Alive*	JOSH

1959	*Bonanza*	**ADAM**
1963	*Wagon Train*	COOPER
1964	*Bewitched*	**SAMANTHA**
	Peyton Place	**ALLISON**
1965	*I Spy*	KELLY (*m*)
1966	*Family Affair*	JODY (*m*)
	As the World Turns	AMANDA
	The Secret Storm	BROOKE (*still a soap favorite*)
1968	*Here Come the Brides*	**JASON** **JEREMY** **JOSHUA**
1970	*The Secret Storm*	INDIA
1972	*Bob Newhart*	EMILY
	The Waltons	OLIVIA
1974	*Good Times*	FLORIDA (*an early place name*)
	General Hospital	CAMERON
	Ryan's Hope	MAEVE (*an early ethnic Irish name*)
1975	*General Hospital*	KYLE
1976	*Bionic Woman*	JAIME
	Charlie's Angels	SABRINA
1977	*Eight Is Enough*	**NICHOLAS**
	The Edge of Night	LOGAN RAVEN
	Search for Tomorrow	KYLIE
1978	*The Avengers*	EMMA
	Diff'rent Strokes	**KIMBERLY**
	WKRP in Cincinnati	BAILEY (*f*)
	Dallas	JENNA
1979	*Charlie's Angels*	**TIFFANY**
	Facts of Life	BLAIR

Year	Show	Character
	Hart to Hart	JONATHAN
		JENNIFER
	The Edge of Night	PAIGE
1980	*Another World*	MIRANDA
		TAYLOR (*m*)
	The Guiding Light	MORGAN (*m*)
	As the World Turns	HALEY
1981	*Dynasty*	BLAKE (*m*)
		KRYSTLE
1981	*Dynasty*	FALLON (*f*)
		ALEXIS
	Falcon Crest	COLE
1982	*As the World Turns*	ARIEL
		JASMINE
	Days of Our Lives	**KAYLA**
	Family Ties	**ALEX**
		MALLORY
	Dynasty	KIRBY (*f*)
	Santa Barbara	SYDNEY (*f*)
	The Young and the Restless	**ASHLEY** (*appeared earlier on* The Doctors)
	Newhart	STEPHANIE
1983	*One Life to Live*	COURTNEY
	Search for Tomorrow	HOGAN
	Dallas	JENNA
	Scarecrow & Mrs. King	AMANDA (*hits prime time*)
1984	*Kate & Allie*	EMMA
	The Cosby Show	THEO
		VANESSA
	Days of Our Lives	**JASMINE**
	Dynasty	BRAD
	Another World	HUNTER

	The Guiding Light	INDIA
1985	Another World	**BRITTANY**
	As the World Turns	HOLDEN
		SIERRA (*m*)
	Days of Our Lives	**SAVANNAH**
	Falcon Crest	CASSANDRA
		JORDAN (*f*)
	The Colbys	MILES
	General Hospital	**JADE**
1986	Matlock	**TYLER** (*m*)
	As the World Turns	**DUNCAN**
	L.A. Law	**KELSEY**
		(*attorney Ann*
		Kelsey's
		surname)*
		GRACE
	General Hospital	CHARITY
1987	Cheers	**SAM**
		REBECCA
	A Different World	JALEESA
	thirtysomething	HOPE
		MELISSA
		BRITTANY
		(*child*)
	Miami Vice	CAITLIN
	As the World Turns	**TAYLOR** (*f*)
	My Two Dads	NICOLE
1988	Murphy Brown	MURPHY
	As the World Turns	CALEB
	Days of Our Lives	LEXIE
		ORION
	General Hospital	COLTON

---

*She bestowed it on the adopted baby daughter she was forced to return to the birth mother, in a heartrending episode that not only launched the name Kelsey but also spawned an important trend toward using mothers' maiden names as first names.

1989	*Anything but Love*	HANNAH
	Days of Our Lives	COLIN
	Baywatch	TREVOR
	The Cosby Show	OLIVIA (*child*)
	The Bold and the Beautiful	**MACY**
	The Young and the Restless	**SKYLAR**
1990	*Beverly Hills 90210*	**BRANDON**
		DYLAN
	thirtysomething	LEO (*baby*)
	All My Children	**CEARA** (*an anything-goes spelling*)
	As the World Turns	**CONNOR** (*f*)
	Days of Our Lives	TANNER
1991	*Blossom*	SIX
	Another World	SPENCER
1992	*Mad About You*	JAMIE (*interesting because her nickname is the male James*)
	Murphy Brown	AVERY (*the show's baby was a boy, but most of its namesakes were girls*)
	Another World	KELSEY
	Days of Our Lives	**AUSTIN** (*appeared earlier on* The Edge of Night *and* One Life to Live)
	Loving	**COOPER**

	One Life to Live	SUEDE
	General Hospital	JAGGER
1993	*All My Children*	KENDALL (*f*)
	As the World Turns	DAMIAN
	Blossom	KENNEDY (*little girl*)
	Dr. Quinn, Medicine Woman	**MICHAELA** (*also called Mike*)
	Hangin' with Mr. Cooper	GENEVA
	Late Night with Conan O'Brien	CONAN
	Melrose Place	SYDNEY (*f*)
	The X-Files	FOX
1994	*Ellen*	PAIGE
	Friends	CHANDLER
		ROSS
	Party of Five	JULIA
		BAILEY (*m*)
		GRIFFIN
		OWEN (*child*)
	Sister, Sister	TIA
	As the World Turns	BETHANY
	The Young and the Restless	**KEESHA**
1995	*Baywatch Nights*	**DESTINY**
	The Guiding Light	ABIGAIL
	Loving	**BRIANNA**
1996	*General Hospital*	JASPER (JAX)
	ER	RILEY
1997	*Buffy the Vampire Slayer*	XANDER
		WILLOW
		CORDELIA
		ANGEL (*m*)
	Just Shoot Me	MAYA
		HANNAH (*child*)

	Mad About You	MABEL (*baby*)
	One Life to Live	ZEUS
	All My Children	**BRADEN**
	General Hospital	VENUS
1998	*Days of Our Lives*	ELVIS (*baby*)
	Boy Meets World	TOPANGA
	Felicity	FELICITY
	Sex in the City	CHARLOTTE
		MIRANDA
		AIDAN
	Charmed	PIPER
	The West Wing	JOSIAH (JED)
	That '70s Show	(MICHAEL)
		KELSO
1999	*The West Wing*	ZOEY
		DONNATELLA
	Passions	SHERIDAN (*f*)
	The Sopranos	CARMELA
1999	*The Sopranos*	MEADOW
		ADRIANA
	Buffy the Vampire Slayer	ANYA
2000	*All My Children*	RAIN
	General Hospital	ZANDER
	The Guiding Light	CATALINA
	The Gilmore Girls	LORELAI (RORY)
		PARIS (*f*)
	CSI	WARRICK
2001	*All My Children*	LORENZO/ENZO
		MIA
	The Guiding Light	ROMEO
	Alias	IRINA
	The Wire	SHAKIMA
		STANISLAUS
	Days of Our Lives	VIOLET
	Reba	KYRA

Multiple Personalities

Some soap names work overtime, pedaling between several different shows. The following are some of the names that have appeared on at least two daytime dramas—some of them as many as five (Olivia, Julia):

MALE	FEMALE	
Aiden	Alexandra	Margo
Austin	Amanda	Miranda
Bo	Angela	Molly
Brady	April	Natalie
Brandon	Brooke	Olivia
Cole	Carly	Ruby
Damian	Charity	Samantha
Derek	Chloe	Taylor
Dylan	Dinah	Tess
Evan	Emma	Tiffany
Grant	Eve	Vanessa
Hart	Felicia	
Ian	Gillian	
Jasper	Grace	
Leo	Hannah	
Lucas	Hope	
Marcus	Isabella	
Miles	Jade	
Ned	Julia	
Pierce	Keesha	
Ryan	Kelsey	
Shane	Lexie	
Tanner	Lila	
Tyrone	Lily	
Zack	Lydia	

2002	*Sex in the City*	**BRADY** (*baby boy*)
	The Young and the Restless	FELIX
	The Guiding Light	SUMMER
	Everwood	BRIGHT (*m*)
		EPHRAM
	CSI: Miami	ALEXX
		HORATIO
		CALLEIGH
2003	*One Life to Live*	RIVER
	Angel	HARMONY
	Arrested Development	(MAE) MAEBY
	Queer Eye for the Straight Guy	KYAN, JAI
2004	*Tru Calling*	TRU

Reality TV Names

Some of the most inventive names to appear on TV in the past few years aren't invented at all, but are the real life names of the real live contestants on reality shows. Some of these reality contestants—think of *American Idol*'s big belter Ruben or *Survivor*'s Colby—are inspiring hundreds of baby namesakes.

Here, some of the names that have come to us via reality television:

ACE	*Real World*
ALESSIA	*Joe Millionaire 2*
ALTON	*Real World*
AMAYA	*Real World*
ANEESA	*Real World*
ARISSA	*Real World*
BRYNN	*Real World*

CHIARA	*Big Brother*
CLAY	*American Idol*
COLBY	*Survivor*
CORAL	*Real World*
DARRAH	*Survivor*
DARVA	*Who Wants to Marry a Millionaire?*
ELKA	*Real World*
EREKA	*The Apprentice*
FANTASIA	*American Idol*
GENESIS	*Real World*
GERVASE	*Survivor*
GHANDIA	*Survivor*
GIADA	*Joe Millionaire 2*
IRALAN	*Real World*
JACINDA	*Real World*
JAREE	*Amazing Race*
JENASCIA	*America's Next Top Model 2*
JERUSHA	*Joe Millionaire 2*
JUDD	*Real World*
KAIA	*Real World*
KAMEELA	*Real World*
KAT	*Real World*
KEL	*Survivor*
LEX	*Survivor*
MALIK	*Real World*
MALLORY	*Real World*
MARCELLAS	*Big Brother*
MONTANA	*Real World*
NELEH	*Survivor*
OMAROSA	*The Apprentice*
OSTEN	*Survivor*
PASCHAL	*Survivor*
PETRA	*Joe Millionaire 2*
PUCK	*Real World*
REICHEN	*Amazing Race*

RUBEN	*American Idol*
RUDY	*Survivor*
RUPERT	*Survivor*
SHII ANN	*Survivor*
SILAS	*Survivor*
SYRUS	*Real World*
TALICIA	*Amazing Race*
TAMYRA	*American Idol*
TIAN	*Amazing Race*
TIJUANA	*Survivor*
TRENYCE	*American Idol*
TRISHELLE	*Real World*
TRISTA	*The Bachelor*
VECEPIA	*Survivor*
XIOMARA	*America's Next Top Model 2*
ZORA	*Joe Millionaire*

They Came from Outer Space

Recent space operas and mythic dramas have added their own eccentric entries (with an emphasis on the letters "z" and "x") into the name game. Among them are Ezri, Jadzi, Xena, and Yara (female) and Callisto, Dax, Fox, Joxer, and Neelix (male).

It Takes One to Play One

Not only do some soap opera characters have some wildly inventive names, but often so do the actors who portray them. A few examples:

FEMALE	MALE
ALLA	AVALON
BLUEJEAN	CRUISE
CHALICE	DAX
FEY	KALE
FUSCHIA	KIN
KAM	KOHL
KIMBERLIN	NYNNO
SABRYN	RAD
SCHAE	REEF
SHELL	SHEMAR
STARLA	STACK
THYME	ZEN
VANITA	

And Tide Was the Surfer Dude Who Had an Affair with Dawn

We even named characters after Procter & Gamble products. Dawn was named after the dishwashing soap and Cal's horse Comet after the cleanser.

—*John Kuntz, scriptwriter for* As the World Turns, *in* Soap Opera Magazine

---

Disney World

Over the years, Disney characters have provided naming inspiration for generations of parents. Before the movie of the same name, for example, Bambi was rarely if ever used as a girl's name, but after the movie's release, and despite the fact that the deer in question was male, there soon were thousands of little girl Bambis across the land. More recently, another name that was influential was that of Ariel, the title character of *The Little Mermaid*.

Here is a list of Disney names that might be considered by prospective parents and that could give their bearers a special connection to the leading purveyor of children's popular culture in America. Be warned, however, that some of these are names of bad guys, and others play pretty minor parts.

A School of Mermaids

As any parent with school-age children knows, names are subject to fashion, and the source for trendy names is often the movies: there may be five Ariels in your daughter's fourth-grade class, because a character by that name was the heroine of Disney's *The Little Mermaid*, in 1989, but just try finding an Ariel in the play group where you deposit your preschooler. (Mulan, anyone?)

—*Brendan Lemon*, The New Yorker

GIRLS

ABIGAIL	*The Fox and the Hound* and *The Aristocats*
ADELAIDE	*The Aristocats*
ALICE	*Alice in Wonderland*
AMELIA	*The Aristocats* and *Treasure Planet*
ANASTASIA	*Cinderella*

ANITA	*One Hundred and One Dalmatians*
ARIEL	*The Little Mermaid*
AURORA	*Sleeping Beauty*
BAMBI	*Bambi* (male character)
BELLE	*Beauty and the Beast*
BIANCA	*The Rescuers* and *The Rescuers Down Under*
CALLA	*The Gummi Bears* (TV)
CALLIOPE	*Hercules*
CARLOTTA	*The Little Mermaid*
CELIA	*Toy Story 2*
CLEO	*Pinocchio*
CLIO	*Hercules*
DAISY	cartoon shorts
DINAH	*Alice in Wonderland*
DORY	*Finding Nemo*
EEMA	*Dinosaur*
ENA	*Bambi*
ESMERALDA	*The Hunchback of Notre Dame*
FELICIA	*The Great Mouse Detective*
FIFI	cartoon shorts
FLORA	*Sleeping Beauty*
HYACINTH	*Fantasia*
JENNY	*Oliver and Company*
KATRINA	*The Adventures of Ichabod and Mr. Toad*
LILO	*Lilo & Stitch*
LUCY	*One Hundred and One Dalmatians*
MARIAN	*Robin Hood*
MIM	*The Sword in the Stone*
MINNIE	cartoon shorts
MOLLY	*TailSpin* (TV)
NALA	*The Lion King*
NEERA	*Dinosaur*
OLIVIA	*The Great Mouse Detective*

PERDITA	*One Hundred and One Dalmatians*
POLLY	*The Rescuers Down Under*
SARABI	*The Lion King*
SARAH	*Lady and the Tramp*
THALIA	*Hercules*
URSULA	*The Little Mermaid*
VANESSA	*The Little Mermaid*
WENDY	*Peter Pan*
WINIFRED	*The Jungle Book*

BOYS

ABU	*Aladdin*
AKELA	*The Jungle Book*
AMOS	*The Fox and the Hound*
ANGUS	*The Adventures of Ichabod and Mr. Toad*
BARBOSSA	*Pirates of the Caribbean*
BARTHOLOMEW	*The Great Mouse Detective*
BASIL	*The Great Mouse Detective*
BORIS	*Lady and the Tramp*
BROM	*The Adventures of Ichabod and Mr. Toad*
BRUNO	*Cinderella*
CASEY	*Dumbo*
CHRISTOPHER	*Winnie the Pooh*
CLAUDE	*The Hunchback of Notre Dame*
CODY	*The Rescuers Down Under*
DEMETRIUS	*Hercules*
DEWEY	cartoon shorts
ERIC	*The Little Mermaid*
GAETAN	*Atlantis, The Lost Empire 2*
GASTON	*Beauty and the Beast*
GIDEON	*Pinocchio*
GUS	*Cinderella*

HUGO	*The Hunchback of Notre Dame*
IAGO	*Aladdin*
JAFAR	*Aladdin*
JAKE	*The Rescuers Down Under*
KENAI	*Brother Bear*
LUKE	*The Rescuers*
MAX	*The Little Mermaid*
MEEKO	*Pocahontas*
MILO	*Atlantis, The Lost Empire 2*
NEMO	*Finding Nemo*
NIGEL	*Finding Nemo*
OLIVER	*Oliver and Company*
ORVILLE	*The Rescuers*
OTTO	*Robin Hood*
PEDRO	*Lady and the Tramp*
PERCY	*Pocahontas*
PETER	*Peter Pan*
PHILLIP	*Sleeping Beauty*
PHOEBUS	*The Hunchback of Notre Dame*
RAFIKI	*The Lion King*
RAMA	*The Jungle Book*
ROBIN	*Robin Hood*
ROSCOE	*Oliver and Company*
RUFUS	*The Rescuers*
SEBASTIAN	*The Little Mermaid*
SIMBA	*The Lion King*
STEFAN	*Sleeping Beauty*
TANANA	*Brother Bear*
THADDEUS	*Toad of Toad Hall*
THOMAS	*The Aristocats*
TIMON	*The Lion King*
TIMOTHY	*Dumbo*
TOBY	*Robin Hood* and *The Great Mouse Detective*
TOD	*The Fox and the Hound*

WALDO	*The Aristocats*
WINSTON	*Oliver and Company*
ZAZU	*The Lion King*
ZEUS	*Hercules*

There's Only One Uma

If you have one of these names, what it means is that when you make a phone call, you'll never be asked "Ving who?" On the other hand, nothing necessarily lasts forever, including uniqueness. There are a lot more Elvises around than there used to be, including a soap opera baby, but there's still only one Elvis. In terms of one-person names, these seem to be permanently assigned to their current owners:

ALANIS Morrisette
ALFRE Woodard
ANANDA Lewis
ARETHA Franklin
ARSENIO Hall
ASHANTI
AVRIL Lavigne
AZURA Skye
BAI Ling
BECK
BENICIO Del Toro
BEYONCÉ Knowles
BIJOU Phillips
BJÖRK
BLU (b. Tiffany) Cantrell
BONO (b. Paul)
BRECKIN Meyer

BUSY (b. Elizabeth; Busy a childhood nickname)
  Philipps
CHARISMA (named after an Avon perfume)
  Carpenter
CHARLIZE Theron
CHER
CILLIAN Murphy
CLEA DuVall
CUBA Gooding Jr.
DELROY Lindo
DEMI (b. Demetria) Moore
DENZEL Washington
DIVA Zappa
DJIMON Hounsou
DOUGRAY Scott
DULÉ Hill
DWEEZIL Zappa
EMO Phillips
ENYA (b. Eithne)
ERYKAH Badu
FAIRUZA Balk
FAMKE Jannssen
HEATH (named for the *Wuthering Heights* character
  Heathcliff) Ledger
IBEN Hjejle
ILEANA Douglas
IMAN
JADA Pinkett
JORJA Fox
JOSS Stone
JUDGE (b. Edward) Reinhold
KEANU (it means "cool breeze over the mountain"
  in Hawaiian) Reeves
KIEFER Sutherland

KOBE Bryant

LAKE Bell

LEBRON James

LEELEE (b. Liliane) Sobieski

LIEV Schreiber

MADONNA

MOBY (born Richard Melville—a descendant of the
author of *Moby Dick*)

MONET Mazur

MONTEL Williams

MYKELTI Williamson

NENAH Cherry

NEVE (her mother's maiden name) Campbell

OPRAH Winfrey

PICABO Street

PINK (b. Alecia)

PLUM Sykes

REESE (b. Laura) Witherspoon

RIDDICK Bowe

ROMA Downey

SADE (b. Helen)

SAFFRON Burroughs

SALMA Hayek

SANAA Lathan

SAVION Glover

SEAL (b. Seal Henry)

SHAKIRA (b. Isabel)

SHALOM Harlow

SHANIA Twain

SHAQUILLE O'Neal

SIGOURNEY (b. Susan) Weaver

SINBAD (b. David)

SKEET (b. Brian) Ulrich

SOLEDAD O'Brien

STAR (b. Starlet) Jones

Much Ado About Naming

With names like Olivia and Julia, Duncan, Sebastian, and other favorites of the Bard of Avon experiencing a revival, you might want to consider a more expansive playbill of Shakespearean choices:

GIRLS

ADRIANA	*The Comedy of Errors*
ALICE	*The Merry Wives of Windsor*
AUDREY	*As You Like It*
BEATRICE	*Much Ado About Nothing*
BIANCA	*The Taming of the Shrew, Othello*
CASSANDRA	*Troilus and Cressida*
CELIA	*As You Like It*
CHARMIAN	*Antony and Cleopatra*
CLEOPATRA	*Antony and Cleopatra*
CORDELIA	*King Lear*
CRESSIDA	*Troilus and Cressida*
DESDEMONA	*Othello*
DIANA	*All's Well That Ends Well*
DORCAS	*The Winter's Tale*
EMILIA	*Othello, The Winter's Tale*

TAYE (b. Scott) Diggs

THANDIE Newton

THORA Birch

TOPHER (b. Christopher) Grace

TREAT (b. Richard) Williams

TYRA Banks

UMA (a Tibetan name chosen by her Buddhist scholar father) Thurman

USHER

VENDELA

VENUS Williams

VIGGO Mortensen

VIN (b. Mark) Diesel

VING (b. Irving) Rhames

WHOOPI (b. Caryn) Goldberg

WINGS (b. Gerald) Hauser

WINONA Ryder

WYCLEF Jean

ZOOEY Deschanel

The Goddess Uma

Uma Thurman has three brothers: Dechen, Ganden, and Mipam. The four siblings all have Tibetan names because their father, Robert A. F. Thurman, the Jey Tsong Khapa Professor of Indo-Tibetan Buddhist Studies at Columbia University, was the first American to be ordained as a Tibetan Buddhist monk by the Dalai Lama, in 1965. Uma means "the Middle Way" in Tibetan and is the name of the mother goddess in Indian mythology.

FRANCISCA	*Measure for Measure*
HELENA	*A Midsummer Night's Dream, All's Well That Ends Well*
HERMIONE	*The Winter's Tale*
IMOGEN	*Cymbeline*
ISABEL	*Henry V*
ISABELLA	*Measure for Measure*
JACQUENETTA	*Love's Labour Lost*
JESSICA	*The Merchant of Venice*
JULIA	*Two Gentlemen of Verona*
JULIET	*Romeo and Juliet*
JUNO	*The Tempest*
KATHARINA (KATE)	*The Taming of the Shrew*
LAVINIA	*Titus Andronicus*
LUCIANA	*The Comedy of Errors*
MARGARET	*Much Ado About Nothing*
MARINA	*Pericles*
MIRANDA	*The Tempest*
NELL	*The Comedy of Errors*
NERISSA	*The Merchant of Venice*
OCTAVIA	*Antony and Cleopatra*
OLIVIA	*Twelfth Night*
OPHELIA	*Hamlet*
PAULINA	*The Winter's Tale*
PERDITA	*The Winter's Tale*
PHEBE	*As You Like It*
PORTIA	*The Merchant of Venice, Julius Caesar*
REGAN	*King Lear*
ROSALIND	*As You Like It*
ROSALINE	*Love's Labour Lost*
TAMORA	*Titus Andronicus*
TITANIA	*A Midsummer Night's Dream*
URSULA	*Much Ado About Nothing*

VIOLA	*Twelfth Night*
VIRGILIA	*Coriolanus*

BOYS

ABRAHAM	*Romeo and Juliet*
ADRIAN	*The Tempest*
ADRIANO	*Love's Labour Lost*
ALONSO	*The Tempest*
ANGELO	*Measure for Measure*
ANGUS	*Macbeth*
ANTONIO	*The Tempest, Two Gentlemen of Verona, The Merchant of Venice, Much Ado About Nothing*
ANTONY	*Antony and Cleopatra*
ARIEL	*The Tempest*
BALTHASAR	*Romeo and Juliet, The Merchant of Venice, Much Ado About Nothing*
BALTHAZAR	*A Comedy of Errors*
BENEDICK	*Much Ado About Nothing*
BENVOLIO	*Romeo and Juliet*
CALIBAN	*The Tempest*
CAMILLO	*The Winter's Tale*
CLAUDIO	*Measure for Measure, Much Ado About Nothing*
CLEON	*Pericles*
CORIN	*As You Like It*
CORNELIUS	*Hamlet*
DEMETRIUS	*A Midsummer Night's Dream*
DION	*The Winter's Tale*
DUNCAN	*Macbeth*
EDMUND	*King Lear*
FABIAN	*Twelfth Night*
FERDINAND	*The Tempest*

FRANCISCO	*Hamlet*
GREGORY	*Romeo and Juliet*
HENRY	Several plays
HORATIO	*Hamlet*
HUMPHREY	*Henry VI, Part II*
KENT	*King Lear*
LENNOX	*Macbeth*
LEONARDO	*The Merchant of Venice*
LORENZO	*The Merchant of Venice*
LUCIUS	*Timon of Athens, Titus Andronicus, Julius Caesar*
LYSANDER	*A Midsummer Night's Dream*
MALCOLM	*Macbeth*
NATHANIEL	*Love's Labour Lost*
OBERON	*A Midsummer Night's Dream*
OLIVER	*As You Like It*
ORLANDO	*As You Like It*
ORSINO	*Twelfth Night*
OWEN	*Henry IV, Part I*
PHILO	*Antony and Cleopatra*

Gulliver versus Romeo

When asked about his son Gulliver's unusual name, Gary Oldman explained to *People* magazine, "I was inspired by the character from *Gulliver's Travels*. My wife {photographer Donya Fiorentino} was a great sport about it." Maybe it was a happy compromise. "I also wanted to name him Romeo," said Oldman, "which would have been doing the boy a favor. Any boy named Romeo is going to get the chicks."

Brit Lit

The annals of British literature, from the pastoral poets of the seventeenth century, through Jane Austen and Dickens, and up to more modern times, are a rich source of imaginative names:

ADELINE	*Lord Byron*
AGATHA	*Evelyn Waugh*
ALETHEA	*Samuel Butler*
ALTHEA	*Richard Lovelace*
AMANDA	*Noel Coward*
AMELIA	*Henry Fielding, W. M. Thackeray*
ANASTASIA	*Charles Dickens*
ANTHEA	*Robert Herrick, Barbara Pym*
ARABELLA	*Charles Dickens*
BATHSHEBA	*Thomas Hardy*
BELINDA	*Alexander Pope*
CANDIDA	*George Bernard Shaw*
CECILIA	*Charles Dickens*
CHARLOTTE	*Jane Austen, Charles Dickens*
CHASTITY	*Evelyn Waugh*

CHRISTABEL	*Samuel Coleridge, Barbara Pym*
CLARICE	*P. G. Wodehouse*
CLARISSA	*Charles Dickens, Samuel Richardson, Virginia Woolf*
CORDELIA	*Evelyn Waugh*
CORINNA	*Robert Herrick*
CRESSIDA	*Barbara Pym*
DAHLIA	*George Meredith, P. G. Wodehouse*
DINAH	*Lawrence Sterne*
DOMENICA	*Evelyn Waugh*
ELECTRA	*Robert Herrick*
ELIZA	*Jane Austen, George Bernard Shaw*
EMMA	*Jane Austen*
ESTELLA	*Charles Dickens*
EUSTACIA	*Thomas Hardy*
EVANGELINE	*P. G. Wodehouse*
FLEUR	*John Galsworthy*
FLORA	*Charles Dickens, Sir Walter Scott*
FORTITUDE	*Evelyn Waugh*
GEORGIANA	*Jane Austen, Charles Dickens*
GUINEVERE	Arthurian legends
HONORIA	*Charles Dickens*
JEMIMA	*Jane Austen, Beatrix Potter*
JULIANA	*Andrew Marvell*
JUSTICE	*Evelyn Waugh*
JUSTINE	*Lawrence Durrell*
LAVINIA	*Charles Dickens*
LEILA	*Lord Byron*
LETITIA	*Jane Austen*
LILIA	*E. M. Forster*
LUCASTA	*Richard Lovelace*
LUCRETIA	*Charles Dickens*
LYDIA	*Jane Austen*
MALTA	*Charles Dickens*

MARIGOLD	*Barbara Pym*
MATILDA	*Charles Dickens*
MAUD	*Alfred, Lord Tennyson*
MERCY	*Charles Dickens, Evelyn Waugh*
MORGAN	Arthurian legends
NELL	*Charles Dickens*
PERDITA	*Evelyn Waugh*
PIPPA	*Robert Browning*
PLEASANT	*Charles Dickens*
PRIMROSE	*Barbara Pym*
ROMOLA	*George Eliot*
ROWENA	*Sir Walter Scott*
SELINA	*Jane Austen*
TAMSIN	*Barbara Pym*
TESS	*Thomas Hardy*
THOMASIN	*Thomas Hardy*
VELVET	*Enid Bagnold*
ZULEIKA	*Sir Max Beerbohm*

BOYS

ALARIC	*Barbara Pym*
AMBROSE	*Evelyn Waugh, P. G. Wodehouse*
AUGUSTINE	*P. G. Wodehouse*
AUGUSTUS	*Charles Dickens*
BARNABY	*Charles Dickens*
BARNEY	*Charles Dickens*
BARTHOLOMEW	*Charles Dickens*
CHEVY	*Charles Dickens*
CRISPIN	*Barbara Pym*
DARCY	
(*surname*)	*Jane Austen*
DIGBY	*Barbara Pym*
DORIAN	*Oscar Wilde*

DUNCAN	*Evelyn Waugh*
EBENEZER	*Charles Dickens*
ELIJAH	*Charles Dickens*
EPHRAIM	*Charles Dickens, Barbara Pym*
EUSTACE	*P. G. Wodehouse*
FELIX	*Barbara Pym, Evelyn Waugh*
FERDINAND	*Charles Dickens*
FITZWILLIAM	*Jane Austen*
GARETH	Arthurian legends
GILES	*Barbara Pym*
GRAY	*W. Somerset Maugham*
GULLY	*Joyce Cary*
HIRAM	*Charles Dickens*
HORATIO	*Charles Dickens*
HUMPHREY	*Tobias Smollett, Evelyn Waugh*
IVOR	*Evelyn Waugh, P. G. Wodehouse*
JASPER	*P. G. Wodehouse*
JEREMIAH	*Charles Dickens*
JOSIAH	*Charles Dickens*
JUDE	*Thomas Hardy*
LEMUEL	*Jonathan Swift*
NICODEMUS	*Charles Dickens*
NICOL	*Sir Walter Scott*
OBADIAH	*Anthony Trollope*
OLIVER	*Charles Dickens*
ORLANDO	*P. G. Wodehouse, Virginia Woolf*
PEREGRINE	*Tobias Smollett, Evelyn Waugh*
QUEBEC	*Charles Dickens*
QUENTIN	*Sir Walter Scott*
REX	*Evelyn Waugh*
RODERICK	*Tobias Smollett*
ROLLO	*Barbara Pym*
RUPERT	*P. G. Wodehouse*
SEBASTIAN	*Evelyn Waugh*

SEPTIMUS	*Charles Dickens, Virginia Woolf*
SILAS	*George Eliot*
TOBY	*Charles Dickens*
TRISTRAM	Arthurian legends, *Laurence Sterne*

IMAGE

W hat's really in a name?

In this section, we examine that Shakespearean puzzle to determine what kind of images are embodied in a name, and how much information those images convey.

Some names have a Traditional image while others feel Creative—that's the easy part. Here we tell you everything you ever wanted to know about the sixty most classic names, and also offer a long list of names with a creative flavor.

In these days of highly inventive baby-naming, we analyze the issue of Unusual Names: How unusual is too unusual for your child? And if you're tired of both usual and creative names, which names have a more straightforward, down-to-earth image?

We explore the implications of nicknames here, too. And if you want a name that will help your child fit in with the crowd as well as stand out, this is where you'll find it.

And we wrestle with that most taboo of American subjects as it relates to names: class. Are there really names that sound classy, and those that don't? We tell all.

What's Really in a Name?

Power, Image, and Names

All names carry an image. That much is indisputable. We perceive some names as sounding stronger, more serious than others, some names as being attractive and intelligent and others not.

But how important, how influential is that image? By your choice of a name, do you really set your child up for being thought of as smart or energetic, sexy or unreliable for the rest of his or her life? Or can a name shape your child's destiny in an even more elemental, insidious way, by conveying power through its very sounds and rhythms?

Through the years and over the ages, from ancient times to the present, there are those who have believed—and who would have you believe—that names are everything, that the image of a name is all-important in determining your child's future.

Primitive people believed that the name was the vessel for the person's soul or spirit. There are many superstitions relating to names and their power to influence someone's life for good or evil, to bless them with riches and a long future, or to drain their very lifeblood from them, hastening their death and even the deaths of those in their families.

It may be easy to dismiss these sorts of traditional beliefs as nonsense, yet as recently as 1937 name expert W. E. Walton wrote: "A person's first name may be a determining factor in his development of personality, acquisition of friends, and in all probability in his success or failure in life."

At the time of this writing we went on the Internet, that thoroughly modern vehicle for the dissemination of information, and checked in at the name site of the Kabalarian Society, which analyzes what it considers the power inherent in over 150,000 names, from P-Nut to Padmavathamma, based on its own Mathematical Principles.

Here is the Kabalarian's reading of Pamela:

> The first name of Pamela creates a rather dual nature. You can appear to be two entirely different people, depending upon what environment you are in. . . . You are inclined to be temperamental and impulsive, overemotional and generous. The beauties of nature, fine music, art and literature you find very inspiring. . . . You must guard against indulgence in any form, particularly in the emotions, and also in the desire for sugars and starchy foods.

Seems wacky? Consider that in Italy, standard baby-naming books carry similar predictions about a child's personality and destiny based on his or her name. A boy named Enrico, for instance, will be calm and reflective and, when he's in love, will be faithful and devoted. His lucky number is one; his best day, Sunday; and his lucky precious metal, gold.

And much closer to home and mainstream social science, UCLA professor Albert Mehrabian has undertaken extensive surveys in which people rate names on six qualities: success, morality, health, warmth, cheerfulness, and masculinity-femininity. His book, *The Name Game*, lists every name with its number rating on each of these characteristics, noting which names are perceived as being highest and lowest in each category.

While this is an interesting exercise, perceptions of names change over time, sometimes quite rapidly. A name that sounds successful, say, or masculine one year might seem anything but a few years later. And our ideas about many of these names vary radically from what Mehrabian's panel decided. Brad, for instance, gets one of the highest ratings, a 90, in success. At what? Surfing? Bruce is seen as one of the most masculine names, yet its widespread image is as anything but.

We can see why Moses and Solomon, Lincoln and Ernest got high marks for morality, but why Herman? Why Filbert and Myrtle? Just because they sound too old to do anything nasty? Charlie indeed sounds cheerful, yet Abigail, which means happiness, gets one of the lowest ratings for cheer. Maggie hasn't got much chance of success, Eleanor's not very healthy, Jessica's not really feminine—gee, this doesn't sound entirely accurate to us.

In surveying the research on the power of names, there is a lot of going back and forth: studies that show one thing about image, and then further studies that show the complete opposite.

One well-publicized study from a few decades ago seemed to demonstrate that having a well-liked name could lead to academic success. Teachers graded the essays of children with popular names such as Lisa and Michael higher than those by children named Elmer and Bertha.

Yet other, much larger, studies disproved the link between names and grades. One analysis of the grades of nearly 24,000 second- to eleventh-graders in a midwestern public school system found no correlation between name popularity or desirability and academic achievement. Another study of 724 high schoolers in the Midwest found no correlation between names and grade-point average, achievement tests, and social competence and empathy tests. Researcher Martin Ford at Stanford reasoned that in some cases having an unusual or undesirable name might have a negative effect on a child's achievement, but it was just as likely that it would build character.

Another highly publicized study from Tulane University showed that hypothetical beauty pageant contestants with attractive names such as Jennifer and Christine won out over contestants with less desirable names such as Ethel and Harriet.

Still another study, which assigned two names found to have a high variation in attractiveness, Christy and Gertrude, to the same actress, found that the names had no effect on how appealing people judged her looks and behavior to be.

Names, some more than others, carry stereotypes that can lead people to make judgments. A 1992 investigation of names in television at SUNY–Stonybrook found that people judged a hypothetical woman named Andrea Wolcot to be highly educated, they saw Kathy and Elisa as waitresses, Ruby was seen as a black jazz singer. Kimberly Channing was seen as a spoiled preppy girl and Marina a gypsy con woman. Avery and Bret get rich, Stanley Nmitski and Clyde Regan are criminals.

But our real-life experiences tend to overshadow whatever judgments we make about names on a theoretical

> Freudian Analysis
> *A human being's name is a principal component in his person, perhaps a piece of his soul.*
>
> —SIGMUND FREUD

> ### On Being a Stanley
> *Stanley is your brother-in-law, your CPA, your cousin in drapes. He collects stamps, washes his car, belongs to Triple A, and keeps a weather eye on the gas mileage. He is, that is, as all of us are, the fiction of his sound, all his recombinant glottals, labials, fricatives, and plosives . . . He is, I mean, the vibrations of his name.*
>
> —FROM A LECTURE BY
> STANLEY ELKIN

basis. Kenneth Steele and Laura Smithwick, psychologists at Mars Hill College in North Carolina, found that people judge certain names as good (David, Jon, Joshua, and Gregory) or bad (Oswald, Myron, Reginald) and tend to assign positive and negative characteristics to people based on those names if, that is, they haven't met or seen the specific individual, and have no other information but the name. Once the subjects in the experiment were shown photos of the theoretical Joshuas and Reginalds, judgments based solely on the names were erased.

Interestingly, a name's most potent influence may be on the person who bears it. A British book called *The Cognitive Psychology of Proper Names* says that the intimate relationship between one's given name and one's sense of identity accounts for the frequency with which psychotics, particularly schizophrenics, forget their names, refuse to tell them, or adopt new ones.

Children tend to be extremely interested in their own names, which springs from their developing sense of selfhood. Educators have found that the name is an ideal vehicle with which to engage children in learning. The first thing most kids can write is their names, and once they learn the letters in their own names they use those as a jumping-off point to other words. Children are attracted to lists containing their own names and interested in differences between their names and their friends' names, which can be a way for them to start learning to read and write.

It's easy to get caught up in the mania over the image and power embodied in a name during the months you're on the hunt for the perfect choice. At the time, it can feel like your child's name is one of the few things you really have control over, and it's essential as one of your first important parenting acts that you make the perfect choice. It can seem as if the name you pick will make all the difference in whether your child will be seen as an intelligent, attractive, creative, interesting person or not.

And yet in your heart, you know that's not true. What's really in a name? A lot, we believe, but not everything. Choosing a great name for your child may be important, but it's nowhere near as important as making him or her feel secure, overseeing his education, and being a loving parent.

Sixty Traditional Names
That Transcend Time

What's the definition of a classic name? One that's not only rooted in history, but that's been consistently well used throughout the ages, finding fans in the twentieth century as it did in the twelfth. Classic names transcend class and religion and nationality to appeal to a wide range of parents, from royals on down to the hoi polloi. A great traditional name is hard to find, not least because there simply aren't that many of them around. Here are our picks for the top sixty Traditionals, thirty for girls and thirty for boys, that work as beautifully today as they have over the centuries.

GIRLS

ALICE. Forever associated with Lewis Carroll's heroine in *Alice's Adventures in Wonderland* and *Through the Looking Glass and What Alice Found There*, Alice still retains an aura of long, streaming hair and pastel-hued ribbon hairbands, which was reinforced by such sentimental songs as *Alice Blue Gown*. Stemming from an ancient German word meaning "nobility," it moved from Alalheidis to the French shortening Adaliz, which arrived in England as Aliz. The name enjoyed enormous popularity following the publication of *Alice's Adventures in Wonderland* in 1865, remaining in the top twenty-five names in this country until 1925, but it then gradually began to fade as a baby name, especially after it took on a blue-collar tinge with the characters Alice Kramden on *The Honeymooners* and Linda Lavin's TV waitress, to be replaced by such variations as **Allison** and **Alyssa**. In England the name has survived as an aristocratic and even royal name and was number six on the most recent *Times of London* most popular names list, which reflects the current taste of the British upper class. Literary-minded parents might favor the name because of the unusual raft of excellent contemporary writers called Alice: the Alices Munro, Sebold, Walker, Hoffman, Adams, McDermott, and Elliott Dark.

ANN, ANNE. Ann is the English form of the Hebrew name Hannah (which means "God has favored me"); in the Old Testament, Hannah was the mother of Samuel. Traditionally, Anne is also believed to have been the name of the mother of the Virgin Mary, which led to its great popularity in the Christian world. The Ann spelling was much more common in the nineteenth century, then was surpassed by the longer (French) version, especially with the birth of England's Princess Anne in 1950. In this country, Ann was in the Top 10 in 1925, but now **Annie**, a short form that was near the top of the Most Popular List around the turn of the twentieth century; **Anna**, the Greek form of the name; and especially the original **Hannah** are much more popular choices.

CAROLINE. This name comes from **Carolina**, the Italian female form of **Charles**, and was introduced to the English-speaking world by Caroline of Ansbach, the German wife of George II, who became Queen in 1727. It was a favorite eighteenth-century name and has moved in and out of favor ever since, to be replaced in the 1930s and 1940s by **Carol,** then was given a high-profile gloss when it was picked by America's royal family, the Kennedys, and by Grace Kelly for her daughter, the Princess of Monaco. **Carolyn** is a twentieth-century variation. The quintessential yuppie name of the eighties, Caroline retains its classy image, but has slipped a few rungs on the fashion ladder.

CHARLOTTE. Charlotte is another Italian female offshoot of Charles, this time via Carlo and **Carlotta.** Before the late eighteenth century it was considered a French name and rarely used in England or America, until Britain's King George III married a German princess named Charlotte-Sophia. Charlotte has had a long reign as a popular literary name, used for the heroines of novels ranging from Goethe's *The Sorrows of Young Werther* to the endearing spider in E. B. White's *Charlotte's Web.* In the early 1990s, it was the number-one girl baby's name in England, and is beginning to be reappreciated in this country as well.

CHRISTINE, CHRISTINA. All the names with this first syllable are derived from the Greek *chrio,* meaning "I anoint." The initial record of these two short forms of **Christiana** dates from the third century, via St. Christina, a martyred Roman noblewoman. It reached the British Isles late in the eleventh century, a time when the name **Christian** was used for both sexes. Christina became a royal name in both Spain and Sweden (Greta Garbo played Queen Christina in one of her best-known films). Christine (the French form) was at the height of its popularity in this country in the 1970s, when it reached number ten on the Hit Parade; these days Christina is the preferred choice.

CLAIRE, CLARE.   Claire, not surprisingly, comes from the Latin word meaning "clear, bright." Its first association was with St. Clare of Assisi, a follower of St. Francis and the founder, in 1212, of a benevolent order called the Poor Clares. Because she reportedly "witnessed" a mass being celebrated a great distance away, Clare was proclaimed, believe it or not, the patron saint of television in 1958 by Pope Pius XII. The name has been quite quietly used in this country, never ascending to the great heights of popularity it has in England, although the Claire spelling seems to be picking up some steam at present, as are its derivatives, **Clarissa** and **Clara**. **Clair** is another accepted spelling.

DEBORAH.   Deborah is the Hebrew word for "bee," an ancient symbol of eternity and later, perhaps because of that insect's musical humming, also came to mean "eloquence." The first mention of this ancient name is in the Book of Genesis, where Deborah was Rebecca's faithful nurse. The later biblical bearer of the name was a formidable judge, poet, and prophetess who predicted the fall of the Canaanites and sang a famously expressive song of triumph when the Israelites were victorious. This name was very popular among the Puritans of the late seventeenth century, partially because the bee was a symbol of industriousness, an admired virtue. Deborah was then revived in the twentieth century, peaking around 1960, when it was second only to Mary, and it seemed that every other kid on the block was a **Debbie**. **Debra** is a twentieth-century variation.

DIANA. One of the most enduring of the ancient goddess names, Diana, which means "divine" in Latin, was the Roman goddess of the moon and of the hunt, represented in myth as both beautiful and chaste. It was not used as an English Christian name until well into the sixteenth century, coming into general use only around 1750, partly because until then some ecclesiastics were hesitant to baptize girls with a pagan name. In America, Diana took even longer to take hold, infrequently used until the middle of the twentieth century, and even then it was the French form **Diane** that was more commonly heard. In contemporary times, it is certain to be associated with Diana, Princess of Wales, for a long while. Despite the Princess's popularity, however, the name's popularity has not been revived, here or in England.

ELEANOR. This name derives from the French Provençal form of Helen, Alienor, which came to England when Eleanor of Aquitaine married King Henry II in the twelfth century, and was popularized when Edward I erected many memorial "Eleanor" crosses to his wife, "Good Queen Eleanor," in the next century. Jane Austen's character **Elinor** Dashwood, the embodiment of sense in *Sense and Sensibility*, publicized that spelling of the name, and Eleanor Roosevelt was its most famous twentieth-century bearer. It was one of the first somewhat staid classic names to be revived by today's stylish parents. Short form **Ellie** has recently hit Britain's Most Popular list.

ELIZABETH. In Hebrew, this name means "God has sworn," and in the New Testament it was borne by the mother of John the Baptist. Her significance as the first person to recognize the impact of Mary's child inspired Christians to honor the name Elizabeth. It became even more widely used via the royal families of England from the fifteenth century on, in particular with Elizabeth Tudor, who ruled the country for half a century, giving her name to the Elizabethan Age—during her reign 25 percent of girls born were named in her honor. The name was transported to this country by the colonists—three Elizabeths arrived on the *Mayflower*—and has had a remarkably consistent popularity: It was number three in 1875 and is still in the Top 10 in many states today. Elizabeth may also have spawned more offshoots and pet names than any other appellation, from **Betty** to **Betsy** to **Beth** to **Libby** to **Lisa** to **Liz**.

EMILY. Emily, which in 1997 became the most popular baby girl's name in America, derives from the Roman family name, Aemilius. It was Geoffrey Chaucer who introduced the name as Emily in "The Knight's Tale" section of *The Canterbury Tales*. It did not come into common use until after 1800, then, stimulated by two renowned writers, Emily Brontë and Emily Dickinson, it became among the most well-used names in both Britain and the United States by 1870. Emily had been climbing steadily toward the top since the early 1980s, its combination of strength and femininity appealing to a wide range of parents.

EMMA. Although Emma has sometimes been used as a short form of Emily, they have completely different origins. Emma comes from the Old German word meaning "universal" or "whole," and, along with many other names, was brought to the English-speaking world by the Normans when Queen Emma, "Fair Maid of Normandy," married the English king Ethelred the Unready in 1002. The literary heroines of Jane Austen's *Emma* and Flaubert's *Madame Bovary* cast further light onto the name. By the end of the nineteenth century, it was in the

British Top 10, then faded until the character of Emma Peel in the massive TV hit, *The Avengers*, brought it back. Always more popular in England than in the United States, it has finally come into its own here as a fresher alternative to Emily.

EVE. The meaning usually attributed to this name is "life-giving," or "breath of life," quite fitting for the first woman, created from one of Adam's ribs. In Genesis, Adam gave names to all the animals, and then to his wife, who was the "mother of all living." However, since, according to the Old Testament, Eve was believed to have brought sin into the world, her name has not been overly popular. And the serpentlike character in the 1950 film *All About Eve* didn't help much either. There is, however, an old tradition that children named Eve are always long-lived, which may account for the fact that the name was used even when Old Testament names were uncommon. At one time it was not unusual to name one twin Eve and her brother Adam. Eve was not used at all in the Puritan colonies, and has never appeared on the Top 50 lists since then.

FRANCES. Frances, which means "free woman," is the feminine form of Francis—although, until the seventeenth century, the two spellings were used interchangeably for both sexes. In England the name did not appear until it was given to Henry VII's granddaughter. Frances became a favorite name among the Tudor aristocracy, then began being used, in the eighteenth century, more democratically. St. Frances (Mother) Cabrini, the first American citizen to be canonized, founded the Missionary Sisters of the Sacred Heart and helped Italian immigrants in America. The name saw its greatest popularity in this country around 1900, when it reached the Top 10 (and when its short form, **Fanny**, was popular in its own right), and now it is being used by some of the hippest Hollywood parents, such as Courtney Love and Robin Wright and Sean Penn.

GRACE. A Puritan-attribute name like Hope, Faith, and Charity, this name's original meaning referred to a person attaining a state of grace in the theological sense, rather than a physical characteristic. In Greek mythology, the Three Graces were nature goddesses who spread joy throughout the world. The name was used in the colonies, particularly the Puritan ones, and reached its high point in the last quarter of the nineteenth century—it was number eleven in 1875, and Grace Kelly came to be seen as the embodiment of its image. Modern parents have embraced this pure and elegant appellation, often using it as a middle name.

HELEN. The most illustrious of all female Greek names, Helen means "the bright one," and it very early on became associated with beauty thanks to Helen of Troy, the daughter of Leda and Zeus, whose exquisite face was said by Christopher Marlowe to have "launched a thousand ships," and whose seizure by the Trojan prince Paris ignited the ten-year Trojan War. In England, the popularity of this name was due originally to St. Helena, the mother of Constantine the Great and daughter of the Old King Cole of nursery rhyme fame. Heard first as **Elena**, the *H* wasn't used until the Renaissance, when the study of classical literature revived Homer's epics and the story of the beautiful Greek queen. Not being the name of a biblical saint, however, Helen disappeared for centuries, suddenly making a comeback in the mid-nineteenth. Since then Helen and the colloquial form **Ellen** have alternated in popularity—Helen reached number three in 1900—although there aren't many babies named either Helen or Ellen these days.

JANE.   Jane is the most common female form of John, developing from the Old French and replacing the earlier Joan. At one time in this country, the use of the name was so widespread that *jane* became a slang term for "girl." Still a popular name in England, it reached its highest point of U.S. popularity in 1925, but has not been on the American Top 50 since then. For a time it was most often seen as half of such double names as Mary Jane and Betty Jane, and then became virtually replaced by such more modern-sounding variants as **Janet**, **Janice**, and **Jeanette**. But of all such similar names as **Jane**, **Joan**, **Jean**, **Janet**, and **June**, Jane stands the greatest chance of being revived.

JEAN.   Jean is, like Jane and Joan, a medieval variant of the Old French Jehann, and at one time its use was almost totally restricted to Scotland, still retaining a Scottish accent today. Its use peaked in this country in the 1920s and 1930s (it reached number nine in 1925), but has been declining ever since, despite the lingering popularity of the song *Jeanie with the Light Brown Hair* and the recycled TV standard, *I Dream of Jeannie*.

JULIA.   Julia is the feminine form of the old Roman family name, Julius, and was a common Christian name among early Romans. Borne by several early saints, it was used by Shakespeare in *Two Gentlemen of Verona* and was popular with the classical and romantic poets, only to be replaced for much of this century by the less euphonic, more straightforward **Julie**. Julia is now, thanks to such attractive influences as the Julias Roberts, Ormond, Stiles, and Louis-Dreyfuss, making a strong return with sophisticated baby-namers, along with its male cognate, **Julian**. **Juliet** and **Juliana** are other chic variations.

KATHERINE. This name goes back to a Greek form, Aikaterine, the meaning of which is unknown. Its popularity in the Western world is due to the story and cult of the martyred fourth-century St. Catherine of Alexandria, who, according to legend, was such a brilliant Egyptian princess that she refuted the arguments of all the wisest men of her country with her defense of Christianity. After being killed with a spiked wheel, her body was carried by angels to Mount Sinai. The **Katherine** spelling is related to the Greek adjective *katharos*, meaning "pure." It is a royal name in England, belonging to the wives of Henry V, Henry VIII (including the formidable Catherine of Aragon), and Charles II, as well as the French Catherine de Medici. The **Catherine** spelling predominates in England and France; **Kathryn**, a twentieth-century form, is still the number-two spelling here; the shortened form **Kate**—a favorite of William Shakespeare's—became one of the standard English names as well early on. Other related names, including **Karen**, **Kay**, **Kathleen**, **Kitty**, and **Kathy**, have had periods of popularity of their own, but today it is Katherine that is being chosen by conservative parents, with the name in all its variations at number seventeen.

LAURA. Laura is a feminine version of **Laurence**, both of which relate to the bay laurel, the leaves of which have long been an emblem of victory. Laura was first popularized in modern English via the love sonnets of the Italian poet Petrarch, which were largely addressed to a woman with that name. It was imported into England and America in the nineteenth century, and was given a thrust into the spotlight by the movie and song *Laura* in the 1940s, remaining in the Top 25 in 1960. It was largely replaced by **Laurie**, **Lori**, **Lauren**, and to a lesser degree, **Laurel**, in recent years, though Laura seems now to be making a comeback in its own right, and in its original form is the most stylish version of the name.

LOUISE.   Louise is the French feminine form of Louis, **Louisa** being the Latin version. They both came into widespread English usage during the seventeenth century, when all things French were exerting a potent influence. Louise had its greatest period of popularity in this country from the end of the nineteenth century until about 1930, and has made a definite return in England in recent years, with some signs of new life stirring on this side of the Atlantic as well.

LUCY.   Lucy is related to the Greco-Roman word *lux*, via the Latin **Lucia**, which means "light." In Roman times, the name was often given to a child born around daybreak. St. Lucy was a fourth-century Sicilian martyr whose cult became very popular in England in the Middle Ages, after which the name moved in and out of favor, increasing greatly in the eighteenth century, and returning again in the counterculture 1960s.

MARGARET.   Margaret comes from the Greek word meaning "pearl," which carries with it the ancient Persian meaning, "child of light." The popularity of the name derives from the third-century St. Margaret of Antioch, one of the four great virgin martyrs and the patroness of women in childbirth, who was said to have been, like St. George, a slayer of dragons—the legend goes that she was swallowed alive by Satan in the form of a dragon, but on making the sign of the cross, burst out of the monster and killed it. Margaret was among the most common names in medieval England, along with Elizabeth, Joan, Agnes, Maud, and Alice. Margaret is another name that was especially popular in Scotland, sometimes considered the national Scottish female name, and was a royal name in both Scotland and England, as well as in Scandinavia and Austria. It did not come into full bloom in this country until the turn of this century, when, despite competition from some of its own variations and nicknames, such as **Margery**, **Peggy**, **May**, and **Daisy**, it remained in the Top 20 for fifty years.

MARY. The New Testament form of **Miriam** (via the Greek **Mariam**), Mary was the mother of **Jesus**, as well as the name of numerous saints and queens of England and Europe. Considered in the Middle Ages to be connected with the sea, it was not in general use before 1200, being considered too sacred for ordinary mortals. But by the time of the English colonization of America, it was the most common name for girls and remained so until it was replaced by Linda in 1948. Mary has been in decline in this country ever since. Until very recently, a quarter of all Irish girls were still baptized Mary. Historically, there were so many Marys that many pet names were invented to distinguish them from one another, some of which—**Marian**, **Molly**, **Polly**, **Minnie**, **Mamie**, **Mae**—became distinctive names on their own. **Maria** is a widespread variant throughout the Western world, while **Marie**, the French form, was popular here in the middle of the twentieth century. These days, Mary is a rarer choice for a baby girl than Madison or Morgan.

RACHEL. In Hebrew, Rachel means "little lamb," a symbol of gentleness and innocence; and the character in the Old Testament, the daughter of Jacob and mother of

Joseph and Benjamin, is described in the Bible as "beautiful and well-favored." Like Rebecca, Rachel has always been common as a Jewish name and began to be used by others at the time of the Reformation. In this country it began to be revived in the 1970s, having reached the Top 10 for the first time in 1995. **Rachael** is an accepted spelling variation.

REBECCA. In the Old Testament, Rebecca (spelled there **Rebekah**) was the beautiful wife of Isaac and the mother of Jacob and Esau, and was one of the few biblical characters to show compassion for animals. The name, which means "knotted chord," symbolizing a faithful wife, was brought to the New World by the English settlers, and was especially well used in New England, where it was often the fifth or sixth most popular name. It was the name adopted by Pocahontas at her baptism, and is also identified with the lovely heroine of Sir Walter Scott's *Ivanhoe*, as well as the eponymous character in the novel and classic film, *Rebecca*. In recent history, Rebecca made a strong comeback— along with other Old Testament stalwarts such as Rachel, Sarah, Samuel, and Benjamin—in the late 1960s and early 1970s, and has been in the Top 50 for the past several years.

SARAH. Sarah has been the leading biblical girls' name for over two decades now, ranking currently at number eight. According to Genesis, it was God who said to Abraham, when his wife was ninety years old, "As for **Sarai** thy wife, thou shalt not call her Sarai, but Sarah shall her name be," and thus the name Sarah (which means "princess") was born. The name came into English popularity after the Reformation, and by the seventeenth century it was often the third most popular name for girls, following Mary and Elizabeth. By the late nineteenth century, it was beginning to sound somewhat dowdy, and was often replaced by its nickname, **Sally**. The **Sara** spelling, by the way, was originally the Greek adaptation.

SUSAN, SUSANNAH. These names are derived from the Hebrew **Shoshana**, which means "lily." In the biblical story of Susanna and the Elders, the beautiful and pure Susannah was saved by the clever stratagems of Daniel, who proved that she had been falsely accused. It was a common name, often spelled **Susanna**, in early America, reaching its greatest popularity in the eighteenth century. The simplified Susan gradually began to take over, zooming way ahead in the 1940s, and still holding the number-four spot in 1950 and 1960, but it is rarely used today. Susannah, however, has definite style power.

VIRGINIA. The first English child to be born in America was christened Virginia, a feminine form of the Roman family name Virginus. Sir Walter Raleigh had called his newly founded colony in the New World Virginia, in honor of Elizabeth I, the "Virgin Queen," and little Ms. Dare was given the name for the same reason. This was an early example of a name becoming used first in America and then spreading to other parts of the world. The name had been borne previously by a young Roman woman who was, according to legend, killed by her own father to spare her from the amorous clutches of a despised political official. Virginia enjoyed a sudden burst of popularity around 1870, which lasted through the 1950s, peaking in the 1920s. With comparable names such as Elizabeth and Katherine becoming overused classics, Virginia may be getting ready to step up to the plate.

BOYS

ALEXANDER. A Greek name that means "defender of men," Alexander has been popular for three thousand years. In Homer's *Iliad* it was said to have been given as a nickname to Paris of Troy for saving his father's herdsmen from cattle rustlers. The name was borne by several characters in the New Testament and some early Christian saints. It was a Macedonian royal name, gaining worldwide fame in the fourth century B.C. via Alexander the Great, who conquered most of Asia Minor, Egypt, and Babylon while still in his twenties and who, after his death, became the hero of a cycle of popular "Alexander romances" similar to those about King Arthur. Alexander became a royal name in Scotland in the twelfth century and has always been a particular favorite in that country, as well as in Russia, and today it is the seventeenth most popular name for boys in America—though combined with its short form, **Alex**, it rates even higher.

ANDREW. Andrew is a Greek name (from Andreas) that means "manly." It is found in the New Testament—borne by the Galilean fisherman who was the first to be called by Jesus to become one of the Twelve Apostles—and St. Andrew is the patron saint of Scotland, Greece, and Russia. The name was quite consistently common from the Middle Ages on, brought to the New World by Scottish immigrants, and was borne by two U.S. Presidents—Jackson and Johnson. Andrew is now one of the most popular boys' names in the English-speaking world, boosted by the royal naming of England's Prince Andrew in 1960, and in one Harvard study it was cited as the boy's name most favored by highly educated mothers. It is now number seven on the most popular list.

BENJAMIN. The biblical name Benjamin was borne by one of the founders of the twelve tribes of Israel, the youngest of the twelve sons of Jacob, who was the favorite of his father and brothers. As a result, at times the name has been used to signify a favored child and also for the son of older parents. It means "son of the right hand," representing strength and good fortune. The name was brought to the Puritan colonies by early settlers and proceeded to become more popular in New England than it was in Britain, especially with the celebrity of Benjamin Franklin. After centuries of waning use, Benjamin made a comeback in the 1960s, not only because biblical names were back, but because of the influence of the leading character in *The Graduate*, and is still popular today, especially in the era of Benjamin Bratt, Ben Affleck, and Ben Stiller.

CHARLES. Charles, a Germanic name that stems from a word (*carl*) meaning "man," was made famous via Charles the Great, better known as Charlemagne, who founded the Holy Roman Empire in the early ninth century. A royal favorite in England and France, the name was so widely used in the Middle Ages that many early historical bearers are identified by such nicknames as Charles the Bald and Charles the Fat. Although it took a while to take off in this country, it reached third place in 1875 and remained in the U.S. Top 10 until 1950, when it started to slip, and is now at number 104. **Charlie** and **Charley** are the more stylish nicknames, with **Chuck** no longer on anyone's agenda. Jodie Foster chose this elegant classic for her son, as did Cynthia Nixon, Russell Crowe, and Chris O'Donnell.

CHRISTOPHER. Deriving from the Greek word meaning "bearing Christ," Christopher's use as a first name developed in honor of the giant-sized third-century martyr, originally called Offeros, who was believed to have carried the infant Jesus, heavy with the sins of the world, on his shoulders across a river to safety—which explains why Christopher is the patron saint of travelers. There was also a medieval belief that if you looked at a picture of St. Christopher you would be protected all day. The name was very popular among early Christians, as it made them feel that they were symbolically bearing Christ in their hearts. In English-speaking countries Christopher moved in and out of favor for centuries, hitting a high in the 1940s (probably due to the beloved, gentle image of Christopher Robin), and is currently the sixth most popular boy's name in America.

DANIEL. Daniel is a biblical name meaning "God is my judge." The Old Testament prophet Daniel was an Israelite slave who garnered great favor for his skill at interpreting dreams, and whose faith protected him when he was condemned to die in a den of lions. The name was popular among Jews, early Christians, and, because of its resemblance to some Celtic names, has been a favorite Irish name as well. It is currently the tenth most popular boy's name in America.

DAVID. David, which means "beloved" in Hebrew, is another Old Testament perennial. In the Bible, David was the second king of Israel, who as a boy killed the Philistine giant Goliath with a slingshot. Considered by some the greatest king of Israel, he was also renowned as a poet, with many of the Psalms attributed to him. The Star of David is the symbol of Judaism and the national emblem of the State of Israel. This name is also very popular in Scotland, where it is a royal name, and in Wales, of which David (also called Dewi) is the patron saint. In this country, it reached as high as number two on the 1960 popularity list, was still number three in 1970, and on most recent lists stood in fifteenth place.

EDWARD. Edward, which means "happy protector," is one of the most abiding of all Old English names, having survived from before the Norman Conquest to the present. It was the name of several Saxon kings and eight English kings, and is now the name of the youngest son of the current queen. The name was an early arrival in the New World—there were several in the Jamestown colony and six Edwards sailed on the *Mayflower*. The Puritans, however, were less enthusiastic about the name, as it was attached to a nonbiblical saint. In more recent times, Edward was in the Top 25 until around 1960, when it started to slip, but now appears to be making a nicknameless (no **Eddie**, no **Ed**) comeback—think Edward Norton, Edward Furlong, and Edward Burns—though **Ned** may be acceptable to some parents.

FRANCIS. This name has an interesting history in that it stems from a nickname. The young Giovanni Bernadone, later to become famous as the nature-loving St. Francis of Assisi, was nicknamed **Francesco**, or "little Frenchman," because his wealthy merchant father traded extensively with France, and because the then-worldly youth spoke French. In 1210, he founded the Order of the Friars Minor, later called Franciscans or Greyfriars because of the color of their habits—twelve traveling preachers who emphasized poverty, humility, and love for all living creatures, and whose ideas spread throughout Europe. St. Francis of Assisi became the patron saint of ecology, and another Francis, St. Francis de Sales, is the patron saint of writers and editors. The name was first used in England in the early sixteenth century and was popular in this country among the early colonists. It peaked in the middle of the nineteenth century, after which it was superseded by its short form, **Frank**, and also began to be used (spelled Frances) as a girl's name, which made it less desirable for boys. In recent years, its masculine use has been pretty much confined to Irish and Italian Roman Catholics.

FREDERICK. Frederick is a name that translates from the Old High German as "peaceful ruler." One not-so-peaceful ruler was Frederick the Great, eighteenth-century king of Prussia, an enlightened despot who was a brilliant soldier and laid the foundations of the powerful Prussian military state. The modern use of the name in English-speaking countries was influenced by the Victorian vogue for Germanic names. In America, it came over with the German immigrants in the 1850s and remained popular until the 1930s, after which it faded. There is now a Society of Freds, trying to restore and defend the dignity of the name.

GEORGE. George comes from a Greek word meaning "farmer," and is linked with the patron saint of England, the legendary dragon-slaying Roman martyr, St. George. In the Middle Ages St. George was closely associated with knighthood and chivalry. From 1714 on, a series of four kings named George ruled England for more than a century, and a George was, of course, the first president of our own country. It was among the five most common names in America from 1830 to 1900, remaining in the Top 10 until 1950, but although it is still way up there in England, most American Georges are not infants but the age of the second President Bush.

HENRY. Henry is a Germanic name, with the fairly irrelevant meaning, "home rule." It was a favorite among the

Norman conquerors who brought it to England in the French form, Henri, which was more or less transliterated into Harry, the normal English usage until the seventeenth century. A British royal name from the eleventh to the seventeenth century, Henry was borne by eight English kings (all nicknamed Harry, just as the present young prince is), and was pretty much restricted to the aristocracy until the widespread popularity of Henry V, the spirited Prince Hal of Shakespeare's *Henry IV*. The name was revived at the end of the nineteenth century when biblical names started to fade. In this country, Harry and Henry were both in the Top 15 at the turn of the century, but neither was even in the Top 50 much after 1950. Still, although Henry has been off the popularity charts for decades, it has recently been picked up by several trendsetting celebs (see Hotties, under Starbabies, p. 109) and is favored by upwardly mobile parents.

JACOB. A name of uncertain origin, Jacob was featured in the Bible as belonging to one of the most important patriarchs in the Book of Genesis, father of twelve sons who each gave his name to a tribe of Israel. Jacob's Ladder refers to a vision seen by the patriarch of a stairway reaching from earth to heaven, a name also given to a ladder-looking plant. In this country, from early colonial times, the name was associated with both the Jewish and German communities—it was the third most popular name among German immigrants. Anti-German feeling during the two World Wars almost wiped out the use of the name in that period, but it came back strong with the Jakes of the Age of Aquarius, and is currently at the very top of the list.

JAMES. James, the Latinized form of Jacob, was the name of two of the Twelve Apostles and three other figures in the New Testament, and James also has the distinction of being the name of more U.S. Presidents than any other. The name was particularly prevalent in Scotland, where it was attached to royalty for over a century. In the seventeenth century, the name, as in James I, for example, was pronounced Jeames (*Jeems*). Still near the top of the list in England—James has now dropped to number twenty-two in America and is more often than not used in full, modern parents eschewing its former nicknames of **Jim** and **Jimmy**, with **Jamie** the only possibly acceptable variation. It was chosen by high-profile couple Sarah Jessica Parker and Matthew Broderick.

JOHN. This name, which is of Hebrew origin, has been throughout history (and until relatively recently in America) the most popular name for boys in English-speaking countries, and its many foreign cognates (such as **Ian**, **Evan**, **Sean**, **Ivan**, **Hans**, **Juan**, and **Giovanni**) have rated equally high in the rest of the Western world. It has been so common, in fact, that it's been used to represent Everyman—from John Bull to John Doe to John Q. Public. John stems from the Hebrew word meaning "God is gracious," and became a well-used name around 1200, largely because of the two prominent saints, John the Baptist and John the Evangelist. In total, however, there are eighty-two canonized St. Johns. In the early years of American history, about a fifth of all men answered to this name, and at the same time in England it was more like one quarter. The pet form **Jack** has been used independently for centuries and is a current favorite among celebrity baby-namers (see Hotties, under Starbabies, p. 109) as well as fashion-conscious parents.

JOSEPH. Joseph is an important name in the Judeo-Christian tradition, both as the Old Testament favorite son of the patriarch, Jacob, who gave him the coat of many colors, and whose brothers sold him into slavery, and also as the righteous carpenter husband of the Virgin Mary; while St. Joseph is the protector of working men. The widespread use of the name dates from the seventeenth century, when foreign forms such as José and Giuseppe also proliferated. After 1900, Joseph was a particular favorite with Catholics, especially those with an Italian heritage, and in this century it has always been among the fifteen most popular names, currently listed at number nine.

MATTHEW. Matthew, which is Hebrew for "gift of the Lord," was one of the four Evangelists, author of the first Gospel in the New Testament, who had been known by the name of Levi before he embraced Christianity. The name was well used from the Middle Ages until the beginning of the nineteenth century, when it began to wane. It came back strongly, partly as the result of such western TV heroes as Marshall Matt Dillon in the sixties, and is still in third place today. **Mathew** is a spelling variation.

MICHAEL. A name that crosses religious and ethnic lines perhaps more than any other in its unparalleled modern popularity, Michael's literal meaning is "Who is like the Lord?" In the Bible Michael is one of the seven archangels (one of only two recognized by Jews, Christians, and Muslims alike), and their leader in battle. Also a conqueror of Satan and the weigher of good deeds and bad at the Last Judgment, Michael became the patron saint of soldiers, as well as of bankers, police officers, and radiologists. His popularity assured the early spread of the name throughout Europe, and it became royal as well via nine Byzantine emperors, five Romanian kings, and a tsar of Russia. Always a favorite in Ireland, where it is often spelled **Micheal** (the nickname **Mick** is sometimes used as a generic, if un-PC, term for an Irishman), its entrance into this country paralleled the heavy Irish immigration of the mid-nineteenth century. Michael knocked Robert out of first place in 1950, and remained there until it was replaced by Jacob in 1999.

NICHOLAS.   Nicholas is a name of Greek origin that means "victory of the people." St. Nicholas is a saint with many charges: Not only is he the patron saint of Greece and Russia, but he is also responsible for the welfare of children, sailors, scholars, brides, bakers, thieves, merchants, and pawnbrokers. There are countless legends concerning his miracles and acts of bravery, such as calming storms and restoring dead boys to life. Santa Claus is an American alteration of the Dutch version of St. Nicholas. Nicholas was the name of five popes, a Danish king, and two emperors of Russia. In early American history, Nicholas was used most frequently by Dutch colonists, and later by German and Greek immigrants as well. Nicholas now stands at its highest point ever in the history of American baby naming, most recently rated at number five.

PATRICK.   A Latin name meaning "of noble birth," Patrick is associated with the saint who was originally named Sucat. Born in England and educated in France, Patrick was sold as a slave in Ireland, eventually becoming the patron saint and apostle of that country, devoting his life to converting the Irish to Christianity. Not surprisingly, then, the name Patrick has been especially linked with Irish immigrants in America, although for a long period of time the Irish reverentially avoided the use of the name. Patrick has been swept along with the present wave of popularity of Irish names, currently climbing back onto the charts.

PAUL. Paul was the name taken by Saul of Tarsus, formerly a vehement persecutor of Christians, at the time of his conversion after a blinding vision on the road to Damascus. There have been five Pope Pauls, and as Pablo and Paolo, the name has been a classic of Latin culture. Paul was hardly used in England until the seventeenth century, the time when it was brought to the colonies, where it remained steadily, but not flashily, bestowed on babies for three hundred years. From 1900 to 1960, Paul ranked a consistent sixteenth to eighteenth place, but it is scarcely heard from today. It has been much more successful in England where, in the 1980s, it reached second place, probably influenced by mothers who had been adoring adolescent McCartney fans.

PETER. Peter, which means "rock" in Greek, has special significance because it is the only New Testament name to be credited to Jesus, who changed the name of Simon to Peter (in the form of Cephos), because he would be the "rock" of the new group of followers ("Thou art Peter and upon this rock I will build my Church."). And St. Peter is the legendary keeper of the keys of Heaven. It was a common name in the Middle Ages, then suffered a setback, as did many New Testament names, with the Protestant Reformation. In Russia, Peter the Great developed his country into a modern nation; in Britain its use was spurred by the fondness for the character, Peter Pan. Peter's high point of popularity here was from roughly 1930 to 1960—though it never climbed very high on any popularity lists—and today it stands just outside the Top 100.

PHILIP. Philip, which means "lover of horses" in Greek, was very popular in the classical period, being the name of the father of Alexander the Great. It was borne by one of Jesus' apostles, but is not thought of as a biblical name. Philip's royal associations include six French and five Spanish rulers, and the present husband of England's Queen Elizabeth. Often spelled with two *l*'s, Philip was most commonly used in modern America pre-1960, and like Peter and Paul, is currently on hiatus.

RICHARD. Richard is a Germanic name meaning "strong ruler." It belonged to three English kings, one of whom, Richard I ("The Lion-Hearted"), was influential in establishing the popularity of the name. In Elizabethan England, Richard usually stood in fourth place among boys' names, and continued to be in roughly the same position in the New World, common enough to become one of the "Tom, Dick, and Harry" trio. After some ups and downs, it reached as high as fifth place in 1950, but is rarely used for the babies of today, showing no signs of the kind of revival seen with James, John, Thomas, and William. Whether this name's decline has been related to the decline of Richard Nixon (who was actually named after Richard the Lion-Hearted), we can only surmise.

ROBERT. Robert is an Anglo-Saxon name, deriving from the far more cumbersome Hreodbeorht, and meaning "bright fame." It was borne by three Scottish kings, most notably Robert the Bruce, who freed Scotland from British domination. The name became so popular in England after 1066 that it developed no less than six major short forms, including **Robin** and **Bob**. Robert was the top name in America for twenty-five years, from 1925 to

1950, and even now stands toward the bottom of the top hundred.

SAMUEL. This Old Testament name has the Hebrew meaning of "heard by God," referring to the fact that Samuel's mother, Hannah, had vowed that if God would give her a male child, she would dedicate him to God, and when she did have a son, it was evidence that her voice had been heard. Samuel was a Hebrew judge and prophet of great historical importance, and the significance of his naming was particularly appealing to women who were under social pressure to populate a new land. By the time of the settling of the New World, Samuel was already quite common in England, and became even more so in the colonies, particularly among the Puritans, at times achieving second place, just behind John, a pervasiveness reflected in the symbol of the United States being called Uncle Sam. It began to decline around 1800, when Old Testament names were beginning to sound fusty, but came back in the sixties and is now in the Top 35, a favorite, along with its short form **Sam**, among fashionable parents.

STEPHEN. Stephen derives from the Greek word meaning "crown," referring to the wreath of leaves awarded to athletic champions in ancient times, and was the name of the first Christian martyr, stoned to death as a blasphemer. His name reflects his martyr's crown, as martyrdom was regarded then as a kind of victory. The feast of St. Stephen is celebrated the day after Christmas. The *ph* spelling preserves the Greek tradition, but the later, streamlined version, **Steven**, has become the more common choice by far in this country (Stephen still reigns in England)—it was in seventh place here from 1960 to 1970, having dropped in recent years out of the Top 50.

THOMAS. Thomas, which means "twin" in Aramaic, was first given by Jesus to an apostle named Judas to distinguish him from Judas Iscariot. One of the Twelve Apostles, he was referred to as the Doubting Thomas because initially he refused to believe in Christ's resurrection. And the fact that this made him seem more human and fallible contributed to the spread of his name. In England Thomas was originally used only as a priest's name, but the martyrdom of St. Thomas à Becket in 1170 established the name as one of the most popular in England, usually the third highest, following John and William, and it reached top place there in the early 1990s. On this side of the Atlantic, Thomas was the second most common name in the Jamestown colony, and has been consistently used ever since.

TIMOTHY. A Greek name meaning "honoring God," Timothy was the companion of St. Paul, to whom he addressed two epistles. The name had been in use among the Greeks at least since the time of Alexander the Great, but was not prevalent in Europe until the sixteenth century, when the revival of classical studies led to the use of the names of antiquity. It reached its high point in the 1960s, when there were lots of little Timmys on TV, and is still well used by modern parents.

WILLIAM. A Germanic name, William has, over the years, been second only to John (which took over in the thirteenth century) as the most widely used British and American boy's name. In the Elizabethan age, 22.5 percent of all males were named William. It first came into vogue via William the Conqueror in 1066, and has never really been out of fashion since. It was number one in this country at the end of the nineteenth century and remained in the Top 10 through 1960, currently ranking number twelve. Now with the British princes Harry and William—the latter called Wills by his late mother—more and more in the spotlight, both their names have taken on an attractive and youthful aura. Many boys named Bill in the last generation have been replaced by those called Will or Willie.

Unusual Names

More and more parents today are interested in giving their children unusual names, with over half the parents who responded to our parenting.com name poll saying they'd picked an unconventional name for their children. The pool of names from which parents are choosing is growing ever wider and deeper, as parents grow more adventurous and individual in their tastes. But even the most open-minded of parents has to ask the question: At what point is a name *too* unusual?

The only possible answer: It depends.

Certainly, the line separating unusual names from "normal" ones is constantly being redrawn these days. With choices such as Madison, Brianna, Kayla, Sydney, Sierra, Savannah, Destiny, Autumn, and Cheyenne among the top names for girls, and Brandon, Tyler, Justin, Dylan, Jaden, Jordan, Cody, Kyle, and Logan edging out the Roberts and Thomases on the formerly staid Most Popular List for boys, there is virtually no distinction between names that are unconventional and those that are widely used.

Today, fewer children receive one of the Top-10 names—and more are given unusual or unique names—

than in years past. In the 1990s, 13 percent of babies received one of the Top-10 names, versus nearly a quarter in the first decade of the twentieth century. Every year, a smaller proportion of the babies born are given Top-10 names, while more and more children get unusual or unique names.

Why does this matter? Because a child's name is only unusual, or not, in the context of the names of other children in his or her community. When a large proportion of the kids have unusual names—as they do in Manhattan, or Hollywood, or in an African-American neighborhood in New Orleans, say—then having an unusual name will make your child feel like one of the crowd. But the same unusual name might make a child stand out, perhaps uncomfortably so, in a conservative small town in New England or the Midwest.

And then there's the question of what kind of unusual the name is. Some name scholars have attempted to differentiate between unusual names that are invented along the lines of current tastes and fashions and those that are outmoded—those that are perceived as attractive, in other words, and those that are not. The not-so-surprising findings: Attractive names, unusual or common, are better.

Of course, who your child is can be central to how he fares with an unusual name. The trouble with that is, your baby's personality can be kind of hard to predict when he or she's only a few hours old. Looks might be one indicator. A child whose looks are likely to make him stand out in a crowd—one with bright red hair, for instance—might do better with a regular-guy name, while a more ordinary-looking kid might welcome the distinction of being called Inigo or Jasper.

But how do all the little Vivianas and Frazers feel about their names? If you name your son Malachy, will he hate

> ### Newt's Name
> *Newt Gingrich spent his last day in Congress on the To-night show. "I'm grateful to the country that a guy like me, with a weird name . . . would be allowed to lead the country like that," the outgoing Speaker told host Jay Leno.*
>
> — *PEOPLE ONLINE DAILY*

you forever? Are you setting up Kendra and Isolde for a lifetime of shame?

Not really, according to psychologists. People with unusual names do not like their names any less than people with ordinary names do, found one study, which said that 18 percent of men and 25 percent of women considered their names unusual. There is some evidence that girls tend to feel better about having uncommon names than boys do. Girls are more likely to have unusual names—there's simply a larger pool of girls' names than boys' names, and girls are given names from the Top 20 less often than boys. Since girls with distinctive names are apt to find that other people like their names, they are more likely to accept the names themselves.

One study found that 40 percent of men and 46 percent of women did not like their names—but half of those women didn't like them because they were too common! An early name study found no difference between neurotic tendencies in girls with unusual names such as Janapea, Vondelier, and Honthalena and those named Dorothy, Helen, and Mildred—although these days, Dorothy, Helen, and Mildred would tend to be the odd ducks.

In dealing with an unusual name, confidence seems to count for a lot. Another study found that women with masculine-sounding names—Dean, Earl, Randy, Zeke, the kind of boyish fare that is becoming standard for girls today—who liked or accepted their names enough to use them, were less anxious, less neurotic, and had more

From *The Namesake* by Jhumpa Lahiri

As a young boy, Gogol doesn't mind his name. For birthdays his mother orders a cake on which his name is piped across the white frosted surface in a bright blue sugary script. It all seems perfectly normal. It doesn't bother him that his name is never an option on key chains or metal pins or refrigerator magnets.

(*but later . . .*)

He's come to hate questions pertaining to his name, hates having constantly to explain. He hates having to tell people that it doesn't mean anything "in Indian." He hates having to wear a nametag on his sweater at Model United Nations Day at school. He even hates signing his name at the bottom of his drawings in art class. He hates that his name is both absurd and obscure, that it has nothing to do with who he is. He hates having to live with it day after day, second after second. He hates seeing it on the brown paper sleeve of the *National Geographic* subscription his parents got him for his birthday the year before and perpetually listed in the honor roll printed in the town's newspaper. At times his name, an entity shapeless and weightless, manages nevertheless to distress him physically, like the scratchy tag of a shirt he has been forced permanently to wear.

Unique Names

In the ever-energetic search for a name that no one else has, many parents have taken to inventing their own. Of course, if you make up a good enough name, what's going to happen is that other people will start using it too—look at Jazlyn, Jaylen, Bryson, and Taryn, a few of the momentarily unique names now rising through the popularity charts. Even naming your baby Unique isn't enough: There were 246 of them born in one recent year.

Certainly the host of celebrities with very special names has promoted the trend. There still aren't many babies named Oprah, Madonna, Uma, or Dweezil. But other formerly one-person names are fast being appropriated by parents in search of something special as well as glossy: witness Calista, Cuba, Demi, Denzel, Keanu, Neve.

Every so often, though, we come across a name that does seem to be truly one of a kind. Some recent examples we've encountered; imitate at your own peril:

Affanita	Germiracle
Beegie	Hazari
Burritt	Ish
Damarquez	JaDerriaille
Deseral	JaKavon
Dez'travion	Jiae
Earlayshia	Keviana
Fantazia	LaTrayvia
Genovela	MaKatelynn

Mandrey	Tyreek
Tem	Xuqio
Traniqualon	Zeenab

leadership potential than women who substituted more feminine nicknames.

Who chooses unusual names? Mothers with less education, according to research by Harvard sociology professor Stanley Lieberson, are more likely to select unusual names for their children, especially for their daughters, than mothers who've graduated from college. He also found that African-American mothers of all classes and educational levels are more likely to choose unusual or unique names than Caucasian mothers.

But today, as personal meaning becomes more important in the choice of a name, as parents look to celebrate ethnic identity and increasingly prize individuality in their children, unusual names are becoming more, well, common.

The upshot: Having an unusual name is likely to become less of a burden, and more of a mark of distinction, over time.

Why Briyana Spells Trouble

The impulse may be benevolent enough. Why not, many parents wonder, find a name that has it all? A name that's familiar, fashionable, attractive, easy to like, and that's also original and creative and—hey, why not go all the way!—completely unique.

Toby in a Tommy World

Like being 6-foot-10 and having to duck through doorways, the curse of dysappellatia colors one's whole existence. It is the sore thumb that never heals. Perennial Top Five targets of schoolyard bullies, the ill-named live in dread of introductions, with the inevitable looks of confusion and the pity they elicit from every Tom, Dick and Holly we meet . . . So—Dave, Nancy, Mike—spare me your patronizing comments about how "neat" it would be to have a "distinctive" name. Maybe now, in the afterglow of our current baby-naming Golden Age—where diversity is celebrated and every playground teems with Baileys and Logans and Skylars—maybe now it's OK. But for those of us arriving in the Eisenhower years, uncommon meant un-American . . . I was a Toby in a Tommy world.

—TOBY MULLER, "GROWING UP TOBY," *LOS ANGELES TIMES MAGAZINE*

And so Abigail, thousands of years after King David's wife, hundreds of years after John Quincy Adams's mother, becomes Abbigayle. Anna morphs into Anah. Hayley (the way child star Mills spelled it) might be Haley, Halley (like the comet), Hailey, or Haylee. Rylee? Kearston? Konnor? Kaine? *Basta!*

Parents today are wild about invented spellings, that much is clear from the rosters of baby names across the country. Variations such as Kaitlyn and Katelynn have become much more prevalent than the original Caitlin, and Ashleigh and Brittney are now accepted names in their own right. Nearly 20 percent of the respondents to our parenting. com survey said they varied the spelling of their child's name.

Today's epidemic of inventive spellings

has its roots in the 1960s and early 1970s, when so many Pattys and Terrys and Sherrys became Pattis and Terris and Sherris. Even the president's daughter jumped on the bandwagon, shedding Lucy for Luci Baines Johnson. Barbra Streisand nudged the trend along when she dropped an *a*, though stars have long favored the dramatic spelling, from Carole Lombard to Jayne Mansfield, Diahann Carroll to Dyan Cannon.

But the trend really caught fire in 1981, when along came the sweet and gentle character Krystle Carrington on the hugely successful show, *Dynasty*. Krystle spawned not only her own perfume, but a rash of characters with creatively spelled names.

Named for Success

If your name is your destiny, chances are the fates never intended for Uma Thurman, Neve Campbell, Keanu Reeves, Skeet Ulrich, Jada Pinkett, Winona Ryder, Charlize Theron, Mykelti Williamson, and Ving Rhames to see their names on a marquee.

Maybe they would be poets, herbalists, hairdressers, or, in the case of Mr. Ulrich and Mr. Rhames, professional athletes, but movie stars? With those names? You must be kidding.

Stranger things happen. In a time when diversity, ethnicity and individuality are celebrated, it is the weird, one-of-a-kind monikers that are not only accepted but embraced by cutting-edge moms—and Hollywood moguls.

—JILL GERSTON,
THE NEW YORK TIMES

There was a soap opera character named Sierra . . . and another called Ceara. One sitcom character was dubbed Synclaire. What's more, the real live actors whose names rolled in the credits also popularized ever-more outrageous spellings, from Margaux (Hemingway) to Tempestt (Bledsoe) to Khrystyne (Haje).

This kind of thing might get you noticed if you're Cybill Shepherd, but if you're little Briyana (or Baylee or Greggory) Smith, your name will often spell trouble. Think of it: "No, that's Briyana, with one *n* and a *y*. No, there's a *y* and an *i*. No, it's pronounced the regular way. Bree-anna. Of course I'm sure."

If you've got a little Briyana of your own, you've doubtless discovered some advantages to counterbalance the problems inherent in an unusual spelling. Your child does stand out from the crowd; the name does feel more "artistic" than the same name with a run-of-the-mill spelling. But we'd wager you'd counsel an expectant parent to hesitate before stepping down your path.

Of course, there are some names that have more than one accepted spelling, such as Catherine, Katherine, and Kathryn, or Anne and Ann. Funny how a few letters can make a difference: Catherine seems gentler somehow than the K versions, Anne more substantial than the too-abbreviated Ann.

Then there are those names whose spelling variations become accepted over time. The original Caitlin, for instance, is more often these days spelled phonetically as Katelyn, or Katelynn, or Kaitlyn. Michaela has quickly, through association with the popular Kayla, become Mikayla or Makayla.

But there's such a thing as getting too inventive with a spelling. Our advice: Consider getting creative with the name instead. Rather than Anah, consider a foreign variant such as Anika, Annina, Anouk, or even Annabel or Ana—all legitimate names with history and substance. Or you might seek a distinctive name with a similar sound—Anthea or Angelica.

213

In the end, the thing to remember is that there is a fine line between cute and cumbersome, out-of-the-ordinary and outlandish, and your child will appreciate you for staying on the right side of it.

Creative Names

Creative names instantly confer an artistic, exotic image on your child. They also mark you as a parent who prizes originality, who wants to instill a love of the inventive and poetic in your little one. These days, the source of Creative Names has expanded to include everything from surnames to place names to foreign names to names that are literally coined by the parents. But the names here are among those that have both a historical basis and an instantly recognizable creative image.

GIRLS

ABRA	ARIADNE
ALESSANDRA	ARIEL
ALLEGRA	ARISSA
ALTHEA	ASTRA
ANAÏS	ATHENA
ANDRA	AUDRA
ANTHEA	AURELIA
ANYA	AURORA
ARAMINTA	AUTUMN
ARDITH	BIANCA

BLYTHE	KAIA
BRYONY	KATYA
CALLA	KYRA
CALLIOPE	LARA
CAMILLA	LARK
CANDIDA	LEILA
CHINA	LELIA
CLEA	LIANA
CLEMENTINE	LILITH
CLIO	LILO
COLUMBINE	LOLA
CRESSIDA	LULU
DAMARA	LUNA
DARIA	MAIA
DELPHINE	MALA
DIANTHA	MARA
EBBA	MARLO
ELECTRA	MERCEDES
ESMÉ	MICHAEL
EVANGELINE	MINTA
FEODORA	MIRABEL
FLAVIA	MIRANDA
FLEUR	MIRRA
FRANCESCA	NADIA
GELSEY	NATASHA
GENEVRA	NERISSA
GISELLE	NESSA
GWYNETH	NEVE
INDIA	NICOLA
IONE	ODELIA
ISA	OLYMPIA
ISADORA	OONA
ISOLDE	ORIANA
IVY	OUIDA
JADE	PALOMA

PANDORA	TANIA
PETRA	TATIANA
PILAR	TEAL
PORTIA	TESSA
QUINTINA	THEA
RAFFAELA	TRESSA
REINE	TRILBY
SABINE	TWYLA
SABRA	TYNE
SASHA	VENETIA
SILVER	VIOLET
SINEAD	WILLA
SKYE	WILLOW
TALIA	ZANDRA
TALLULAH	ZARA
TAMARA	ZELIA

BOYS

ADRIAN	CHRISTO
ALEXI	CLAY
ALISTAIR	COSMO
AMYAS	CRISPIN
ANATOL	CROSBY
ANDRÉ	DAMIAN
ANDREAS	DANTE
ANTON	DARCY
ASH	DARIUS
ATTICUS	DIMITRI
BARNABY	DONOVAN
BASIL	DORIAN
BEAU	ELLERY
BENNO	EMMETT
BOAZ	FINN
CHENEY	GARETH

GARSON	MILO
GRAY/GREY	MISCHA
HARDY	MOSS
HART	NICO
INIGO	OMAR
IVO	ORION
JAGGER	ORLANDO
JAMESON	ORSON
JASPER	PABLO
KAI	PHILO
KILIAN/KILLIAN	PHINEAS
KINGSTON	QUENTIN
LEANDER	QUINCY
LEONARDO	RAFAEL/RAPHAEL
LIONEL	RAOUL/RAUL
LORENZO	REMY
LORNE	ROONE
LUCIAN	SEBASTIAN
MARIUS	TARQUIN
MERCE	TRISTRAM
MICAH	ZENO

No-Nonsense Names

Maybe you're sick of fashion. Fed up with fads. Perhaps all the creativity and invention with names is beginning to feel like anything but that to you. For your child, you want a straightforward, down-to-earth, no-nonsense name. You want a name with history, but also one that's honest, that's not putting on airs. Some of the names here—let's face it, Hilda—are a little flat-footed. But many sound appealingly simple and fresh compared with the rich diet of Dakotas and Donatellas the world of baby-naming has been feasting on.

GIRLS

ABIGAIL	CHARLOTTE
AGATHA	CLARA
ALICE	CLARE
ANNA	CLAUDIA
ANNE/ANN	CONSTANCE
BARBARA	CORA
BEATRICE	DEBORAH
CAROLINE	DIANE
CATHERINE	DOROTHY

Are Margarets Smarter?

Margarets cannot help being the best at everything—and catching hell or oblivion for it. Some scholars have observed the phenomenon as early as third grade. A Margaret will invariably be winning spelling bees, while the entire class can be seen mouthing the word, "miss."

—LOIS GOULD, "THE MARGARET FACTOR,"
THE NEW YORK TIMES MAGAZINE

EDITH	JOSEPHINE
ELEANOR	JUDITH
ELIZABETH	JULIA
ELLA	KATE
EMILY	KATHERINE
ESTHER	KAY
EVE	LAURA
FAITH	LEIGH/LEE
FLORENCE	LOUISE
FRANCES	LUCY
GRACE	MARGARET
HARRIET	MARIAN
HELEN	MARIE
HILDA	MARTHA
HONOR	MARY
HOPE	MILDRED
IRENE	MIRIAM
JANE	MONA
JANET	NORA
JEAN	NORMA
JOAN	PATIENCE
JOANNA	PRUDENCE

220

RACHEL	SALLY
REBECCA	SARAH
ROSE	WILLA
RUTH	WINIFRED

BOYS

ALBERT	MAX
ALFRED	MOE
ARTHUR	MOSES
BEN	NAT
CAL	NED
CARL	NEIL
CHARLIE	NICK
DAVID	NORMAN
DREW	PAUL
ERNEST	PHILIP
FRANK	RALPH
FRED	RAY
GEORGE	ROBERT
GUS	ROGER
HAL	ROY
HAROLD	SAM
HARRY	SAUL
HENRY	SIMON
HOWARD	SOL
HUGH	TED
JACK	TIM
JAKE	TOM
JAMES	VICTOR
JOE	WALTER
JOHN	WILL
KURT	

The Nickname Game

Before we even get into the subject, we have to establish the fact that when we talk about nicknames we're not really talking about nicknames. Nicknames are those descriptive, usually derogatory terms like Fatso, Freckles, Four-Eyes, Skinny and Stretch, Bones and Baldy, which, outside the worlds of rap music and organized crime, have pretty much moved off into the well-deserved purgatory of Politically Incorrect cruelty.

When we say nicknames now, we're actually talking about pet names (which itself has a rather unpleasant puppyish connotation) or diminutives, like Bill and Barbie and Ken.

Modern parents usually have strong feelings for or against the use of a nickname for their child. Over the past decade or so, there has been a pervasive trend toward using children's names in full—especially when it comes to the standard classic names—rather than the short forms that have traditionally been attached to them. There are far more baby Elizabeths, for instance, than there are baby Bettys or Betsys or Beths, just as Jameses now tend to out-

> ## Slim Tim
>
> *[Tim Henman] is the first human called Tim to achieve anything at all . . . The name lacks gravity. It's easy enough to see how it happened: the Tims of the world had all their ambitions crushed, all their aspirations dashed, by being called "Timmy" during childhood. The association with "timid" and "timorous" . . . was obviously too strong to bear.*
>
> —MARTIN AMIS,
> *THE NEW YORKER*

number Jimmys and Jims; and Williams, Edwards, and Victorias also reign across the playgrounds of America.

But be warned that this strike for children's dignity can easily be thwarted, despite any resoluteness to stick with the undiluted original. If and when your eight-year-old Susannah gets a phone call from a friend asking for Susie, there's not very much you can do about it, even if you do say, "Hold on, I'll get Susannah."

What's a parent to do? If you really hate nicknames, the best tack may be to choose a name that seems to be nickname-proof. If what you object to is not nicknames in general but a particular nickname, you might try choosing an unusual one, archaic or foreign, off the bat, before the kids in the playground have a chance to turn Edward into Eddie. More guidance and suggestions follow.

Of course, it may be the nickname you're really after, choosing to name a child Joseph to get to the down-to-earth, easygoing Joe, opting for Katherine because you love Kate. Just be warned that even nickname-names tend to morph all on their own, with Joe somehow descending into Joey and Kate turning into Katie. Parents who deliberately give their children an informal name such as Annie or Jamie may find those names buttoning themselves up into Ann and James.

The only certainty with nicknames seems to be that, no matter what you do, they have a life of their own.

Short & Sweet

Since there was such a limited supply of first names in past centuries—at one point, for example, 57 percent of the female population of England was named either Mary, Anne, or Elizabeth—and it wasn't unusual to give more than one child in a family the same name, it's hardly surprising that a great diversity of imaginative diminutive names sprang up to make it easier to distinguish among all the same-named people. Over the years, many of these have simply faded away. But some, we think, are worth reconsidering and resurrecting.

GIRLS

BARRA	*for*	Barbara
BEAH		Beatrice
BESS		Elizabeth

BETTA	Elizabeth
CARO	Caroline
CASSIE	Catherine
CHARTY	Charlotte
DAISY	Margaret
DEBS	Deborah
DORO	Dorothy
FEENY	Josephine
FRANKIE	Frances
GRETA	Margaret
IBBY	Isabel
IMMY	Imogen
KAT	Katherine
KAY	Katherine
KITTY	Katherine
LETTIE	Letitia
LIBBY	Elizabeth
LISSA	Melissa
LIVVY	Olivia
LOTTA	Charlotte
LOTTIE	Charlotte
LULU	Louise
MAGO	Margaret
MAISIE	Margaret
MALLY	Mary
MAMIE	Mary
MANDA	Amanda
MELLY	Melanie
MINNIE	Mary
MOLL	Mary
NELL	Eleanor, Helen
NESSA	Vanessa
PATIA	Patricia
PIPPA	Philippa

POLLY	Mary
SADIE	Sarah
SUKIE	Susan
TILLIE	Matilda
TORY	Victoria
VITA	Victoria
ZAN	Alexandra

BOYS

BENNO	*for*	Benjamin
BRAM		Abraham
CHAZ		Charles
CHRISTY		Christopher
DEZI		Desmond
DIX		Richard
DUNN		Duncan
GAZ		Gary
GORE		Gordon
GRAM		Graham
HITCH		Richard
JEM		Jeremy
JOCK		John
KIT		Christopher
LAURO		Laurence
LEX		Alexander
NED		Edward
PIP		Philip
RAFE		Ralph
ROBIN		Robert
SEB		Sebastian
SIMS		Simon
TAD		Theodore
TELLY		Theodore

TIP	Thomas
TOLLY	Bartholomew
WILLS	William
ZAN	Alexander
ZANDER	Alexander

No-Nickname Names

D o you hate nicknames, or just hate the idea that someone other than you is going to decide what your child is actually named by shortening Elizabeth to Lizzie or creating some similarly unwanted short form? Then you might do well to consider choosing a name that doesn't *have* a nickname, one that already is a short form or that's too succinct to be abbreviated further. Here are some no-nickname options:

GIRLS

AMBER	CLAIRE
APRIL	COURTNEY
AVA	DAISY
BLAIR	DALE
BLANCHE	DREW
BLYTHE	FAITH
BREE	FAY
BRETT	GAIL
BROOKE	GREER
BRYN	HEATHER
CHELSEA	HOPE

INGRID	PILAR
IVY	PIPER
JADE	PORTIA
JOY	RAE
LEIGH	RUBY
MAEVE	SAGE
MORGAN	SKYE
NORA	TIFFANY
PAIGE	TYNE

BOYS

AARON	DUANE
ADAM	ELI
ADRIAN	ETHAN
AMOS	FINN
AUSTIN	FLYNN
BAILEY	FRASER
BEAU	GLENN
BLAKE	GRANT
BO	GRAY
BRADY	GROVER
BRAM	GUY
BRETT	HARRY
BRICE	IAN
CARL	JAY
CHASE	JUDD
CLAUDE	JUDE
CLAY	JUSTIN
CODY	KENT
COLE	KIRK
DALLAS	KYLE
DAMON	LARS
DEAN	LLOYD
DREW	LUKE

LYLE	ROSS
MARK	ROY
MILES	SEAN
MORGAN	SETH
NEAL	SHANE
NILES	THOR
NOAH	TOBY
NOEL	TODD
PALMER	TROY
QUINN	WALKER
REED	WILEY
REEVE	WYATT
REX	ZANE

Fitting In/Standing Out

This is one of our most popular lists, and one that's much more difficult to construct than it seems at first sight. As you probably realize if you've been hunting for the right name for more than a few days, most names fall on one wrong side or another of the golden mean that will allow your child both to fit in with peers, and stand out among them. Scroll down any index of names and the problem becomes instantly apparent: Aba, too weird; Abena, too weird; Abida, too weird; Abigail, too normal! Yet many parents are looking for a name that is right smack in between, which we hope you will find on this list. Because so many parents are interested in this category, we've tried to be as inclusive as possible—and as a result, you might find some of *these* names too weird or too normal. But there's also a good chance you'll find a choice among them that strikes the perfect note.

GIRLS

ADRIENNE	AMELIA
ALEXA	ANNABEL
ALICE	ANTONIA

ANYA	LAUREL
AVA	LEAH
BERNADETTE	LILA
CAMILLE	LOLA
CAROLINA	LOUISA
CELESTE	LYDIA
CELIA	MAIA/MAYA
CELINE	MARGARET
CHARLOTTE	MARGOT
CHLOE	MARIANA
CLAIRE	MARTINE
CLARISSA	MAY
CLAUDIA	MERCEDES
DAISY	MEREDITH
DELIA	NATASHA
DINAH	NELL
EDIE	NORA
ELIZA	PHOEBE
EMMELINE	POLLY
EVE	PRISCILLA
FELICITY	ROMY
FRANCESCA	RUBY
GEMMA	SABRINA
GEORGIA	SERENA
GILLIAN	SIMONE
HOPE	STELLA
INDIA	SUSANNAH
IVY	TAMARA
JADE	TESS
JOCELYN	TOBY
JULIA	VALENTINA
JULIANA	VIOLET
JULIET	WILLA
KITTY	WILLOW

BOYS

ADRIAN	LEO
BARNABY	LUCAS
CALEB	MALCOLM
CALVIN	MILES
CARSON	MILO
CLAY	NED
DEREK	NOAH
DERMOT	NOEL
DUNCAN	NOLAN
EMMETT	OTIS
FLYNN	OWEN
FREDERICK	PATRICK
GABRIEL	QUENTIN
GORDON	QUINN
GRADY	REED
GRANT	REUBEN
GRAY	SEBASTIAN
GREGORY	SETH
GRIFFIN	SIMON
HARRY	SPENCER
HAYDEN	THEO
HOLDEN	TREVOR
ISAIAH	TRUMAN
JACKSON	WALKER
JASPER	WYATT
JONAH	ZANE
JULIAN	

Americans like to pretend that class doesn't exist. We often designate someone "working class" or "upper-middle class" according to how much money they make, rather than how they behave or how they talk or what they name their children.

Class in names? Never heard of it. That's what we claim, anyway. Yet, our feelings about names, whether we like them and consider them appropriate for our children, often have more to do with class than we care to admit, even to ourselves.

There are distinct class patterns and tastes in baby-naming in the United States, as detailed by researchers who've examined what parents of different incomes and educational levels name their children and why. Parents who can be defined as middle or upper class, either by profession or education, are more likely to choose traditionally rooted names and to name children after family members than working-class parents.

Sociologist Alice Rossi found in a landmark study that 83 percent of middle- and upper-class parents named at least one child for a relative, versus working-class parents who used a family name only 37 percent of the time.

Boys are more likely than girls to get family names and firstborn boys are more likely to be named after relatives than boys born later. In recent years, parents have been more apt to name children after grandparents on both sides of the family tree than after themselves.

Upper-class parents try to disassociate themselves from lower-class parents by choosing different names, say researchers. But the lower class tries to catch up by adopting those names later. And as names become popular among the lower classes, the upper class abandons them and moves on to fresh, higher ground.

Harvard professor Stanley Lieberson found that white mothers with higher education levels prefer different names from white moms with less education. The high-education moms Lieberson studied preferred girls' names that connote strength: those that end in an *n* sound, biblical names, and names with long-standing traditional roots. For their sons, they like Old Testament names.

Mothers with less education, on the other hand, were more apt to like new or invented girls' names that end in an *ee*, *a*, or *l* sound. They preferred conventionally feminine girls' names, but chose boys' names they thought sounded strong.

Among African-American mothers in Lieberson's study, education did not make a significant difference in name preferences. For more details, see African-American names, page 298.

But Lieberson's work on class and names was done in the 1980s, and the class status of names shifts over time. Some of the specific names preferred by Lieberson's high-education mothers in 1985—Megan and Ryan, for instance—have moved down the class ladder since then, while the more classic boys' names such as William, James, and Thomas, preferred by lower-education mothers, have moved up.

Figuring out the class status of names in a society where nobody likes to talk about class can be difficult at best. A humorous book called *The Distinctive Book of Redneck Baby Names* makes a stab at defining names at the low end. Two nicknames strung together—Joe Bob, say, or Johnnie Mae—makes for a redneck name. So do initial names like J.W. or nickname-names such as Ouisie.

Humorous but too easy. How to peg the class standing of more ordinary names?

One general rule seems to be that names that sound rich—names that signify expensive things such as Tiffany, Lexus, Bentley, or Crystal, or names that sound like the surnames of the British nobility such as Ashley or Courtney—are in fact downwardly mobile. And more down-to-earth, less pretentious names—Josephine, Patrick, Sophie, Harry—are moving up.

In England, where class informs every aspect of everyday life, British parents inevitably talk about class in the same breath that they discuss baby names. More important than whether a name is in style or out in Britain is whether it's considered upper class or not.

Consistent use by royalty automatically gives a name an upper-class seal of approval: Names such as Charles, Elizabeth, William, Henry, and Anne, conferred consistently on royal babies over the ages, are unimpeachably upper class. Other traditional royal names—Alexandra, Charlotte, Victoria, and James, for example—are also well established on the upper-class roster. Even less traditional names borne by nobility—Beatrice and Eugenie for instance, Marina and Angus and Zara—are now firmly upper class.

Other names are true class nomads: Harry and Abigail, for instance, once undeniably upper, became working class by the end of the nineteenth century, though now both have recovered favor with the upper classes. Samantha, once an impeccably aristocratic name, became tarnished after it was popularized by the television witch—and an American witch at that. Being branded "American"—invented, silly, untraditional—is about as low as a name can sink in status in Britain.

Some of the most thoroughly upper-class names in England are so stodgy—and, some might say, ugly—that they will never be in danger of becoming too widely used. More than one British parent has said that the most upscale name you can give your daughter is Henrietta. For boys, Hugh and Piers are right up there, along with Hamish.

A name can be counted as upper or not depending on niceties (or not) of spelling: Deborah, Geoffrey, and Stephen are upper class; Debra, Jeffrey, and Steven decidedly not. Likewise, nicknames can make the difference in a name's class status: Kitty is an upper-crust nickname for Katherine while Kath is non-upper; Ned is an accepted upper-class abbreviation for Edward; Ed and Eddie are not. And pronunciation can be significant: Ralph, pronounced *Rafe* as in Fiennes, is upper, but not when pronounced *Ralf* as in Kramden.

One well-known British arbiter of class, *The Official Sloane Ranger Handbook*, divides those names appropriate for Sloanes—sort of the English equivalent of Yuppies—from those that were not. Acceptable girls' names, according to the book, include Emma, Lucinda, Sarah, Diana—"almost any name ending in 'a' except Tanya." Harriet, Georgina, Charlotte, and Caroline are Sloane; Jennifer and Jane are not. Daisy, Flora, and Pansy are Sloane; Lily and Heather un-Sloane. For boys, plain English or Scottish names are considered Sloane-worthy: Henry, Charles, Peter, Simon, William, Alistair, Archie.

In the United States, Yuppies as such may be dead, but

Yuppie names are not. There are names that are favored by young urban professional parents, parents who are the American definition of upper-middle class. These names have some style or dash, but are not invented; they're traditional, but not boring. Be warned, however. If you're a Yuppie-equivalent yourself, many of these names will be far more popular among your peers than they seem judging from their standing on popularity lists. Emma, for instance, seems to be today's standard-issue girl's name among Yuppie parents.

Yuppie Names

GIRLS	
ALEX	EMMA
ALEXANDRA	FAITH
ALICE	FELICITY
ALLEGRA	FLORA
AMELIA	FRANCES
ANNA	FRANCESCA
ANNIE	GABRIELLE
ANTONIA	GEMMA
CAROLINE	GEORGIA
CATHERINE	GRACE
CHARLOTTE	HALLIE
CHLOE	HANNAH/HANA
CLAIRE	HILARY
ELEANOR	HOPE
ELENA/ELANA	ISABEL
ELIZA	ISABELLA
ELIZABETH	JOANNA
ELLA	JULIA
EMILY	JULIANA

JULIET	OLIVIA
KATE	PHOEBE
KATHERINE	POLLY
LAURA	PRISCILLA
LEAH	RACHEL
LILY	REBECCA
LOUISA	ROSE
LUCY	ROSEMARY
MADELEINE	RUTH
MARGARET	SARAH
MARTHA	SOPHIA
MIA	SOPHIE
MIRANDA	SUSANNAH
MOLLY	TESS
NATALIE	TESSA
NATASHA	VIOLET
NELL	VIRGINIA
NINA	ZOE
NORA	

BOYS

ALEX	EVAN
ALEXANDER	GRAHAM
ANDREW	GRAY
BENJAMIN	HARRY
CHARLES	HENRY
CHRISTOPHER	HUGH
COLIN	IAN
COOPER	JACK
DANIEL	JACKSON
DAVID	JAMES
EDWARD	JONATHAN
EMMETT	JOSEPH
ETHAN	JULIAN

LEO	PETER
LIAM	PHILIP
LOUIS	QUENTIN
MALCOLM	REID
MATTHEW	SAM
MAX	SEBASTIAN
MILES	SIMON
NATHAN	SPENCER
NATHANIEL	THOMAS
NED	TIMOTHY
NICHOLAS	TOBIAS
OLIVER	WALKER
OWEN	WILL
PARKER	WILLIAM
PATRICK	ZACHARY
PAUL	

Royal Names

Where the royals still reign, the question of class and names becomes a bit clearer, for names that are used by the royal families automatically have class. In general, these tend to be old, well-established names, passed down through the family, though in recent years there have been some breaks with tradition: Princess Anne's daughter is named Zara, for instance, while Princess Stephanie's third child, born out of wedlock and fathered by her bodyguard, is Camille. In fact, many of the choices on this list, while time-honored, also have a surprisingly off-beat quality. Consider these—mostly from the British royal family, but with some Scottish and other European royal names mixed in—for your own little prince or princess.

GIRLS

ADELA	GABRIELLA
ADELAIDE	GERTRUDE
AGNES	GRACE
ALBERTA	HELEN
ALEXANDRA	HELENA
ALICE	HENRIETTA
AMABEL	ISABEL
AMELIA	ISABELLA
ANNE	JANE
ARABELLA	JOAN
AUGUSTA	JULIA
BEATRICE	JULIANA
BENEDIKTE	LOUISA
BIRGITTE	LOUISE
CAMILLE	LUCY
CAROLINE	MARGARET
CATHERINE	MARINA
CHARLOTTE	MARY
CHRISTIAN	MATILDA
CHRISTINA	MAUD
CLAUDINE	MAY
CONSTANCE	OLGA
DAVINA	OLIVIA
DONADA	PAULINE
DOROTHEA	PHILIPPA
EDITH	ROSE
ELEANOR	SARAH
ELIZABETH	SOPHIA
ELLA	STEPHANIE
EMMA	VICTORIA
EUGENIE	WILHELMINA
FEODORA	ZARA
FINNUALA	

BOYS

ALBERT	GEORGE
ALEXANDER	HAROLD
ALFRED	HENRY/HARRY
ANDREW	HUGH
ANGUS	JAMES
ANTONY	JOHN
ARCHIBALD	LEOPOLD
ARTHUR	LOUIS
CHARLES	MALCOLM
CHRISTIAN	MICHAEL
COLIN	NICHOLAS
CONSTANTINE	PATRICK
DAVID	PAUL
DUFF	PETER
DUNCAN	PHILIP
EDGAR	RICHARD
EDMUND	ROBERT
EDWARD	STEPHEN
ERNEST	THOMAS
FINLAY	VICTOR
FRANCIS	WALTER
FRANKLIN	WILLIAM
FREDERICK	

SEX

Gender identity as it relates to names has become an ever-evolving, increasingly delicate subject. Whether you're expecting a girl or a boy, whether you know the sex of your child-to-be or not, the gender implications of names undoubtedly play an important role in your name discussions and will be central to the perception of your child's name for years to come.

In *Naming a Daughter*, we look at how giving a frankly feminine or a gender-neutral name is apt to affect your daughter's self-image. And we analyze the possible reasons behind parents' preferences and choices for their daughters' names—to help you do the same.

In *Naming a Son*, we approach the same subjects from a male angle. Are there any decidedly masculine names left for boys? Can you find a name that breaks free from the conventional male mold, yet isn't drifting into female territory?

And in our section on *Unisex Names*, we investigate the history, the linguistics, and most important, the gender identity of unisex names today.

Naming a Daughter

All gender issues inherent in raising a daughter today present themselves when choosing a girl's name.

Do you want to give your daughter a traditionally female name, and if so, does that mean confining her to a set of conventional expectations? If you call her Lucinda, say, or Allegra, will people stereotype her as a frilly, hyperfeminine girl? And if they do, what exactly is wrong with that?

Many feminist parents today want to give their daughter an androgynous or even frankly masculine name, liberating her with a kind of gender-free image. When Harvard gets the application, when Merrill Lynch surveys the résumé, no one will guess that Campbell or Christopher is a girl—and that can only be to her advantage. Or can it?

Other parents say it's time to leave that girls-must-be-boys thinking behind, and reembrace femininity along with strength, and energy, as well as ruffles. Parents want the world to be opened up to their daughters, but there's an appreciation for success beyond the conventional male model of corporate ladder-climbing. Success is not only money and power, but creativity, individuality, personal satisfaction.

Studies have found that girls' names are more prone to the whims of fashion than boys' names; they're more decorative, less conventional, more likely to be invented or to be based on diminutives. People find novelty more appealing in girls' names than in those for boys. Linguistically, girls' names tend to have more syllables, are more likely to end in a vowel, and to have an unstressed first syllable than boys' names. And according to name scholar Leonard Ashley, while many of the favored girls' names have meanings that relate to appearance and personality, the male names whose meanings relate to looks—Albert, Claude, Augustus—are mostly out of fashion.

These style and linguistic differences carry a deeper meaning. The theory of "phonetic symbolism" holds that the sound and structure of girls' names makes them lighter, weaker, and less threatening than boys' names. "The divergent tastes underlying naming patterns for boys and girls reflect a tendency to assign a lesser role to women," wrote Harvard professor Stanley Lieberson in the *American Journal of Sociology*.

The more popular the girl's name, the more likely it is to embody conventional feminine characteristics. Sociologists rate names on how strong, how intelligent, how good, sincere, and energetic people think they sound, and the gender gap is widest between the most popular boys' and girls' names, which were thirty-two points apart on these qualities, versus eleven points with less popular names. Popular girls' names score higher than less popular ones on goodness, intelligence, and sincerity, but lower on connotations of strength and activity.

Highly educated mothers, according to Harvard's Lieberson, are less likely to give their daughters names in the conventional female mode, and more likely to choose girls' names that connote strength, goodness, activity, sincerity, and intelligence.

And what of Dad's preferences in naming a daughter? They're likely to vary from Mom's, studies show. Women are more likely than their husbands to choose unusual or fashionable names for girls, and to choose unusual names for their daughters rather than their sons.

The eminent name researcher Edwin Lawson did a study comparing men's and women's reactions to full girls' names—Barbara, Susan, Deborah—versus short forms such as Barb, Sue, and Deb and affectionate names like Barbie, Susie, Debbie. The men and women were asked to rate the various forms on characteristics such as good, strong, active, sincere, intelligent, calm.

Women ranked affectionate names—Barbie and Debbie—lowest in all categories. Men ranked affectionate names lowest in the Strong and Active categories, but *highest* in the Good, Sincere, and Calm categories, and tied with formal names in Intelligence. Formal names were ranked highest by men for strength, highest by women for goodness and sincerity. Women ranked short forms like Deb and Sue as highest in strength, activity, and intelligence.

"Women . . . reject the image of the immature, dependent 'baby doll' female," writes Lawson. "But why do men accept it? We can only speculate that it is more satisfying to the male ego to perceive women in this way. Dependent, immature women may represent less of a threat to male sensitivities."

Now that you know *why* you and your mate seem to be arguing so much over girls' names, perhaps you can move closer to making an enlightened choice for your daughter.

Feminissima Names

If these names were dresses, they would be pale pink, with ruffles and lace and big bows and sprigs of flowers strewn on every available square inch. They are the sweetest of the sweet, the most feminine of the feminine names.

What makes these names Feminissima rather than merely Feminine? Three or more syllables sometimes do it. Soft sounds—*s*'s and *f*'s—can also push a name over the edge from Feminine to Feminissima. Names that by their meaning suggest ultrafeminine qualities, like Allegra and Lacey, are Feminissima. Very exotic names—especially Latin ones such as Raffaela and Gabriella—qualify. And sex-goddess names—from Salomé to Marilyn to Madonna—also connote an exaggerated femininity.

You can hardly give your daughter one of these names without suggesting a little girl with ringlets and rosy cheeks, the kind of child who plays only with dolls (with ringlets and rosy cheeks) and cries if her Mary Janes get scuffed. Her name will make boys want to go out on blind dates with her, and other girls see her as a potential threat even before they meet her.

Does that mean that giving your girl a Feminissima name will automatically make her a spineless jellyfish? Quite the opposite. There is something modern about these hyperfeminine names, something liberating about the possibility of an Angelica being chosen vice-president over an Alix. Just as the notion of a female Tyler with long hair and high heels has the appeal of the unexpected, so has that of a Felicia in a business suit or sweat pants.

FEMINISSIMA NAMES

ADORA	EMMALINE
ADRIANA	EVANGELINE
ALEXANDRA	FAWN
ALLEGRA	FELICIA
ALYSSA *(and*	FIFI
variations)	FRANCESCA
ANGELICA	GABRIELLA
ANGELINA	GEORGIANA
ANNABELLA	GISELLE
ARABELLA	HEATHER
ARIANA	HYACINTH
ARIEL	ISABELLA
AURORA	JOSETTE
BABETTE	JULIANA
BARBIE	LACEY
BELINDA	LANA
BLOSSOM	LARISSA
CAMILLA	LETITIA
CAROLINA	LILIANA
CASSANDRA	LISABETH
CECILIA	LOUELLA
CECILY	LUCIANA
CHERIE	LUCINDA
CHRISSIE	MADONNA
CHRISTABEL	MARCELLA
CICELY	MARIETTA
CLARISSA	MARILYN
CRYSTAL	MARTITIA
DAWN	MELISSA
DESIRÉE	MELODY
DOLLY	MERRY
ELISSA	MIRABELLE

MISSIE	SUZETTE
MONIQUE	TABITHA
ORIANA	TAFFY
PRISCILLA	TATIANA
RAFFAELA	TEMPEST
ROSALINDA	TIFFANY
SABINA	TRICIA
SALOMÉ	VALENTINA
SAMANTHA	VANESSA
SCARLETT	VENUS
SELENA	YVETTE
SERENA	

Feminine Names

By far the largest group of girls' names is made up of Feminine names: names that are clearly feminine without being too fussy, sweet without being syrupy, soft without being limp. Many of the most popular girls' names of recent years can be found on this list. Style has favored these decidedly feminine names, along with androgynous names, over either ultrafeminine or no-nonsense female names.

The advantages of a Feminine name are several. Most of these names are easy to recognize and easy to like: Your child will hear again and again what a pretty name she has, and that's pleasing as well as ego-boosting. Also, kids like names that are sexually unambiguous; they like labels that clearly identify them as a girl or a boy. And most of these names are familiar, either because of their classic status or because they have been popular in recent times.

What of the future for Feminine names? Some, like

Many names are almost gone: Gertrude, Myrtle, Agnes, Bernice, Hortense, Edna, Doris, and Hilda. They were wide women, cotton-clothed, early rising. You had to move your mouth to say their names, and they meant strength, spear, battle, and victory. When did women stop being Saxons and Goths? What frog Fate turned them into Alison, Melissa, Valerie, Natalie, Adrienne, and Lucinda, diminished them to Wendy, Cindy, Suzy, and Vicky?

—HUNT HAWKINS,
*MOURNING THE DYING
FEMALE NAMES* FROM
THE DOMESTIC LIFE

Katherine and Elizabeth, are virtually timeless, but many of the names in this group have been so fashionable for several years that they verge on the clichéd. If you want to stay away from a name that is already too trendy, be sure to cross-reference any you like here with the What's Cool list in the Style section. One general observation: Many of the extremely euphonic feminine names—Jennifer, Christina, and so on—are on their way out, while more offbeat feminine names, like Annabel, Daisy, and Savannah, sound newer and stronger.

FEMININE NAMES

ABIGAIL	ALANA/ALANNA
ADELA	ALEXA
ADELAIDE	ALEXANDRA
ADELINE	ALEXIS
ADRIENNE	ALICIA
AILEEN	AL(L)ISON

AMANDA	CHELSEA
AMBER	CHLOE
AMELIA	CHRISTA
AMY	CHRISTIANA
ANDREA	CHRISTINA
ANGELA	CHRISTINE
ANNABEL	CLARICE
ANNETTE	CLAUDETTE
ANTONIA	CLEMENTINE
APRIL	COLETTE
ARAMINTA	COLLEEN
ARLETTA	CORDELIA
AUDRA	CORNELIA
AUDREY	CYNTHIA
BEATRICE	DAISY
BEATRIX	DANIELLA
BECCA	DAPHNE
BELLE	DARLA
BENITA	DARLENE
BERNADETTE	DEANNA
BIANCA	DEBORAH
BONNIE	DEIRDRE
BRIDGET	DELIA
BRONWYN/BRONWEN	DELILAH
CAITLIN/KAITLYN	DENISE
CAMILLE	DIANA
CANDACE	DINAH
CARA	DOMINIQUE
CAROLINE	DONNA
CATHERINE/	DOREEN
KATHERINE	DORIA
CECILE	DOROTHEA
CELESTE	EILEEN
CELIA	ELAINE
CHARMAINE	ELENA

ELISE	JASMINE
ELIZA	JEANETTE
ELIZABETH	JENNA
ELOISE	JENNIFER
EMILY	JESSA
ESMÉ	JESSICA
EVA	JOANNA
EVELYN	JOCELYN
FERN	JULIA
FIONA	JULIET
FLORA	JUSTINE
FRANCINE	KATHLEEN
GABRIELLE	KEZIA(H)
GAY	KIMBERLY
GELSEY	KIRSTEN
GEORGIA	KRISTIN
GILLIAN	LAILA
GINA	LARA
GLORIA	LAURA
GLYNIS	LAUREL
GRETCHEN	LAUREN
GWENDOLYN	LEATRICE
HALEY/HAYLEY	LEILA
HELENA	LEONORA
HELENE	LIA
HENRIETTA	LIANA
HIL(L)ARY	LILA
HOLLY	LILIAN
IMOGEN(E)	LILY
INGRID	LINDA
IRIS	LISA
ISABEL	LIZA
JACQUELINE	LOLA
JANICE	LORETTA
JANINE	LORNA

LORRAINE	ODETTE
LOUISA	ODILE
LUCIA	OLIVIA
LUCY	OPHELIA
MADEL(E)INE	PALMA
MARA	PALOMA
MARCIA/MARSHA	PAMELA
MARGO	PANDORA
MARGUERITE	PANSY
MARIA	PATRICE
MARIEL	PATRICIA
MARINA	PAULETTE
MARLENE	PAULINA
MARYA	PAULINE
MAURA	PEGEEN
MAUREEN	PENELOPE
MEGAN	PETRA
MELANIE	PHILIPPA
MELANTHA	PHOEBE
MERCEDES	PIA
MIA	PILAR
MICHELLE	POLLY
MIRANDA	QUINTINA/QUINTANA
MOLLY	RAMONA
MONICA	REBECCA
NANCY	REGINA
NANETTE	RENATA
NAOMI	RENÉE
NATALIE	RHEA
NESSA	RITA
NICOLA	ROCHELLE
NINA	ROSA
NOELLE	ROSALIE
NOREEN	ROSALIND
ODELIA	ROSAMOND

ROSANNA	TAMAR
ROSEMARY	TAMARA
ROWENA	TANYA
ROXANNE	TARA
RUBY	TESSA
SABINE	THEODORA
SABRA	T(H)ERESA
SANDRA	THOMASINA
SAVANNAH	TINA
SELENA	VALERIE
SERENA	VENICE/VENETIA
SHANA	VERONICA
SHANNON	VICTORIA
SHARON	VIOLET
SHEENA	VIRGINIA
SHEILA	VIVIAN
SHERRY	WENDY
SIMONE	YASMINE
SONDRA	YOLANDA
SONIA	YVONNE
SOPHIA	ZANDRA
STELLA	ZARA
STEPHANIE	ZELIA
SUSANNAH	ZENA
SUZANNE	ZOE
SYLVIA	ZORAH
TALIA	

No-Frills Names

These are the denim skirts of girls' names: clearly not fit for boys, but as straightforward, down to earth, and—sometimes—blunt as you can get while still being female.

One readily apparent difference between these and the

more feminine girls' names is that they are shorter: fewer letters and syllables, fewer embellishments. Many end in consonants rather than vowels, which gives them a stronger sound. They're almost like generic labeling: Yes, they say, this is a girl, but that's all we're going to tell you.

The No-Frills names here fall into two groups: those with a straightforward sound—direct and to-the-point names like Jean, Lynn, Ruth—and those with a no-nononsense image: Constance, Gladys, Mildred.

NO-FRILLS NAMES

ADA	DIANE
ADELE	DORA
AGATHA	DORCAS
AGNES	DORIS
ALICE	DOROTHY
ANNA	EDITH
ANN(E)	EDNA
BARBARA	ELEANOR
BERNICE	ELLA
BESS	ELLEN
BETH	EMMA
BLANCHE	ENID
CARLA	ESTELLE
CAROL	ESTHER
CASS	ETHEL
CEIL	ETTA
CHARLOTTE	EUNICE
CLAIRE	EVE
CLAUDIA	FAITH
CONSTANCE	FAY
CORA	FRANCES
CORINNE	FREIDA
DELLA	GAIL

GERALDINE	LEAH
GLADYS	LEIGH
GRACE	LENORE
GRETA	LESLIE
GWEN	LOIS
HANNAH	LOUISE
HARRIET	LUCILLE
HAZEL	LYNN
HEIDI	MADGE
HELEN	MAE/MAY
HESTER	MAEVE
HILDA	MARGARET
HONOR	MARIAN
HOPE	MARIE
HORTENSE	MARTHA
IDA	MARY
INA	MAUD(E)
INEZ	MAVIS
IRENE	MAXINE
JANE	MEG
JANET	MILDRED
JEAN	MIRIAM
JILL	MONA
JOAN	NELL
JOANNE	NOLA
JOSEPHINE	NORA
JOY	NORMA
JOYCE	OLIVE
JUDITH	PATIENCE
JULIE	PAULA
JUNE	PAULINE
KAREN	PEARL
KATE	PHYLLIS
KAY	PRUDENCE
KIM	RACHEL

RHODA	THELMA
ROBERTA	TRUDY
ROSE	VELMA
RUTH	VERA
SALLY	VERNA
SARA(H)	WANDA
SELMA	WILLA
SOPHIE	WINIFRED
SUSAN	ZELDA
SYBIL	

Naming a Son

It's a fact: Parents name boys differently than the way they name girls.

Boys are more likely than girls to be named after family members, to be given more traditional names, as well as less apt to be given names that are currently fashionable, found the eminent sociologist Alice Rossi in her landmark study of middle-class naming patterns. As evidenced by their names, said Rossi, boys are expected to be the symbols of family continuity and prestige.

Things have changed in the few decades since Rossi's study, but not entirely. More boys than girls are still given the top-ranked names, and fewer boys get unconventional or invented names; yet although creating new names for boys is a growing trend, we're still more serious when we name our sons, and we tend to give them more serious names.

Why? Well, partly because even the most liberal among us are still a little bit sexist. We may bear our sons' future career success and earning power more closely in mind than we do our daughters', and so give them more straightforward traditional names. And we might shy away from newer names as a tad androgynous, with only the conventional male names carrying the requisite masculine punch. Dads tend to take this consideration especially seriously. Moms push harder for less traditional names, but men are more likely to prefer widely used, historically based names, especially for sons.

The trouble is, as any parent who's searched for a boy's name soon discovers, there simply are not that many old-fashioned, down-to-earth, no-frills masculine names. And the ones that do exist tend to be used for so many thousands of males, decade after decade after decade, that they begin to feel like generic brands. There's Michael, the number-one boy's name for four decades, David and Joseph and John, William and James and Robert, Thomas and Charles.

The boys' names that straddle the boundary between the old-line men's club and hipper, more nouveau choices tend to get very popular indeed. These include Jacob and its short form Jake, which has overtaken Michael for the number-one spot. Christopher is another longtime favorite that blends traditionalism with style. Many other boys' names well-used in recent years tend to offer this same combination: Matthew, Nicholas, Zachary, Daniel, Jonathan, Ryan, Justin, Alexander, Benjamin, Ethan, Joshua.

Over the past several decades, we've kept changing our minds about how masculine and traditional we want our sons' names to be. The fifties and early sixties were strict Bobby-Billy-Johnny territory. Then, with the anti-establishment, "down with male chauvinist pigs" era, we turned to names that symbolized a softer, less aggressive brand of masculinity, to androgynous nickname-names such as Jody and Jamie, and to Victorian gentleman names such as Lindsay, Whitney, and Morgan—yes, for boys.

And increasingly, for girls too, which seemed to cause a sort of backlash in tastes in boys' names. As more girls took over names formerly reserved for boys—Shannon and Shawn, Casey and Taylor—parents began to turn back to the male names that were unequivocally identifiable as such. Yuppie parents in the eighties "rediscovered" such old-time masculine favorites as Andrew and Henry, and also turned once more to old sources for names that were clearly male, yet carried some originality.

One ever-more-popular source has been the Bible, particularly the Old Testament, for names ranging from Caleb to Nathaniel to Noah. And the formerly fusty grandpa names, brought out of mothballs, have also been major hits, with Max and Sam leading the pack.

Now there seems to be yet another swing, this time back to less conventional boys' names, though most of them are rooted firmly in male territory. For now, that is: Any boy's name, even the old-timers like Thomas and Christopher, seems to be fair game for girls these days. And the most stylish new boys' names share something— a flavor, a sensibility—with their female counterparts. It may seem clear, to the modern American ear, that Tyler and Tanner are boys' names and Taylor is primarily a girls', that Mason is for boys yet Madison and Mackenzie are for girls, but linguistically these names are all joined at the hip.

This is a real divergence from times past, when linguists analyzed boys' and girls' names as being very different from one another. The cultural origins of the most widely used traditional boys' names, for instance, were more likely to be Greek, Hebrew, and English, while several of the leading girls' names had Latinate roots.

And then there are the sounds themselves. One linguistic analysis showed that 87 percent of the Top 100 boys' names ended in a consonant. Favorite girls' names are also much more likely than boys' to end with the "ee" sound, which tends to make the name sound like a more childlike diminutive.

These linguistic investigations confirm what most of us assume: That traditional boys' names "sound" stronger than girls' names. And other studies show that boys' names, particularly popular boys' names, rate higher in such qualities as strength, intelligence, and energy than girls' names. Still another study showed that for whites, less educated mothers are most likely to favor boys' names that connote strength, while more educated mothers choose names rooted in history. And African-American mothers of all educational levels are more likely to give their sons unusual or invented names than are white mothers. What does all this mean for naming your son? It always helps, especially when dealing with an issue as powerful and complicated as gender identity, to try to untangle your feelings and prejudices when you discuss names. These are likely to differ from one partner to another, and to clash with the opinions of people from another generation, such as parents who are offering name advice, solicited or not.

A boy with a less-than-conventional male name will certainly feel at home in today's more liberal atmosphere. Compared with even a decade ago, boys' names are becoming decidedly less macho and more adventurous. Top-50 lists are crowded with such gentle choices as Tristan and Elijah, Gabriel and Cameron.

If you like this sort of bordering-on-androgynous name, the one caveat we offer is that you consult the text and list in the Unisex section on the gender status of the names you like. Several names have recently crossed the border from mainly boys' to mainly girls' choices, and female-ward is the direction in which names tend to move, bad news for the boys' camp. Your son will defi-

Ralphitis

For years, Ralphs have suffered not-so-subtle discrimination. Every other dog in a TV commercial is named Ralph. "To ralph" is slang for "to vomit," as my third-grade classmates reminded me ceaselessly. The most famous Ralph in the world was a wife-abusing bus driver with a hair-trigger temper. And when Hollywood finally produced a leading man named Ralph—the actor Ralph Fiennes—we promptly learned he pronounced his name "Rafe." There are those who will mention Ralph Lauren as a credit to our name. I think not. The guy (who was born Ralph Lifshitz, choosing to keep the lesser of two evils) has made a fortune recycling British snob appeal, all of it undoubtedly an attempt to compensate for the fact that his family named him Ralph.

—*Ralph Gardner Jr.*, The New York Observer

nitely not like sharing his name with his female classmates, and we advise you to beware of using a name that's becoming popular for girls.

The traditionally male and borderline names are easy choices. You can't go wrong with one of these old standbys—unless you hate the idea of giving your son a standard-issue name. As we said before, there are relatively few of these names, and those that exist tend to be extraordinarily popular. So if it's fresh ground you want to till, you'll have to look elsewhere.

Like where? Foreign rosters are an increasingly popular choice, for new variations on the conventional names.

Alejandro, Marco, Kristof: these are fresh twists on familiar material. Surname-names, especially ones that authentically spring from your family tree, are another good source.

It is somewhat dicier, in the end, to give your son an unusual or unique name than it would be to give one to a girl. There's some evidence that boys have a more difficult time fitting in with unusual names, and are less likely than girls to feel good about those names. But attractiveness is the bottom line: Choose a likable name that, unusual or popular, your son will have an easy time carrying through life.

All-Boy Names

While some cutting-edge parents may be starting to use conventionally male names for their daughters, these traditionals are still firmly in the boys' camp. There have long been girls named Michael, for instance, yet that didn't stop Michael from being the number-one boys' name for nearly half a century. The names here are the standard, classic names, perhaps not wildly exciting but always reliable. Boys tend to fare well with these sturdy, classic names. No one ever gets teased for being called David, and no little Frank is ever mistaken for a girl on the basis of his name. Here is the all-boy selection:

ADAM	ANTHONY
ALAN/ALLAN/ALLEN	ARTHUR
ALBERT	BENJAMIN
ALEC	CARL
ALEXANDER	CHARLES
ALFRED	CHRISTOPHER
ANDREW	DANIEL

DAVID	NATHANIEL
DOUGLAS	NEAL/NEIL
EDWARD	NED
ERIC	NICHOLAS
FRANK	NORMAN
FREDERICK	OLIVER
GEORGE	PATRICK
GERALD	PAUL
GORDON	PETER
GREGORY	PHILIP
HARRY	RALPH
HARVEY	RAYMOND
HENRY	RICHARD
HUGH	ROBERT
JACK	ROGER
JACOB	RONALD
JAMES	ROY
JEFFREY	RUSSELL
JEREMY	SAMUEL
JOHN	SEBASTIAN
JONATHAN	SIMON
JOSEPH	STEPHEN
JOSHUA	STUART/STEWART
JUSTIN	THEODORE
LAWRENCE	THOMAS
LEO	TIMOTHY
LEWIS/LOUIS	TOBIAS
LUCAS/LUKE	VICTOR
MARK	VINCENT
MARTIN	WALTER
MATTHEW	WARREN
MAX	WILLIAM
MICHAEL	ZACHARY
NATHAN	

Tough Guys, Not-So-Tough Names

Aren't professional athletes, he-man football players and hockey goalies and teammates, supposed to have names like Jake and Joe and Boomer? Well, some of them do, but more and more these days, they have less conventionally masculine monikers. Carmelo, for instance, or Sage. LeBron, or Madre. In fact, there are so many athletes with unmacho names that the roster was far too enormous to include in its entirety. Here, some athlete name highlights, undoubtedly inspiring sports fans everywhere to get more inventive with their own little quarterbacks' names.

AENEAS *Williams*
ALONZO *Mourning*
AMAZ *Battle*
AVION *Blake*
BRETT *Favre*
BRONSON *Arroyo*
BROOKS *Kieschnick*
CADE *McNown*
CARMELO *Anthony*
CENTRAL *McClellion*
CORTEZ *Hankton*
COURTLAND *Bullard*
DANE *Sardinha*
DAUNTE *Culpepper*
DEION *Saunders*
DELTHA *O'Neal*
DeMINGO *Graham*
DEUCE *McAllister*
DMITRI *Young*
DONOVAN *McNabb*

DORSETT *Davis*
EMLEN *Tunnell*
FRANCO *Harris*
GERONIMO *Gil*
JACOBY *Rhinehart*
JACQUEZ *Green*
JOFFREY *Lupul*
KEENAN *McCardell*
KENDRELL *Bell*
KEYSHAWN *Johnson*
KIJANA *Carter*
KIKO *Calero*
KORDELL *Stewart*
KOREN *Robinson*
LANGSTON *Walker*
LAVERRANUES *Coles*
LEBRON *James*
LONDON *Fletcher*
MADRE *Hill*
OLIN *Kreutz*

PASQUAL *Coco*

PEERLESS *Price*

PEYTON *Manning*

PRESTON *Wilson*

PRIEST *Holmes*

RALEIGH *Roundtree*

RAYNOCH *Thompson*

RECHE *Caldwell*

ROMAN *Gabriel*

RONDE *Barber*

RORY *Sabbatini*

SANTANA *Moss*

SENECA *Wallace*

SIMEON *Rice*

STERLING *Hitchcock*

TACO *Wallace*

TAI *Streets*

TAKEO *Spikes*

TALMAN *Gardner*

TIGER *Woods*

TIKI *Barber*

TORI *Hunter*

TRENT *Dilfer*

TYOKA *Jackson*

WADE *Miller*

WARRICK *Dunn*

You've got to peek into the diaper to determine the sex of many a baby these days, because their names are not going to give you a clue. Dylan, Dakota, Morgan, Bailey, Jordan, Alex, Taylor—any of these trendy-named kids could be either a boy or a girl.

In Germany, a name code dictates that the gender of a child has to be recognizable based on the first name. But in the United States, anything goes, and this sort of one-name-fits-all unisex naming grows only more popular every year.

According to the 2002 Social Security statistics on over 3 million babies' names, male Jordans outnumber females about two to one—but there were plenty of each. Eleven thousand boys were named Jordan to six thousand girls. With Cameron, the balance tips further toward the boys, with just over ten thousand male Camerons to about twelve hundred females. With Taylor, the balance tips in the other direction, with eleven thousand girl Taylors to under two thousand boys. And girl Morgans outnumber boys more than ten to one, at over eight thousand to just 693. Dakota has twice as many male bearers as female, while Bailey claims more than four times as many girls—

and that's not counting popular feminized spellings such as Baylee and Baileigh. Among the new ambisexual names, there are about four thousand female Jaden/Jaydens to 10,500 males.

Over time, most androgynous names move to the girl column. One study that compared unisex names in 1960 and 1990 from Pennsylvania records found that in those thirty years, none shifted from a majority of girls to boys, but ten moved the other way: Morgan, Noel, Jaime, Kendall, Casey, Taylor, Shannon, Kerry, and Jan. Names that had been designated boys' names in the 1940s but girls' by 1960 were Alexis, Robin, Jamie, Kim, Lynn, Kelly, Dana. None shifted the other way.

One linguistic study showed that people's preferred names—the names they like to be called as opposed to those they were given—are moving in the direction of male names, which are more likely than female ones to be monosyllabic, end in a consonant, and stress the first syllable. But another study analyzing most popular names over the years says names in general are becoming more feminine, with more syllables and softer sounds.

Linguists say names have gender markers, even when they're invented. The *a* ending usually signals a girl's name, though recent favorites Joshua, Noah, Elijah, and Jonah are evidence of the softening trend in boys' names. Androgynous geographic names such as Dakota, Montana, and Sierra also often end in an *a*. The *d* ending—David, Richard—is almost always a boy's name, while the *sh* beginning is most often used for girls.

Since androgynous names are about gender identity, if you're interested in this kind of name, it makes sense to think about what this says about who you hope your child will become. Parents who favor unisex or masculine names for their daughters may want to encourage their girls to take on characteristics once thought of as male:

strength, ambition, athleticism. And giving a son an androgynous name may signal that you don't want your boy to be a traditional male, that you would prefer that he be sensitive and creative rather than aggressive and macho.

Why today's boom in androgynous names? The new generation of feminist parents and working mothers is one reason. The fashion for surname-names, family names, place names, and names with personal meaning is another. Plus androgynous names fit in with the burgeoning search for ever-more-unusual names. Naming your daughter Thomas or your son Avery will definitely make him or her stand out in a crowd, though perhaps not as positively as you wish.

The sexual shifts names are undergoing today are not unprecedented. Alice, Anne, Crystal, Emma, Esmé, Evelyn, Florence, Jocelyn, Kimberly, Lucy, and Maud all were originally male names. Christian was a feminine name in the Middle Ages, as was Douglas in the seventeenth century and Clarence in the eighteenth. A king of East Anglia in the seventh century was named Anna.

There is a long history of appealing heroines with boyish names: from Jo in *Little Women* to Lady Brett in *The Sun Also Rises*. Irene Dunne played a Ray in one movie, and Audrey Hepburn a Reggie; Bette Davis, Stanley; Olivia de Havilland, Roy; Janet Leigh, Wally; and Jane Russell, Nancy Sinatra, and Anne Baxter all Mikes.

Today, the stars themselves are more likely to have the boyish names: witness Reese Witherspoon, Cameron Diaz, Drew Barrymore, Whitney Houston, Daryl Hannah, Jamie Lee Curtis, James King, Jules Asner, and Dakota Fanning.

Sometimes, a name that sounds tired for a boy, like Sydney, becomes fresh and crisp when applied to a girl. Names that can be wimpy for a boy, such as Brooke or Blair, can confer a brisk kind of strength on a girl.

But androgynous names often appeal more to parents than to children themselves. Little boys dislike having the same name as female playmates, and often find the androgynous name even more troublesome down the road. Little girls likewise tend to dislike unisex names in early childhood, when most children seem to prefer all things sexually distinct, from their clothing to their toys to their names. However, most grown-up women with androgynous names say that once they reached adolescence they began to appreciate the sexual ambiguity as well as the sex appeal of their names.

In the sixties, the big trend was toward cute nicknames that sounded just as right for boys as girls: Jody, Toby, Jamie. In the eighties, unisex nicknames for more sexually distinct proper names took center stage: Chris, Nicky, Alex. Today, the field has widened to include surname-names of all ethnicities, place names, and all-boy names—Gregory, Zachary—for girls. Below are some categories of unisex names.

The True Unisex Names

The pool of True Unisex Names, those that work as well for girls as for boys, is growing rapidly, with many formerly all-boy choices—Aidan, Tyler, Jaden, for instance—crossing over to the girls' side. What customarily happens is that, once a name starts to be used for girls, it soon becomes too feminine for boys. That happened in recent years with such choices as Whitney and Courtney and Lindsay. But that trend seems to be stabilizing as boys' names in general become more androgynous, and as the line between the genders becomes more blurred.

Some of these choices (Paris, Taylor) are distinctly

more girlish; others (Hunter, Tyler) more boyish, while others (Jordan, Alex) truly straddle the line. And then of course there are hundreds of more unusual surnames and place names and word names, detailed in the Style section of this book, that can be used for both sexes. What follows are names widely used for boys as well as girls:

ADDISON	DREW
AIDAN	DYLAN
ALEX	ELLIOT
AMERICA	EMERSON
ARMANI	EVAN
ASA	FRANCES/FRANCIS
ASHTON	GENE/JEAN
ASPEN	GERRY/JERRY
AUGUST	GLENN
AVERY	HARLEY
BAILEY	HUNTER
BLAINE	JADEN
BLAKE	JALEN
BRETT	JAMIE
BROOKLYN	JAYDEN
CAMERON	JESSE/JESSIE
CARSON	JO/JOE
CASEY	JORDAN
CASSIDY	JUSTICE
CHRIS	KAI
CHRISTIAN	KEIL
COREY	KENDALL
DAKOTA	KENNEDY
DALE	KYLE
DALLAS	LANE
DARYL	LEE/LEIGH
DELANEY	LEXIS
DEVIN	LOGAN

LONDON	REMI/REMY
LOREN	RICKI/RICKY
LUCA	RILEY
MARLEY	RORY
MASON	ROWAN
MICAH	SAGE
MICKEY	SAM
MONTANA	SAWYER
MORGAN	SCOUT
NICKY	SEAN/SHAWN
NOAH/NOE	SHANNON
PARIS	SHEA
PARKER	SKY
PAT	SKYLER
PAYTON	SPENCER
PRESLEY	TERRY
QUINN	TRISTAN
RAY/RAE	TYLER
REAGAN	

Boys to Girls

Many girls' names are feminized versions of male names: Carol, Caroline, and Charlotte (not to mention Carla, Charla, and Charlene) all derived from Charles, for instance. We've heard some pretty bad male-to-female inventions (Davette comes to mind) but the names on this list are gently old-fashioned and may be a good way to name a daughter after a male ancestor or lend a masculine note to her name without going all the way to David.

ALANA/ALANNA	ALFREDA
ALBERTA	ANDREA
ALEXANDRA	ANTONIA

AUGUSTA	JESSICA
BERNADETTE	JOHANNA
CARLA	JORDANA
CAROLINE	JOSEPHINE/JOSEPHA
CHARLOTTE	JULIA/JULIANA
CHRISTINE	JUSTINE
CLAUDIA	LAURA
CLEMENTINE	LAUREN
CORNELIA	LEONA
DANIELLE	LOUISE
DAVIDA	LUCY
DENISE	MARCELLA/MARCIA
DOMINICA/	MARTINA
DOMINIQUE	MAXINE
EDWINA	MICHAELA
ERICA	MICHELLE
ERNESTINE	NICOLE
EUGENIA	PATRICIA
FRANCES/FRANCINE	PAULA
FREDERICA	PAULINE
GABRIELLE	ROBERTA
GEORGIA/GEORGINA	SIMONE
GERALDINE	STEPHANIE
HARRIET	THEODORA
HENRIETTA	VALENTINA
ISIDORA	VICTORIA
JACOBA	WILHELMINA/WILLA
JACQUELINE	YVONNE

Androgynous Starbabies

AARON	*Robert De Niro*
AIDAN *(girl)*	*Faith Daniels*
AIDAN *(boy)*	*Scott Hamilton*
ARUN *(girl)*	*Dave "The Edge" Evans*
AUGUST *(girl)*	*Garth Brooks*
AUGUST *(boy)*	*Lena Olin, Jeanne Tripplehorn*
BAILEY *(girl)*	*Melissa Etheridge*
BAILEY *(boy)*	*Anthony Edwards, Tracey Gold*
BILLIE *(girl)*	*Carrie Fisher*
BILLY *(boy)*	*Helena Bonham Carter & Tim Burton*
DAKOTA *(girl)*	*Melanie Griffith & Don Johnson*
DAKOTA *(boy)*	*Melissa Gilbert, Chuck Norris*
DYLAN *(girl)*	*Robin Wright & Sean Penn*
DYLAN *(boy)*	*Pierce Brosnan, Pamela Anderson & Tommy Lee, Joan Cusack, Catherine Zeta Jones & Michael Douglas, Tracy Austin, Kenneth "Babyface" Edmunds*
ELLIOT *(boy)*	*Robert De Niro*
ELLIOTT *(girl)*	*Alexandra Wentworth & George Stephanopoulos*
FINLAY *(boy)*	*Corbin Bernsen & Amanda Pays*
FINLEY *(girl)*	*Angie Harmon & Jason Sehorn*
FINLEY *(boy)*	*Sadie Frost*
MASON *(girl)*	*Kelsey Grammer*
MASON *(boy)*	*Cuba Gooding Jr., Laura San Giacomo, Josie Bisette & Rob Estes*
MONTANA *(girl)*	*Judd Hirsch*
MONTANA *(boy)*	*Richard Thomas*
NOAH *(girl)*	*Billy Ray Cyrus*
NOAH *(boy)*	*Jason Alexander, Kim Alexis, Scott Weiland*
PARIS *(girl)*	*Michael Jackson*

PARIS *(boy)*	*Pierce Brosnan, Blair Underwood*
PRESLEY *(girl)*	*Tanya Tucker*
PRESLEY *(boy)*	*Cindy Crawford*
RILEY *(girl)*	*Howie Mandel*
RILEY *(boy)*	*Mare Winningham, David Lynch*
SAGE *(girl)*	*Lance Hendriksen*
SAGE *(boy)*	*Tracey Gold*
SAM *(girl)*	*Denise Richards & Charlie Sheen*
SAM *(boy)*	*Tracy Pollan & Michael J. Fox, Emily Mortimer*
SCOUT *(girl)*	*Demi Moore & Bruce Willis, Tom Berenger*
SCOUT *(boy)*	*Tai Babilonia*
SPENCER *(girl)*	*Debbe Dunning*
SPENCER *(boy)*	*Cuba Gooding Jr., Gena Lee Nolan, Cynthia McFadden*

The Trouble with Taylor

Androgynous names abound: *Ashley* used to be a boy's name, as fans of *Gone with the Wind* remember. (Ashley Wilkes was played by Leslie Howard; now even Leslie is a girl's name.) Taylor, Cameron, and Madison can be borne by male or female. This means it is harder for prospective employers to tell a job applicant's sex when reading a résumé, a possible reason for the choices.

—WILLIAM SAFIRE, "WELCOME BACK, SARAH," *THE NEW YORK TIMES MAGAZINE*

TRADITION

It may seem ironic that, in the face of all the new adventurousness in choosing children's names, Tradition is one of the fastest-growing sections of this book. But for many parents, the quest for novelty and creativity is coupled with a search for personal meaning— for history and ethnic identity. And these qualities are anything but mutually exclusive, with many of the most exciting new names coming from our own pasts or cultural backgrounds.

There's much that's new in this section.

We delve into American naming history from colonial times to the present. And we take a new look at the often-separate African-American naming traditions, tracing today's African-American name choices back to roots in slavery and early naming practices that blended customs from Africa with the developing American culture to produce a name lexicon that's distinctive and unique.

We offer here a greatly expanded selection of ethnic names, hundreds of selections from European cultures as well as African, Arab, and Hebrew names. Here also is information on Jewish naming traditions, as well as a wide range of saints' names.

A Concise History of American Baby-Naming

In the few centuries since the earliest colonial settlements were established in this country, our stock of names has grown from the limited number of Anglo-Saxon standards that came over on the *Mayflower* and other early vessels to a vast stewpot composed of flavors from different cultures and of names created on our native soil. A look back at our naming history can provide inspiration to today's baby namer as well.

Colonial Period & Eighteenth Century

As you may remember from fourth-grade history, the first English-speaking settlement, called the Raleigh Colony, was established on the mid-Atlantic coast in 1587, and although it soon vanished, we're lucky enough to have some of its name records. Of the ninety-nine men who settled there, twenty-three were named John, fifteen Thomas, and ten William, plus a sprinkling of biblical names as well. On the *Mayflower*, there was a similar proportion of Johns, Williams, Edwards, and Richards, but also men named Resolved, Love, and Wrestling. (A boy born midvoyage was appropriately called Oceanus Hopkins.) In the later Massachusetts Bay Colony, 21 percent of the females were called Mary, 17 percent were Elizabeth, and 15 percent Sarah.

When it came time for the settlers to name their own children, a lot of these old traditional standards faded in favor of biblical names, from both the Old and New Testaments. The Good Book was scrutinized in the search for names of admirable figures, parents believing that such names could shape the characters of their children. It was not unusual to find really extreme examples, like Eliphalet and Bezaleel, but the most commonly used by the Puritans and other colonists—most of which still sound righteous today—were:

GIRLS

ABIGAIL	RACHEL
DEBORAH	REBECCA
ELIZA	RUTH
HANNAH	SARAH
JEMIMA	SELAH
LYDIA	SUSANNAH
MARTHA	

BOYS

AARON	ELIHU
ABIJAH	ELIJAH
BENJAMIN	EZEKIEL
DANIEL	GIDEON
DAVID	IRA
EBENEZER	ISAAC

JEDEDIAH	NATHANIEL
JONATHAN	SAMUEL
JOSHUA	SETH
MOSES	SOLOMON

In their pursuit of ever-more upright, upstanding names, the Puritans went even further, choosing meaningful "virtue" names (for the most currently viable, see page 43), especially for girls. Some of the more radical names (to modern ears) were Desire, Love, Increased, Renewed, Silence, Humility, Fear, Experience, Hopewell, Mindwell, and Thankful—the last being among the commonest names given to New England girls before 1750.

Of course, names varied from colony to colony. In Virginia, the settlers continued to follow British patterns, with two-thirds of the girls being called either Mary, Elizabeth (often recorded as Eliza), Sarah, or Anne. In New England it became a very common practice to name children after their parents—in one town 74 percent of first-born daughters shared their mothers' names and 67 percent of the boys bore their fathers'.

Toward the end of the seventeenth century, there was an influx of European immigrants, who brought their native favorites with them, adding still more diversity to the pot. Among the German and Dutch contributions were Frederick, Johann, Mathias, and Veronica, while the Scots added a multitude of Andrews, Archibalds, Alexanders, and Duncans, the Welsh brought over such names as Owen and Hugh, and the Irish imported Patrick and Patricia, among others.

One of the most significant developments of this time was the increased use of a middle name—by the turn of the eighteenth century, one in four Harvard students had one, whereas previously this had been a rarity. After the Revolutionary War, the wave of biblical names began to recede, replaced by such newly popular names as Charles, George, Frederick, Francis, and Augustus, and such imported royal names as Charlotte, Caroline, and Sophia, as well as a revival of the Robert-Henry-Edward breed.

The distinctively American custom, which continues to thrive today, of using surnames as first names, also took firm hold. Not only were family names moved into first place, but there was an expanded use of the surnames of both historical and contemporary notables for newborn boys. Some that came to the fore in the eighteenth and nineteenth centuries were:

BRADFORD	LINCOLN
BRYAN	MARSHALL
CALHOUN	MASON
CLAY	MAXWELL
CLEVELAND	MONROE
CLINTON	MORRIS
CORNELL	NELSON
CURTIS	OTIS
DEXTER	RANDOLPH
EVERETT	WARD
FRANKLIN	WARREN
GRANT	WASHINGTON
HAYES	WAYNE
JACKSON	WEBSTER
JEFFERSON	WESLEY
LEE	WINTHROP

Another trend of this time was the legitimizing of pet forms. Whereas boys and girls had for centuries been called by nicknames (in order to separate the large numbers of Johns, Marys, Margarets, etc. from one another), now those diminutives became the names with which they were christened. This led to an explosion of new girls' names, helping to even out the previously unbalanced numbers—between 1700 and 1750 there had been twice as many boys' names as girls', and three times more biblical names for boys. Among the newly sanctioned girls' names were:

ABBY	LULU
ANNIE	MAISIE
BESS/BESSIE	MAMIE
BETSY	MILLY
BETTY	MINNIE
CARRIE	MOLLY
DAISY	NANCY
ELSIE	NELL
HATTIE	PEGGY
JENNY	POLLY
JESSIE	SADIE
KITTY	SALLY
LETTY	WINNIE
LUCY	

The eighteenth century also saw upper-class parents taking an interest in Latinized forms of women's names. Mary was now as apt to be Maria, and names like Sophia, Anna, Juliana, and Cecilia came into widespread use.

Nineteenth Century

From the end of the eighteenth century, and into the nineteenth, parents began to favor boys' names drawn from the classics (Homer, Horatio, Horace) and chivalrous-sounding Anglo-Saxon and Arthurian names (Arthur, Alfred, Harold, Edmund), with corresponding girls' names such as Enid, Elaine, Edith, Audrey, and Vivian. The Scottish names discovered in the novels of Sir Walter Scott also enjoyed a surge of popularity, heroic names like Kenneth, Donald, Ronald, Roland, Guy, Quentin, Roy, Douglas, and Bruce. Girls were often named after other romantic literary characters, including Beatrice, Agnes, Julia and Juliet, Lavinia, Rosalind, Clarissa, Gwendolyn, and Maud. Flower and other nature names began to come into fashion, such as Rose, Violet, Lily, Iris, Hazel, and Myrtle, as well as gem names like Pearl, Opal, and Ruby, not to mention the months April, May, and June. Another route to a broader base of girls' names was the feminization of male names. Enter Henrietta, Harriet, Georgia, Charlotte, Edwina, Josephine, Theodora, and others (for a more complete list, see page 274).

This was a period of increasingly widespread immigration, a fact reflected in the foreign input and influences on American names—although if a name became anything resembling a stereotype of a certain group, it soon tended to be avoided, as in the Irish examples of Pat and Mick (Patrick and Michael). This resonated in class distinctions as well—names considered to belong to servants, such as Nora and Bridget, were shunned by middle- and upper-class parents.

Other trends of the nineteenth century: Sons continued to be named for fathers, and there was a greatly accelerated use of the "Junior" form, as well as an even more prevalent use of middle names. This led to the flourishing of combined girls' names such as Marianne, Rosemary, Annabel, Pollyanna, and so on. Expanding populations, urban living, and a turning away from biblical names created a need for new names. For boys, one rich source proved to be the surnames of English and Scottish nobility, some examples of which were:

BARRY	HARVEY
BRENT	HERBERT
CHESTER	HOWARD
CLARE	PERCY
CLARK	SIDNEY
CLIFFORD	STANLEY
CRAIG	STUART
GRANT	

At this time, children had achieved an elevated importance in society and, consequently, more attention was now given to their names, with a decreased use of repeating the parents' or grandparents' name in favor of one that would be uniquely chosen for that child, a trend that would come into full bloom in our own century. The names that were most popular in the third quarter of the nineteenth century showed a variety of sources for the girls' names, while the boys' remained the old classics. These were, in order of popularity:

GIRLS

MARY	EDITH
ANNA	FLORENCE
ELIZABETH	MAY
EMMA	HELEN
ALICE	KATHERINE

BOYS

WILLIAM	HARRY
JOHN	JAMES
CHARLES	GEORGE

FRANK   JOSEPH
ROBERT   THOMAS

Twentieth Century

All the movements mentioned above gradually coalesced
in the present century to form an almost infinite number
of names available to the prospective parent. At the turn
of the century, the most popular list for males was virtually the same as it had been twenty-five years before, with
the addition of Samuel and Arthur, but for girls there
were several changes. Mary remained in first place, as it
would until 1950, but there were new entries on the
scene: Ruth, Margaret, Dorothy, Mildred, and Frances
had now entered the Top 10.

The 1920s and 1930s saw major shifts in the naming
landscape. One of the hottest trends of this period was
what can be thought of as freckle-faced-kid names, for
both girls and boys. These were "Our Gang" comedy
names that came complete with button noses and over-
bites. Many of them were nicknames for perennial favorites—Billy or Willie for William, for example, or
Margie, Maggie, or Peggy for Margaret. For the first
time, media stars were affecting baby naming, as in Jean,
Marion, Norma, Myrna, Shirley, and Virginia. Other female fads included names ending in the letter *s* (Doris,
Phyllis, Iris, Lois); and names with the suffix "een" or
"ine"—Irish ones like Eileen, Pegeen, Maureen, Noreen,
Kathleen, and Colleen, and more Gallic specimens such
as Arlene, Nadine, Maxine, Pauline, and Marlene. Even
more fashionably French were Annette, Paulette,
Claudette, Jeanette, Georgette, and Nanette, not to mention Rochelle, Estelle, and Isabel.

In 1925, although the official top names for girls were Mary, Barbara, Dorothy, Betty, and Ruth, a more colloquial list of popular choices would be:

BETSY	PATSY
BINNIE	PEGGY
DOLLY	PENNY
GWEN	POLLY
KATHLEEN	SALLY
KITTY	TRUDY
MARY ANN	WINNIE

For boys, the usual Anglo-Saxon stalwarts still ruled the official popularity lists, but more representative of the period were:

BARNEY	HAL
CALVIN	HOMER
CHESTER	MICKEY
CLEM	NED
DEXTER	WILBUR
ELMER	WILLIS
FRANKLIN	

During the mid-thirties through the forties, some of the fustier-feeling names like Dorothy, Shirley, Ruth, George, Frank, Edward, and Clarence fell off the Top 10, to be replaced by Carol, Judith, Joan, Ronald, David, and Linda, which, in 1948, would finally topple Mary from first place. Other new names were moving in as well, more sophisticated names for kids whose parents envisioned them triumphing over the Depression and growing up to wear glamorous gowns, drink martinis and use cigarette holders, and live in elegant Hollywood-inspired mansions. Television was still in a neonatal state, so no one could foresee that these would become the sitcom mom and dad names of the next generation:

GIRLS

ANITA	LORRAINE
ARLENE	LYNN
AUDREY	MARILYN
BERNICE	MARJORIE
BEVERLY	NANCY
CYNTHIA	NATALIE
DEBORAH	NORMA
DIANE	PAMELA
ELAINE	PAULA
ELLEN	RENEE
GAIL	RHODA
HELENE	RITA
JANET	SANDRA
JILL	SHEILA
JOANNE	SUSAN
JOYCE	SYLVIA
LOIS	ZELDA

BOYS

ALAN	HARVEY
BARRY	HOWARD
CARL	IRA
CHRISTOPHER	JOEL
ELLIOT	KENNETH
EUGENE	LAWRENCE
GERALD	MARTIN
HAROLD	MICHAEL

MITCHELL	ROGER
NEIL	RUSSELL
NORMAN	STANLEY
PAUL	STEVEN
PETER	VINCENT
PHILIP	WARREN

Post–World War II America was a time of bubbling optimism and a major baby boom that spawned a whole new generation of cuter, younger, glossier names for kids who would play with Betsy Wetsy dolls and watch *Howdy Doody*, oblivious to the treacherous times just past. These names reflected a collective lust for a new way of life, the good life in the sprawling suburbs. In 1948, Linda had leaped into the number-one spot for girls and Sharon and Karen were neck-and-neck at numbers nine and ten. The boys' list still showed Robert in top place, but Michael, a biblical name that had been out of favor for two hundred years, catapulted to second place, with other new names appearing, including Gary, Dennis, Douglas, and Bruce.

The above were representative of what we call Beach Boy names, cool monikers that hit the shores in the late fifties and early sixties and were the personification of surfer machismo. These righteous dudes included:

BRAD	GARY
BRIAN	GLENN
CHAD	GREG
CRAIG	JEFF
DARREN	KEITH
DARRYL	KEVIN
DEAN	KIRK
DENNIS	LANCE
DOUG	RICK
DUANE/DWAYNE	SCOTT

TERRY	TROY
TODD	WAYNE

Some of the newly popular girls' names of the fifties, many of which remained in vogue through the Kennedy administration, were:

AMY	JANICE
BRENDA	JULIE
CHARLENE	KIM
CHERYL	LISA
CHRISTINE	MICHELLE
DARLENE	ROBIN
DENISE	TERRY
DONNA	TINA
HEIDI	WENDY
HOLLY	

It was in the fifties that television began to have a great impact on names, first of all introducing a whole posse of long-forgotten western names like Jason, Joshua, and Jeremy (see page 135), and helping to make the American name supply ever-less-regional in scope. An even greater name revolution came during the Age of Aquarius, when sexual stereotypes were being reexamined and dispelled as men grew their hair to their shoulders and women abandoned their bras, and names became equally androgynous. In deference to the then-current credo of "Do your own thing," new names were invented, familiar forms of old names became perfectly acceptable, and the spelling of traditional names became a contest of creativity: the Karens and Craigs gave way to Caryns and Chastitys, Kellys and Clouds. The ultimate trendy name of the sexually liberated sixties was actually a relaxed nickname name, preferably ambigender. We saw a lot of the following:

CANDY	MARCY
CAREY	MARNIE
CASEY	MINDY
CINDY	RANDI
COREY	RICKI/RICKY
JAMIE	SHARI
JESSE	SHELLY
JODY	SHERRY
JONI	STACY
KELLY	TAMMY
KERRY	TAWNY
LORI	TRACY
MANDY	

The sixties was also the era of invented hippie names, not so different from the people, place, nature, and word names that seem to be making a comeback right now (see Style section). Among those that seemed the grooviest for flower children were:

AMERICA	PHOENIX
BREEZE	RAIN
CHE	RAINBOW
CHINA	RIVER
CLOUD	SEAGULL
DAKOTA	SEQUOIAH
GYPSY	SKY
HARMONY	SPRING
LEAF	STAR
LIBERTY	STARSHINE
LIGHT	SUMMER
MORNING	SUNSHINE
OCEAN	TRUE
PEACE	WELCOME

The seventies saw not only a revival of pioneering American names (Annie, Becky, Jenny, Jessie, Katie, Maggie, Molly, Ethan, Jed, Jesse, Luke, Shane, Zane), but also biblical names like Adam, Aaron, Benjamin, Jacob, Samuel, Jonathan, Rachel, Rebecca, and Sarah were born again, even if the parents choosing them weren't. Those who didn't want to reach back to the frontier or the Bible for their roots looked to their own or other people's ethnic backgrounds for inspiration. Names derived from the Irish or French became particularly popular, even for parents who had no connection to those countries. Thus were born thousands of Erins, Kellys, Kevins, Megans, Ryans, Seans, Shannons, and Taras. For girls, the French twist was the rage, with names such as Danielle, Michelle (given a huge boost by the Beatles song), and Nicole.

Other little girls were liberated from female stereotypes with names previously reserved for effete upper-class gentlemen: Ashley, Blake, Brooke, Courtney, Kimberly, Lindsay, and Whitney. Similar in tone, though they had always been girls' names, were Tiffany and Hayley. At the opposite end of the scale was a group of girls' names as purely feminine as lavender sachet. These were the wildly popular Victorian valentine names, many of which would remain popular through the nineties, which included Alexandra, Alyssa, Amanda, Jennifer, Jessica, Melissa, Samantha, Vanessa, and Victoria, along with their male counterparts Justin, Brett, Alexander, and Nicholas.

And then came the eighties, the era of Yuppie-Gekko-greed, Reaganomics, Cabbage Patch Kids, and Calvins. It was also the decade of a new baby boomlet and of the first generation of mothers more likely to work outside the home than to stay home with their kids. Feminism made concrete, upward mobility, and a strong emphasis on image all conspired to influence naming trends of the era.

In 1980, Jennifer still reigned supreme. The Top 10 girls' names of that year formed a transitional bridge between the soul-searching seventies and the neoconservative Reagan-Bush era. They were:

1. JENNIFER
2. AMY
3. MELISSA
4. KIMBERLY
5. SARAH
6. MICHELLE
7. HEATHER
8. AMANDA
9. ERIN
10. LISA

By the middle of the decade, most of these names vanished from the Top 10 list. At decade's end, only the two most timeless—Sarah and Amanda—would remain. Other classic names, which evidenced the refined taste and traditional values prized in the decade, were restored, with legions of eighties babies named Katherine, Elizabeth, Emily, William, Daniel, Andrew, and Christopher. Working mothers and feminist dads sought in the eighties a different kind of naming equality from the previous decade's, giving both daughters and sons upwardly mobile androgynous names such as Jordan and Morgan and Alex and Blake. Ashley, one such name that emerged for children of both sexes during the seventies, enjoyed a meteoric rise for girls throughout the eighties, reigning at number one for much of the decade.

When the eighties and some of its more superficial values ended with a crash, several of its naming trends survived, with a decidedly nineties twist. The veneer of old money was replaced by a more solid emphasis on genuine family histories, with names that honored real ancestors rather than those that conjure up phony WASP pedigrees. Ethnic names and surnames, as well as place names and nonglitzy family names, became more fashionable than the slick choices of the eighties, directions we see continuing well into the millennium.

African-American Names

History and Traditions

Consider LaKeisha.

LaKeisha is a quintessential African-American name, one well-used by African-American parents for their children, but by virtually no one else, not white Americans, not Africans, not Europeans. It doesn't exist in any conventional naming dictionary, and many people, including name experts, believe it is made up. "Created," decrees one popular name book. Another incorrectly declares it to be a combination of "the popular La prefix" with Aisha, the name of Muhammad's favorite wife and one that's often used, in many variations, by African-American parents.

But most name books simply disregard LaKeisha, along with the entire subject of African-American names, as well as the thousands of names favored by African-Americans. Why? Ignorance plays a major role in the issue, with everyone from name scholars to African-American parents—and of course, most especially the general public—largely unaware of the history and traditions of African-American names. Not much has been written on the subject, and research has been spotty, confined to slave names, for instance, or modern African-American naming practices, but rarely considering the entire sweep of black naming history.

Thus, the misunderstanding of LaKeisha, a name that embodies many of the primary influences that have shaped African-American names over the centuries.

Take that "La" at the beginning. Hundreds of African-American names, male as well as female ones, start with "La," a practice that can be traced back to the vigorous Free Black community in nineteenth-century Louisiana, where the French "La" prefix was affixed to many names, first as well as last.

Keisha derives not from Aisha but from Keziah, a biblical name. Keziah was one of the daughters of Job—Jemima was another one—whose name was popular among slaves who adopted Christianity and favored Old Testament names. Although Puritans used the name Keziah, it was not widely used by Southern whites, which made it fair game for blacks.

This is key: The black naming tradition has always, in America, been separate from the white one, distinct in its references and choices. It is a tradition influenced by Africa, influenced by Europe and American whites, and, more recently, influenced by the Muslim culture. But it is, most dramatically, a tradition unto itself, uniquely African-American.

At the core of the African-American naming culture are variety and invention. You can see that in LaKeisha: It takes something from here, something from there, shakes the spelling up a bit, to arrive at a name that's new and special. This diversity can be traced to the first Africans to arrive as slaves in America in the seventeenth and early eighteenth centuries. They arrived with African names but were immediately renamed by their new white masters. The first generation of African-American infants also tended to be named by the slave owners. Whites endeavored to give each of their slaves a unique name, one borne by no other slave on the plantation, in order to simplify work assignments and provision distribution. And they also looked for names that were not, by and large, used by the white community.

Some of the favorites of these early times were names from classical Greece and Rome. Southern plantation owners admired those ancient cultures, and fancied their own as being similar. Before 1800, classical names accounted for 20 percent of those given to slaves. While these are certainly noble names relating to heroic characters, the attitude of the slave owners in bestowing them, according to one scholar, may have been "whimsical, satiric or condescending in intent." Following are some of the most widely used classical names:

FEMALE

CLEOPATRA	MINERVA
DAPHNE	PHOEBE
DIANA	SAPPHO
DIDO	THISBE
FLORA	VENUS
JUNO	

MALE

ADONIS	HERCULES
AUGUSTUS	JUPITER
BACCHUS	NERO
CAESAR	POMPEY
CATO	PRIMUS
CICERO	SCIPIO
CUPID	TITUS
HANNIBAL	VIRGIL
HECTOR	

Because the slave owners needed a large pool of names, they allowed the continuation of some African names and naming practices, even though many accounts suggest they tended to be threatened by African names and traditions. In colonial times, as many as 15 to 20 percent of slaves in the two Carolinas bore African names, most notably day names, which relate to the day of the week on which the person is born. Prior to 1750, according to the scholar John Inscoe, 14 percent of African-American babies were given pure African names at birth and 25 percent were given names influenced by African names. The West African day names were:

	Female	Male
SUNDAY	QUASHEBA	QUASHEE
MONDAY	JUBA	CUDJOE
TUESDAY	BENEBA	CUBBENAH
WEDNESDAY	CUBA	QUACO
THURSDAY	ABBA	QUAO
FRIDAY	PHEBE/PHIBBI	CUFF/CUFFEE
SATURDAY	MIMBA	QUAME/KWAME

Some of these names were changed to English cognates: Cudjoe to Joe, Quaco to Jack, Juba to Judy, Abba to Abby, Phebe to Phoebe. And then the entire day-naming tradition was translated into English, by slave owners and slaves alike. Names were chosen that signified days of the weeks, months of the year, and special holidays. Some Anglicized day names that were used, primarily for boys but for girls as well, include Monday, Friday, Christmas, Easter, March, and July.

Place names were also commonly used in early days for slaves, often signifying a site of importance to the slave owner but sometimes relating to a place meaningful to the African-American parents. Sometimes, in keeping with the African tradition of using an event of the day of the child's birth to inform the name choice, the originating place of an important ship might dictate the name. Between 1720 and 1740, as many as one in four male slaves were given place names. The only ones noted for females were Carolina, Angola, and Cuba. The male choices from that time include:

ABERDEEN	CURRITUCK
AFRICA	DUBLIN
ALBEMARLE	GLASGOW
AMERICA	LONDON
BALTIMORE	NORFOLK
BARBARY	RICHMOND
BOSTON	WILLIAMSBURG
CAROLINA	WINDSOR
CONGO	YORK

Most avant-garde, to our twenty-first-century ears, were the word names used for and by African-Americans, signifying everything from virtues, à la the Puritan naming tradition, to weather. The use of these kinds of names relates to the African belief in the power of a name to shape personality or influence fate or impart a desirable quality, although some of them sound distinctly pessimistic. Some virtue and word names that have been recorded among early African-Americans are:

FEMALE

CHARITY	HOPE
DIAMOND	JEWEL
EARTH/EARTHA	LOVE
HONOR	MOURNING

OBEDIENCE

QUEEN

PATIENCE

TEMPERANCE

PROVIDENCE

MALE

CALIFORNIA GOLD

MAJOR

DUKE

MISERY

FORLORN

PLENTY

GOODLUCK

PRINCE

HARDTIMES

SQUIRE

JUSTICE

SUFFER

KING

VICE

LOWLIFE

EITHER

CHANCE

PLEASANT

FORTUNE

RAINY

FREEZE

STARRY

LIBERTY

STORMY

After 1800, two changes significantly altered African-American naming patterns. One was that many slaves had been in the United States for a generation or two, and began naming their own children, often using names of kin. This served to shrink the pool of names used, as well as to reinforce family ties among African-Americans. Interestingly, blacks tended to name babies after grandparents, an African tradition, and also a way to extend a family's roots back to African forebears, while whites of the same period tended to name after parents first. Grandparents sometimes chose an infant's name, another African custom. The other major nineteenth-century change was the conversion of many blacks to Christianity, and their subsequent adoption of biblical names. For males, the use of biblical names doubled from 1720 to 1820, from 20 to 40 percent. Popular choices for both sexes included:

FEMALE

DELILAH	LEAH
DORCAS	RACHEL
ESTHER	REBEKAH
HAGAR	RHODA
HANNAH	TAMAR
JEMIMA	ZILPAH
KEZIAH	

MALE

ABEL	ISHMAEL
CAIN	LAZARUS
ELIJAH	MOSES
EPHRAIM	NOAH
EZEKIEL	SAMSON
HEZEKIAH	SHADRACH
ISAAC	SOLOMON
ISAIAH	ZACHARIAH

This move toward biblical names meant that blacks and whites now shared the same names more often than ever before, although African-American choices still tended to diverge from white ones. The use of the older "slave names"—the day names, place names, classical names—declined as biblical names rose to the fore, and when they were used it was as a kin name. After 1865, blacks often dropped names too closely identified with slavery, Pericles becoming Perry, Willie formalizing to William.

By the early part of the twentieth century, black and white names in America were as closely related as they would ever be. There were some similarities as well as some differences in popularity lists, but most significantly, roughly the same proportion of black and white children received one of the top names. During this period, in other words, African-Americans stayed as close to convention and chose from as narrow a selection of names as whites did.

Still, there were variations. A detailed survey of the most popular names given to black females in Augusta, Georgia, in 1937, shows many overlaps with the white popularity list of that time, but with more informal and familiar forms—Lillie instead of Lillian, for example, and Janie not Jane. These short forms reflect the subordinate position of blacks in society, at that time, according to more than one expert:

1. MARY	12. LOUISE
2. ANNIE	13. ELIZABETH
3. MATTIE	14. ELLA
4. CARRIE	15. JULIA
5. ROSA	16. LULA
6. LILLIE	17. LIZZIE
7. EMMA	18. MARIE
8. MAMIE	19. SUSIE
9. HATTIE	20. ALICE
10. SARAH	21. JANIE
11. FANNY	

Black and white naming patterns began to widely diverge during the 1960s, with the rise of Black Nationalism and ethnic identity. While for decades black parents had been more likely than whites to choose unique names for their children, in the sixties everyone's taste for individual names rose—but African-American parents' desire for one-of-a-kind names increased even more. During this period black parents began looking to Muslim and African names for their children, but also took the roots of those native names and made them their own. Perhaps more significantly, for names if not for black culture, this was when the full-blown trend toward invention began.

From 1973 to 1985 in New York, 31 percent of black girls and 19 percent of black boys were given unique names—names that were not used for any other child of their sex and race in that state and that year—according to data collected by Stanley Lieberson, a sociology professor at Harvard. Similarly, in 1989 in Illinois, 29 percent of African-American girls and 16 percent of boys received unique names, according to another study by Lieberson. Although no newer data have been published, our guess is that those numbers have only increased with time.

For whites, the tendency to choose unique names drops off as the child's mother's education rises, according to Lieberson. But for blacks, the mother's education does not affect the chances that she'll choose an individual name for her child. African-American mothers of varying educational levels, says Lieberson, tend to choose names more similar to each other than do Caucasian mothers of the same education level. "Race," says Lieberson, "is a more powerful influence than class on the naming of children." The race effect is strongest on girls' names: roughly twice as significant as on boys' names, which tend to overlap more in popularity.

Popular African-American Names

Many African-American parents draw from the general pool of names for their children, and indeed many of the same names—Taylor and Ashley for girls, for instance, and Christopher and Michael for boys—are most popular for children of all races. Some African-American parents give their children African or Muslim names, or at least names that have their roots in those cultures: The enormously popular Ayeesha in all its variations, for instance, comes from Aisha, the name of the Prophet Muhammad's favorite wife.

But there is another group of names that can be considered truly African-American, names that spring uniquely from the tradition and culture of blacks in America and that are widely used by black parents today. Among these are names with historical antecedents in the African-American community: Keisha, for instance, embodies both the biblical slave and New Orleans Free Black traditions, as detailed earlier. Malik, a stylish boy's name, relates to the Muslim name and also bears a phonetic resemblance to the extraordinarily popular (for all races) Michael as well as to Malcolm, favored because of Malcolm X. Some African-American names relate to black pride: Ebony and Raven, for instance. Others are associated with black celebrities: Jada, for example, as in Pinkett Smith, and Tyra, as in supermodel Banks. Nia relates to one of the days of Kwanzaa.

Then there are names that are used differently by African-American parents than by those of other races. Among whites, for instance, Jordan is more popular for girls than for boys, but for black parents in Texas Jordan was the number-three name for *boys*, certainly due to the popularity and masculine appeal of Michael Jordan. Educator Marcus Garvey has inspired thousands of name-sakes, making his first name one of the most popular for boys in the African-American community. Other names more popular for boys among black parents than white parents include Xavier, Darius, Isaiah, Elijah, Jeremiah, André, and Desmond.

For girls, the list is longer. Jasmine is the number-one name for African-American girls in Texas, for example, but much further down on the list for white girls. Other names black parents like more than white parents do: Jada, Jayla, Destiny, Asia, Desirée, Felicia, Alexandria (as opposed to Alexandra), Andrea, and Angel.

And then there are names that white parents favor that African-American parents reject. For girls, notable examples in this category include Emily, Sarah, Hannah, and Elizabeth. For boys, they include Andrew, Alexander, Benjamin and Thomas.

Having a name that's perceived as typically "black" can be a problem for job seekers, according to a disturbing new study. Researchers from MIT and the University of Chicago business school submitted five thousand résumés with identical credentials for advertised jobs. The only difference was that some of the résumés bore names commonly perceived as African-American—Tamika and Rasheed, for instance—while others had "white" names such as Gregg and Emily. The results: the theoretically white applicants received one response for every ten résumés mailed, while the "black" applicants received only one response in fifteen.

One interesting thing about the differences between the white and black popularity lists is that, in many ways, African-Americans start the naming trends that whites adopt much later. Because creativity is more accepted among African-Americans for baby names, several trends only now clicking in among white parents—toward invented names, for instance, and place names and more un-usual Old Testament names—have been well-established among black parents for years.

But the most widespread and enduring overall African-American naming tradition is diversity and invention. Many names that might be considered African-American are, by their very definition, unique, and therefore difficult to corral onto a list. But here is a selection of African-American favorites:

GIRLS

AALIYAH	IMANI
ALEXANDRIA	INFINITY
ALEXIA	IVORY
ALONDRA	JADA
ANDREE	JAKEISHA
ANGEL	JALEESA
ASIA	JAMAICA
CAMIKA	JAMEEKA
CHANDRA	JASMINE
CHANELLE	JAYLA
CHANTAL	KALINDA
CHARISMA	KATIAH
CHARLAYNE	KATRINA
CHARLISE	KENDRA
CHARMIAN	KESHIA
CHERISE	KIANA
DANICA	KIARA/KIERA
DASHAY	KIERRA
DEJA	KYESHA
DESIREE	LaKEISHA
DESTINY	LaSHAUNA
DIAMOND	LaTEISHA
EBONY	LaTOYA

LETONYA
MARQUISHA/
   MARKEESHA
MIATA
MISHAYLA
NAKARI
NASHIRA
NIA
NIARA
PRINCESS
RASHANDA
RASHIDA
RAVEN
SABRIELLE
SAMISHA
SARONDA
SHAKEISHA
SHAKIRA
SHALISA

SHANAY
SHANIQUA
SHANISE
SHEVON/CHEVONNE
TAISHA
TAMIKA
TAMISHA
TANISHA
TASHAWNA
TAWANNA
TIA
TIARA
TYRA
VALETTA
XAVIERA
YASMIN
ZELEKA
ZORA

BOYS

ALIKA
ANDRÉ
ANTAWN/ANTON
ANTWON
ARIES
ASHANTE
BRAWLEY
BRYANT
CLAYTON
DAMON
DANTE
DARION
DARIUS

DARNELL
DASHAWN
DEION
DENZEL
DESMOND
GERMAINE/JERMAINE
GERVAISE
HARLEM
IMARI
ISAAC
ISAIAH
ISHMAEL
JAHAN

JALEEL/JALIL	NILE
JAMAD	ORION
JAMAR	ORLANDO
JAMEL	OTIS
JARREL	PRINCE
JAYLON	QUINCY
JUWAN	RASHAUN
KADEEM	REGINALD
KAMAR	SHAMAR
KENDRICK	SHAQUILLE
KESHAWN	SHAUN/SHAWN
KYAN	SHEMAR
LAMAR	STERLING
MALIK	TARIQ
MARCUS	TARON
MARIUS	TARRYL
MARQUIS	TAUREAN
MONTEL	TERRIL/TYRELL
MORGAN (*for boys;*	TEVIN
Caucasians use	TYRONE
this more often	XAVIER
for girls)	

Muslim/Arabic Names

Muslim names usually derive from those of the Prophet Muhammad, his descendants or immediate family. There are five hundred variations of the name Muhammad itself; taken together they become the most common boy's name in the world. Other popular Arabic names, such as Karim and Kamil, denote one of the ninety-nine attributes of God listed in the Koran.

A number of African-Americans have adopted Islamic beliefs and taken Arabic or Muslim names. Notable examples include Muhammad Ali, Kareem Abdul-Jabbar, and playwright Imamu Amiri Baraka. But non-Muslim black parents can also choose to use Arabic names, in their original form or as the basis for an invented variation.

GIRLS

ABIDA	HINDA
ABIR	IAMAR
ADARA	IMAN
ADIVA	JAMILA
AISHA	JENA
AKILAH	JINAN
ALAIA	KALIFA
ALIYA	KALILA
ALMIRA	KAMILAH
ALTAIR	KARIDA
AMINA	KARIMA
AMIRA	KHADIJA
ARA	KHALIFA
ATIFA	LAILA
AYASHA	LEILA
AZA	LOELIA
AZIZA	LUJAYN
BARAKA	MAJIDAH
BATHSIRA	MARIAM
CALA	MOUNA
FAIZAH	NABILA
FATIMA	NAILA
GHALIYA	NAIMA
HABIBAH	NEDIRA
HAFSAH/HAFZA	NIMA
HAMIDA	NUMA
HANIFA	NUR
HATIMA	OMA

RADIAH	SAMYA
RAJA	SANA/SANNA
RAZIYA	SHADIYA
RIDA	SHAFIQA
RIHANA	SHAHAR
RIMA	SHARIFA
SABA	TABINA
SADIKA	TALIBA
SADIRA	TAMASHA
SAFIA	ULIMA
SAHAR	YAMINA
SAHARA	YASMEEN
SALIHA	ZADA
SALIMA	ZAHIRA
SALMA	ZULEIKA
SAMIRA	

BOYS

ABDUL	HAKEEM
ABDULLAH	HALIMA
AFIF	HAMAL
AHMAD/AHMED	HAMID
AKBAR	HANA
AKIL	HANIF
ALI	HASHIM
AMIR	HASSAN
ARNAN	HUSAIN
AZIZ	IBRAHIM
BAHIR	JAFAR
BILAL	JAMIL
DAWUD	JUMAH
FARID	KADAR
FARRAN	KAMALI
FAYSAL	KAMIL

KARIM	RAMI
KASIM	RASHID
MALIK	SADIK
MEHMET	SALIM
MUHAMMAD	SHARIF
NURI	TAHIR
OMAR	YASIR
RAFI	YAZID
RAHMAN	ZAKI

African Names

African names used by black American parents are drawn from a wide range of languages and cultures, from Swahili to Bantu, from Ethiopian to South African. Here is a selection of names that fit well into the American culture at large:

GIRLS

ABBA	ASMINA
ABEBA	ASURA
ABEBI	AYANA
ABINA/ABENA	AZMERA
ADA	BINTA
AFRIKA	CAMISHA
AFYA	CHINAKA
AKINA	CHINARA
AKUA	DALILA
ALITASH	DAURA
AMARA	DAYO
AMINATA	EFIA
ARUSI	FANA
ASHAKI	FAYOLA

HASINA	NANTALE
IMAN	NAYO
ISSA	NEEMA
JAHA	NIA
JANI	NKEKA
KAHINA	NOBANZI
KAMARIA	ONI
KANIKA	OZORO
KATURA	PANYA
KAYA	RAMLA
LATEEFAH	SALAMA
LISHAN	SANURA
LULU	SHANI
MAKINA	SUMA
MARIAMA	TABIA
MARJANI	TARANA
MASIKA	TISA
MONIFA	ZUWENA
NADIFA	

BOYS

ABASI	JAHI
ADOM	JELANI
AKONO	JIMIYU
ANKOMA	JUMA
ATSU	KALEB
AZIBO	KALUME
AZIZI	KAMUZU
BENO	KITO
BOMANI	KOJO
CHUMA	KWAMI
EBO	KWASI
HANISI	LABAAN
JABARI	LEBNA

MANU	RAJABU
MAZI	ROBLE
MONGO	RUNAKO
MUSA	SIMBA
OBASI	TABAN
ODION	TANO
OJO	YULISA
OMARI	ZAHUR
PAKI	ZANI
RAFIKI	ZURI

Erica to Erykah

Long before Afrocentric R&B chanteuse Erykah Badu made a big name for herself . . . she was known as Erica Wright. "I didn't want to have the slave name anymore," says Badu. . . . "So I changed the spelling of my first name because the 'kah' is Kemetic {ancient Egyptian} for 'the inner self.' "

—PEOPLE

Names from Across the Ocean

Let's say your roots are Italian and you'd like to give your child a name that reflects your ethnic heritage, but want to go beyond names like Maria and Mario to find others that reflect the expressive beauty of the Italian language. What we offer here is a greatly expanded, much wider variety of choices from primarily European cultures, ranging from names that have long been familiar in this country, such as the French Madeleine and Marguerite, say, to bolder, more original choices like Manon and Musette. For lists of names that are currently most popular in these countries, see pages 90 to 104.

Celtic Names

Celtic names are, as a group, among the most appealing to parents today. But pronunciations can be pesky. Here, we offer wide-ranging lists of names native to Ireland, Scotland, and Wales, with pronunciation guides where pertinent.

Scottish Names

GIRLS

AILSA (*AYL-sa*)
AINSLEE
ALEXINA
ALWYNE
AMABEL
AMILIA
ANNELLA
BARABAL
BETHIA
BEVIN
CAIT
CAITRIONA,
 CATRIONA
 (*Ka-TREE-nuh*)
DAVINA
EDINA
EILIDH (*I-lee*)
EITHNE (*EN-ya*)
ELSPETH
ESMÉ
EUNA
FINELLA/FENELLA
FINOLA
FIONA
FLORA
GREER
IDONEA
IONA/IONE
ISLA
ISOBEL/ISHBEL

JACOBINA
JAMESINA
KEITHA
KENNA
KIRSTY
KYLA
LILEAS/LILLIAS
LORNA
MAIRI (*MAH-ree*)
MALVINA
MARIOTA
MARSALI
MAURA
MOIRA (*MOY-ra*)
MORAG
MUIREALL
 (*MOOR-uh-yel*)
NAIRNE
NESSA
PENUEL
PETRINA
ROBINA
ROSINA
ROWENA
SELVACH
SENGA
SEONA (*SHAW-nuh*)
SHEENA
SHONA

SILE (*SHEE-luh*) THEODOSIA
SINE (*SHEE-nuh*) TRIONA
SORCHA (*SOHR-ra*)

BOYS

ADAIR	DUGALD
ALASDAIR	DUNCAN
ALPIN	EACHANN
ALWIN	(*YAH-han*)
ANGUS	EWAN/EUAN
ARCHIBALD	FARQUHAR
ATHOL/ATHOLL	FERGUS
AVLAY	FIFE
BAIRD	FINAN
BALDWIN	FINGAL
BEATHAN	FINLAY
BLAIR	FRASER
CALUM/CALLUM	GAVIN
CAMERON	GEORDIE
CAMPBELL	GILLEAN (*GILL-*
CLYDE	*yan*)
COLIN	GORDON
COLL	GRAHAM/GRAEME
CONALL	GREGOR
CORMAC	GUINN
COSMO	HAMISH
COSPATRIC	IAIN (*EE-ayn*)
CRAIG	INNES
CRISPIN	IVAR/IVOR
CUTHBERT	JOCK
DOUGAL (*doo-UHL*)	KEIR
DREW	KEITH
DUFF	KYLE

LACHLAN
 (*LAK-lan*)
LAIRD
LENNOX
LOGAN
MACAULEY
MacDONALD
MAGNUS
MALCOLM
MANIUS
MUIR
MUNGO
MUNRO
MURRAY/MORAY
NAIRNE
NIALL
NICOL

NINIAN
OSSIAN (*USH-en*)
PADRUIG (*PA-trik*)
RORY
ROSS
SEAMUS
 (*SHAY-muhs*)
SETON
SIM
SORLEY
STEWART/STUART
SWAIN
TAM
TAVIS/TAVISH
TORQUIL
UILLEAM

Irish Names

GIRLS

AILIS (*AY-lish*)
AINE (*AWN-ya*)
AISLING (*ASH-ling*)
AOIFE (*EE-fah*)
AUGUSTEEN
BIDELIA
CATRIONA
 (*Kat-REE-na*)
CIARA (*KEER-ra*)
CLODAGH
 (*KLOH-da*)
DARINA

DEIRDRE
EABHA (*AY-va*)
EITHNE (*ETH-na*)
FIONNUALA
 (*Fin-NOO-la*)
GRANIA (*GRAW-nyah*)
ISEULT (*EE-sult*)
JUNO
LAOISE (*LEE-sha*)
MAEVE (*Mayv*)
MAIRE (*MAH-ree*)

MAJELLA
MAOLIOSA
  (*Ma-LEE-sah*)
MELLA
MUIREANN
  (*MEER-an*)
NIAMH (*NEE-av*)
ORLA
ROISIN (*Roh-sheen*)

SAOIRSE (*SEER-sha*)
SILE (*SHEE-la*)
SINE (*SHEEN-ah*)
SINEAD (*Shin-AID*)
SIOBHAN
  (*Shi-VAUN*)
SORCHA (*SOR-ra*)
TALULLA

BOYS

AENGUS, AONGHUS
  (*EYN-gus*)
AIDAN (*AY-dan*)
ALASTAR
AODH (*AY*)
BRAN (*Brawn*)
CHRISTIE
CIAN (*KEE-an*)
CIARAN (*KEER-an*)
COLM, COLUM
  (*KUHL-uhm*)
CONNERY
CONNOR, CONOR
DIARMAID (*DEER-mit*)
DONAGH (*DUN-a*)
EAMON (*AY-mun*)
ENEAS (*Ey-NEY-as*)
EOIN (*OH-in*)
FAOLAN (*FEH-lan*)
FARQUHAR (*FAR-har*)
FARRY

FINN
FINNIAN
IVAR
JARLATH
KEIR (*Care*)
KIERAN
KILLIAN
LIAM
LORCAN
MICHEAL (*MEE-haul*)
NIALL (*NEE-al*)
ORAN (*OH-ran*)
OWNY
PADRAIG (*PAWD-rig*)
QUINLAN
RIAN (*REE-an*)
RIORDAN
  (*REER-dawn*)
SEANAN (*SHAW-nawn*)
SEARLAS (*SHAR-las*)
SEOIRSE (*SHORE-sha*)

SIVNEY
SORLEY
TIERNAN (*TEAR-nan*)

UILLIAM (*OOL-yuhm*)
UINSEANN (*IN-sun*)

Welsh Names

GIRLS

AELWYN, AYLWYN
AERON
   (*AY-ron*)
ANEIRA
ANWEN
ARDDUN
ARIANELL
   (*a-ree-AHN-el*)
ARIENWEN
   (*a-ree-AHN-wen*)
AURON (*AYR-on*)
BETHAN
   (*BETH-an*)—a
   popular Welsh
   nickname for
   Elizabeth
BRANWEN,
   BRONWEN,
   BRONWYN
BRIALLEN
BRYN, BRYNN
CATRIN (*KAHT-rin*)
CORDELIA
DELYTH

DILYS (*DIL-iss*)
DWYN
ELERI (*EL-eh-ree*)
FFION, FFIONA (*Fee-on, fee-OH-nah*)
FFLUR (*Fleer*)
GLENYS, GLYNIS
GWENIVERE
GWENLLIAN
GWYNETH
IOLA (*YOH-lah*)
LLEULU (*HLYOO-loo*)
LLINOS
MARGED (*MAHR-ged*)
MORWENNA
NERYS (*NER-iss*)
NESTA
NIA
OLWEN (*AHL-wen*)
RHIAN (*RHEE-an*)
RHIANNON
   (*Rhee-AHN-nun*)
RHONWEN

SIAN (*Shan*)
TEGAN (*TEG-ahn*)
VENETIA

WALLIS
WINNE

BOYS

AED (*Ayd*)
AEDDON (*AYD-un*)
ALUN
BEVAN
BRAN
CADOC (*KAHD-oc*)
CAI (*Kay*)
CELYN (*KEL-in*)
CIAN (*KEE-an*)
COLLEN
DAFYDD (*DAH-vith*)
DEWI
ELIAN
EMLYN
EVAN
GARETH
GLYN
GRIFFITH
GWILYM (*GWIL-im*)
HEW (*Hyoo*)

IAGO
IEUAN (*YAY-un*)
IOLO (*YOH-loh*)
IVOR
JEVAN
LLEWELLYN,
  LLYWELYN
LLIO
MORGAN
NYE
OWAIN, OWEN,
  EWAN
PADRIG (*PAHD-rig*)
PRYS (*Prees*)
RHYS
SIARL (*Sharl*)
SION (*Shon*)
SULIEN (*SIL-yen*)
TEILO (*TAY-loh*)
TREFOR (*TREV-ohr*)

Dutch Names

GIRLS

ANNEKE
ANOUK
BEATRIX

DEMI
ELINE
ELISABETH

EVA	MARGARETE/
FEMKE	MARGRIET
FRANCISCA	MARIEKE
GERDA	NAOMI
GREET/GRETA	ROMY
IRIS	SANNE
JOHANNA	SASKIA
JULIANA	SOFIE
KATRYN	TESSA
KLARA/KLAARTJE	VALENTYN
LOTTE	WILHELMINA

BOYS

ADRIAAN/ADRIAEN	GERRIT
ANDRIES	HANS
ANTON	HENDRIK
ANTONIUS	IZAAK
BART	JAAP
BAS	JACOBUS/COBUS
BENEDIKT	JAKOB
BRAM	JAN
CASPAR	JEROEN
CLAUS	JOHANNES
COOS	JOOP
CORNELIS/CEES	JOOST
DAAN	JOREN
DIDERIK/DIEDERIK	JORIS
DIRK	JURGEN
FLORIS	JUSTUS
FRANS	KAREL
FREDERIK	KEES (*Kayz*)
GASPAR	KLAAS
GEERARD	LARS
GEERD	LAURENS

LUCAS	REIGNIER
MAARTEN/MARTIJN	ROBIN
MATHYS	RUBEN
MAX	RUTGER
MENNO	SANDER
NIELS	SEBASTIAAN/BAS
NIKOLAAS/NICOLAES	SIMON
OTTO	TON
PIETER/PIET	WILLEM

French Names

France has a strict name law instituted under Napoleon, which calls for Christian children to get saints' names, Jewish children to receive Old Testament names, and all children to receive names that will not make them the subject of ridicule. But things seem to be getting somewhat lax of late. Two of the trendiest names: Océane (yes, like Ocean) for girls and Zinnedine, after the hottest 1998 World Cup soccer player, for boys.

GIRLS

ABÉLIA	ANAÏS
ADELINA	ANDRÉE
ADRIENNE	ANGE
AIMÉE	ANGÉLIQUE
ALAINE	ARABELLE
ALBANE	ARIANE
ALEXANDRINE	ARLETTE
ALIZÉE	ARMELLE
AMANDINE	AUDINE
AMÉLIE	AURÉLIE
ANABELLE	AURORE

BERNADETTE	FABIENNE
BERNADINE	FELICITÉ
BERTHILDE	FERNANDE
BERTILLE	FLEUR
BIBIANE	FRANCE
BLANCHE/	FRANÇOISE
BLANCHETTE	GABRIELLE
BRIGITTE	GAELLE
CAMILLE	GENÈVE
CECILE	GENEVIÈVE
CELESTE	GEORGETTE
CERISE	GERMAINE
CHANTAL	GISELE
CHLOÉ	HÉLOÏSE
CHRISTIANE	INDRA
CLAIRE	ISABELLE/ISABEAU
CLARICE	JACINTHE
CLAUDE	JOËLLE
CLAUDIE	JOSETTE
CLÉMENTINE	JULIENNE
CLOTHILDE	LAURE
COLETTE	LAURENCE
COLOMBE	LÉA
CORINNE	LÉONIE
DELPHINE	LIANNE
DOMINIQUE	LILIANE
DYNA	LISETTE
EDWIGE	LOURDES
ELIANE	LUCIENNE
ELODIE	LYDIE
ELOISE	MADELEINE
ELORIANE	MAELYS
ÉMILIE	MAEVA
EUGÉNIE	MANON
EULALIE	MARGUERITE

MARINE	PHILIPPINE
MARJOLAINE	RACHELLE
MARTHE	RÉBEQUE
MARTINE	RÉGINE
MATHILDE	REINE
MAUDE	ROMAINE
MAXIME	SABINE
MELICE	SALOMÉ
MELISSANDE	SANDRINE
MICHELINE	SÉRAPHINE
MIGNON	SÉVERINE
MIRABELLE	SIDONIE
MIREILLE	SIMONE
MONIQUE	SOLANGE
MORGANE	SOLENE
MUSETTE	SYLVIE
NICOLETTE	TENILLE
NOËLLE	THOMASINE
NOEMIE	VANINE
OCÉANE	VENISE
ODETTE	VÉRONIQUE
ODILE	VICTOIRE
ORIANNE	VIOLETTE
ORLEANE	ZÉNOBIE
PATRICE	ZOÉ

BOYS

ADALARD	ANATOLE
ADRIEN	ANDRÉ
ALAIN	ANSELME
ALEXANDRE	ANTOINE
ALUIN	ANTONIN
AMBROISE	APPOLINAIRE
AMÉDÉE	ARISTIDE

ARMAND	GERMAIN
AUBERT	GRÉGOIRE
AUGUSTE	GUILLAUME
BAPTISTE	GUY
BARDIOU	HENRI
BARTHÉLMY	HERVÉ
BASILE	HONORÉ
BASTIEN	JACQUES
BAUDIER	JÉRÉMIE
BELLAMY	JOURDAIN
BENOIT	JULIEN
BLAISE	LAURENT
CÉSAR	LAZARE
CHRISTOPHE	LÉO
CLAUDE	LUC
CLÉMENT	LUCIEN
CONSTANTINE	MARC
CORENTIN	MARIUS
CORNEILLE	MATHURON
DAMIEN	MATTHIEU
DENYS	MAXIME
DIDIER	MELCHIOR
DION	MICHEL
ÉMILE	ODILON
ÉTIÉNNE	OLIVIER
FABIEN	PASCAL
FABRICE	PATRICE
FÉLIX	PHILIPPE
FLORIAN	PIERRE
FRANÇOIS	PROSPER
FRÉDÉRIC	QUENTIN
GASPARD	RAINIER
GASTON	RAOUL
GAUTIER	RAPHAEL
GEORGES	REMI/REMY

ROMAIN	THIBAULT
SÉBASTIEN	THIERRY
SERGE	VIRGILE
SILVAIN	YANIS
TANCRÉDE	YOHAN
TANGUY	YVES
THÉOPHILE	ZINNEDINE

ACCENTuating the Positive

When one of us sent out announcements upon the arrival of a daughter we named Chloe, we were quite surprised to receive back several cards addressed to both Chloé and Chloë. It had never occurred to us to use the forms reflecting the name's Greek origin and heavy French usage. In fact, very few American parents who choose the name Chloe do use an accent, unless they want to establish the French pronunciation—clo-AE, rather than clo-EE—which, in this country, runs the risk of sounding pretentious. On the other hand, as in the cases of such celebrities as Renée (not REE-NEE) Zellweger and Beyoncé (which would otherwise rhyme with sconce) Knowles, the French *accent aigu* is used precisely to emphasize the correct pronunciation of their names. As for the many other accented French and other imports: Noëlle, André, Esmé, Anaïs, Zoë, José, Desirée, Aimée, Salomé, Brontë, et al., the bottom line is they might add a nice, little decorative fillip and sense of authenticity, and clarify the pronunciation of your child's name, but they also might prove to be a clumsy encumbrance, rarely used by other people who don't have umlauts on their keyboards. The option is yours.

In recent times, other forms of punctuation have entered the naming field: apostrophes and periods. Singer/actress Brandy called her daughter Sy'rai, and there are singers India.arie, and rappers Will.i.am, apl.d.apl, Li'l Kim, and several other L'ils. What's next? We hope it's not a question mark.

Those Wild and Crazy Germans

A court in northern Germany recently ruled that parents had the right to invent names, as long as the child could still be "individualized" and there was no threat of him being humiliated because of his name. Baby naming is closely regulated in Germany: First names must be recognized as such and must identify the child's gender. Ambisexual names such as Toni or Kai have to be followed by a middle name that clearly identifies the baby's sex.

German Names

GIRLS

AGNA	BERTITA
ALOISA/ALOISIA	BIANKA
AMALIA/AMALIE	BIRGITTE
ANGELIKA	BRIGITTA
ANJA	CAROLA
ANNELIESE	CHRISTA
ANTONIA	CONSTANZA

CORINNA	LENI
EBBA	LILI/LILLI
ELEONORE	LIN
ELKE	LORELEI
EMELIE	LUCIE
EVA	LUISE
FLORENTIA	LUZI
FRANZISKA	MAGDA
FREYA	MAGDALENE
FRIDA	MARGRETE
FRITZI	MARTHE
GERDA	MATHILDE
GERTA/GISELLE	MINA
GRETA	MINNA
GRETCHEN	MITZI
HANNE/HANNI	MONIKA
HEIDI	OTTILIE
HELGA	RENATE
ILSA/ILSE	ROLANDA
IMMA	STEPHANINE
INGE	SYBILLA
JACOBINE	TILDA
KÄETHE	TRINE
KAMILLA	ULLA
KARLOTTE	URSULA
KATJA	UTA
KLARISSA	VERONA
KLEMENTINE	VERONIKE
KORINNA	WILHELMINA
KORNELIA	ZELLA
KRISTIANA	ZITA

BOYS

ABALARD	GÜNTHER/GÜNTER
ALARIC	GUSTAV
ALBRECHT	HANS
ALOIS	HASSO
ANDREAS	HEINRICH
ANSELM	HELMUT
ANTON	HORAZ
ARIUS	HORST
ARNO	HUGO
AUGUST	JAKOB
AXEL	JOHANN/JOHANNES
BALTHASAR	JOSEF
BENEDIKT	JURGEN
BENNO	JUSTUS
BRUNO	KASIMIR
CASPAAR	KASPAR
CLAUS	KLEMENS
CLEMENS	KONRAD
DIETER	KONSTANTIN
DIETRICH	KURT
DOMINIK	LORENZ
EGON	LOTHAR
EMIL	LUKAS
ERICH	MAGNUS
FABER	MARIUS
FELIX	MARKUS
FLORIAN	MATTHAEUS/
FRANZ	MATHIAS
FRIEDERICH	MAX
FRITZ	MELCHIOR
GEORG	NIKOLAUS
GOTTFRIED	OSKAR
GREGOR	OTTO

RAINER	VALENTINE
ROLF	VIKTOR
RUPERT	VINCENS
SANDER	WALDO
STEFAN	WERNER
THADDAUS	WILHELM
THEOBOLD	WOLFGANG/WOLF
TOMAS	ZEPHYRIN
ULF	

Greek Names

GIRLS

ACACIA	CALLA
ACANTHA	CASSIA
ADELPHA	CHLOE
AEOLA	CLIO
ALETHIA	COSIMA
ALIDA	CRESSIDA
ALPHA	CYNARA
ALTHAIA	DAMARA/DAMARIS
ALYSIA	DELIA
ANATOLA/ANATOLIA	DELPHINE
ANEMONE	DEMETRIA
ANTHEA	DIANTHA
ARIADNE	DORCAS
ARTEMIS	ECHO
ASTA	ELECTRA/ELEKTRA
ATHENA	ELENA/ELENI
BASILA	EUDOCIA
CALANDRA	EUDORA
CALANTHA	EUGENIA
CALISTA	EULALIA

GAEA	PANDORA
IANTHE	PENELOPE
IOANNA	PHAIDRA
KALLIOPE	PHOEBE
KORA	RHEA
KOREN	SABA
LALIA	THADDEA
LARISSA	THALASSA
LEANDRA	THALIA
LELIA	THEA
LYDIA	THEODORA
MAIA	THEODOSIA
MELANTHA	THEONE
MELINA	XANTHE
NEOLA	XENIA
NEOMA	ZELIA
NERISSA	ZENOBIA
ODESSA	ZITA
OLYMPIA	ZOE
PALLAS	

BOYS

ALEXANDROS	CLETUS
ALEXIOS	CONSTANTINE
ANDREAS	COSMO/KOSMOS
ARGOS	CYRIAN
ARISTEDES	DAMIANOS
ARSENIOS	DARIUS
ARTEMAS	DEMETRI/DEMETRIOS
BARNABAS	ELIAS
BASIL	GEORGIOS
CHRISTIANO	GREGORIOS
CHRISTOS	HOMER
CLAUDIOS	ILIAS

IONNES	PETROS
KRISTIAN	PHILO
LEANDER	PLATO
LOUKAS	SANDROS
MARKOS	STAMOS
MATTHIAS	STAVROS
MAXIMOS	STEPHANOS
NEMO	THANOS
NICO/NIKO/NIKOS	THEODOROS
NIKODEMUS	TITOS
ORION	VASILIS
PERICLES	ZENO

Italian Names

Italian baby-naming books do not merely offer a list of names and root meanings. Rather, each name comes with a detailed character analysis as well as lucky days, numbers, colors, and gems. Names are almost like minihoroscopes. Name your son Enzo, for instance, and you're sure to get a boy who's sweet and romantic, who loves music and art; a Martino will be prudent and economic.

GIRLS

ALESSIA	DONATA
AMALIA	ELETTRA
AMBRA	EMILIANA
ANTONELLA	FABRIZIA
ARIANNA	FLAVIA
CANDIDA	GIANNA
CHIARA	GIOIA
CLELIA	GIOVANNA
DANILA	GRAZIANA

ILARIA	ODILIA
ISOTTA	ORIANA
LIA	PALMA
LILIANA	PETRONILLA
LUCA	PIA
LUCIA	RAFFAELA
MADDALENA	RENATA
MARCELLA	ROMANA
MARZIA	ROSARIA
NICOLETTA	VIOLETTA
NOEMI	

BOYS

ADAMO	GIUSEPPE
ALDO	GUIDO
AMEDEO	LEONARDO
ANSELMO	LORENZO
ARTURO	MARCO
AURELIO	MARIO
BERNARDO	MATTEO
CARLO	ORAZIO
CESARE	OTTAVIO
COSIMO	PAOLO
DOMENICO	PIETRO
ELIO	RAOUL
ENZO	ROCCO
ERASMO	RUGGIERO
FRANCESCO	TEO
GIACOMO	UMBERTO
GIANNI	VITO
GIORGIO	

Scandinavian Names

AGATA	GERDA
AGNA	GUDRUN
AGNETHE/AGNETA	GUNILLA
AMMA	GUNN
ANNELI	HANNA
ANNELIESE	HEDDA
ANNIKA	HEDVIG
ANTONIA	HELGE
ARNA	HJORDIS
ASA	IDONY
ASTA	INGA/INGE
ASTRID	INGER
AUDNY	INGRID
BARBRO	JAKOBINE
BENEDIKTA	JANA
BERIT	JANNIKE
BIRGIT	JENSINE
BRITT	KAREN/KARIN/
CARINA	KARENA
DAGMAR	KARITA
DAGNY	KAROLINA
DISA	KERSTIN
EBBA	KLARA
EDDA	KOLINA
ELISABET	KRISTINA
ELKE	LAILA
ELSE	LENA
ESTER	LINNEA
FREJA/FREYA	LIS
GALA	LIV

LOVISA	SANNA
MAI	SIGNY
MAJ	SIGRID
MAJA	SILJA
MALENA	SIV
MARGIT	SOFI/SOFIA/SOFIE
MARGRETA	SOLVEIG
MARIT	SONJA
MARKETTA	SUNNIVA
MARNA	SVANNI
MÄRTA	SVEA
MERETE	TEKLA
META	THORA
MIA	TILDA/TILDE
MONIKA	TYRA
NANNA	ULLA
NEA	ULRIKA
ODA	URSULA
OLA	VALESKA
OLEA	VANJA
PELLA	VERONIKA
PERNILLA	VIKTORIA
PETRINE	VILMA
PIA	VITA
RAGNA	VIVEKA/VIVECA/
RAKEL	VIVICA
RUNA	VOR

BOYS

AKSEL	ANTERO
ALVIS	ARI
ANDERS	ARNE
ANDOR	ARVID
ANDREAS	ASMUND

AUDUN	HALLE
AXEL	HALSTEN
BARDO	HANNU
BARTHELEMY	HARALD
BASILIUS	HEMMING
BENEDIKT	HENRIK
BJØRN	HILLEVI
BO	IB
BORJE	INGEMAR/INGMAR
CHRISTER	ISAK
CLAES/CLAUS	IVAR/IVOR
DAG	JAKOB
EDVARD	JARL
EERO	JENS
EETU	JOHAN
EILIF	JORAN
EIRIK	JORN
ELOF/ELOV	JØRTEN
EMIL	JOSEF
ERIK	KAARLE
ESAIAS	KAI/KAJ
EYOLF	KALLE
FINN	KARL
FREDERIK/FREDRIK	KLEMENS
GEORG	KNUT/KNUTE
GERD	KONRAD
GJORD	KONSTANTIN
GORAN	KORT
GREGER/GREGERS	KRISTOFFER
GUNNAR/GUNDER	LARS
GUNTHER	LASSE
GUSTAV	LAUNO
HAAKON/HAKAN/	LAURIS/LAURITZ
HAKEN	LEIF
HAGEN	LENNART

LORENZ/LORENS	ROALD
MAGNUS	ROLF
MIKKEL	SOREN
MIKKO	STAFFAN
MORTEN	STEN
NELS	STIAN
NIELS	STIG
NIILO	SVANTE
NILS	SVEN
NJORD	SVERRE
ODIN	TAIT
OLAF/OLOF	THOR
ORJAN	TOR
OSKAR	TORSTEN
OVE	TRYGVE
PAAVO	TYR
PEDER	ULF
PELLE	VALDEMAR
PER	VALENTIN
RIETI	VERNER
RIKARD	VIGGO

Slavic Names

GIRLS

ADELINA	ANASTASIA
AGATÁ	ANASTAZIE
ALENA	ANEZKA
ALIDA	ANIELA
ALINA	ANTONINÁ
ALINKA	BARA
ALZBETA	BASIA
AMALIA	BRONYA

CELINA	KAMILÁ
DANIKA	KAROLINÁ
DASHA	KASIA
DOMINIKA	KATERINA
DOROFEI	KATINKA
DOROTA	KATYA
DOSIA	KILINA
ELZBIETA	KINGA
ESTZER	KIRA
EWÁ	KLAUDIA
FANYA	KORDULA
FEODORA	LARA
FILIPA	LARISA
FORTUNATA	LICIA
FRANZISKA	LIDÁ
FYODORA	LIDIA
GALA	LIDMILA
GALINA	LILLÁ
GIZELA	LUBA
GRAZYNA	LUDMILA/LUDMILLA
HALINA	LUIZA
HANÁ	MAGDÁ
HEDVIG	MAJA
ILKA	MARCELINA
ILONA	MARGIT
IRINA	MARIKA
IVANNA	MARINÁ
IZABELLÁ	MASHA
JAGÁ	MAVRA
JANÁ	MILDA
JAROMIRA	MILENA
JELENA	NADYA
JONNA	NASTASIA
JOZEFINA	NATALYA
JUDITA	NATASHA

NINA	SONYA
OKSANA	STEFANIÁ
OLÁ	SVETLANA
OLENA	TALYA
OLEXA	TAMARA
OLGA	TANYA
OTILIE	TATIANA
PELAGIA	TEODORA
POLINA	VALESKA
RADA	VARVARA
RAINA	VERA
RAISA	WANDA
ROMANA	YELENA
ROZA	ZANETA
RUZENA	ZINA
SARI	ZOFIA
SASHA	ZUZANNA
SIBILIA	

BOYS

AKIM	ARTEMI
ALEKSANDER	BARTO/BARTOS
ALEXEI	BAZYLI
ALEXEJ	BÉLA
ALYOSHA	BENEDYKT
AMBROZ	BORIS
ANATOLI	BORYS
ANDRAS	CEZAR
ANDREI	DARIUSZ
ANDREJ	DIMITRI/DMITRI
ANTONIN	DMITRO
ANZELM	DOBRY
ARKADI	DOMINIK
ARSENI	EELIA

EVGENI/EUGENI	KOLYA
FABIAN	KORNEL
FERENC	KRYSTOF
FILIP	LAJOS
FLORIAN	LÁSZLÓ
FYODOR	LAVRO
GABOR	LECH
GASPAR	LEONTI
GEORGI	LEOS
GREGOR	LEV
GRIGORI	LÓRÁNT
GYORGY	MAKSIM
HAVEL	MAREK
IAKOV	MIKHAIL
IDZIO	MIKLOS
IGOR	MIKOLAS
ILYA	MILAN
IMRE	MILOS/MILOSZ
IVAN	MIREK
IZYDOR	MISHA
JACEK	MORIZ
JAKUB	NIKITA
JALU	NIKOLAI
JAN	NOE
JÁNOS	ÕDÕN
JAREK	OLEG
JAZON	PAVEL
JENÖ	PIOTR
JERZY	RODION
JIRI	ROMAN
JOSEF	SÁNDOR
KÁLMÁN	SASHA
KAMIL	SAVVEL
KAROLY	SEMYON
KAZIMIR	SERGEI

SEVASTIAN	VASILI
STASIAK	VENEDIKT
STEFAN	VIDOR
STEPAN	VILEM
SZYMON	VILMOS
TIBOR	VLADIMIR
TIMOFEI	VLAS
TOMAS/TOMASZ	WITOLD
TOMEK	YAKOV
TYTUS	YEGOR
URBAN	YURI
VACLAV	ZAREK
VADIM	ZBIGNIEW
VALENTIN	ZOLTÁN
VANYA	

Spanish Names

GIRLS

ADELA/ADELINA	APOLONIA
ADRIANA	ARACELI
AFRICA	ARANTXA
AIDA	AQUILINA
ALBA	AURELIA
ALEJANDRA	BEATA
ALETA	BEATRIZ/BEATRIX
ALIDA	BEGONIA
ALITA	BELIA
ALMA	BELICIA
ALOISIA	BENICIA
AMALIA	BIBIANA
ANA	BLANCA
ANTONIA	CALIDA

CAMILA/CAMELIA	ESPERANZA
CARIDAD	ESTEFANÍA
CARLOTA	ESTRELLA
CARMELA	EULALIA
CARMEN	FABIANA
CATALINA	FABIOLA
CATARINA	FAUSTA/FAUSTINA
CELESTINA	FELICIA
CHARA/CHARO	FELICIDAD
CHELA	FELIXA
CINTIA	FERNANDA
CLARITA	FILIPA
CLELIA	FILOMENA
CLIO	FLOR
CONSTANZA	FRANCISCA
CONSUELO	GENOVEVA
CORAZON	GIANINA
CRUZ	GISELA
DALILA	GRACIA
DAMIANA	GRACIELA
DAMITA	GUADALUPE
DAVINA	IDALIA
DELFINA	IDONIA
DEMETRIA	ILEANA
DOLORES	IMELDA
DOMINGA	INÉS/INÉZ/YNÉZ
DULCE	ISABELA
EDITA	ISOLDA
ELECTRA	IVONNE
ELEONORA	JACINDA/JACINTA
ELOISA	JADA
EMELIA	JAVIERA
ENGRACIA	JAZMIN
ENRIQUA	JOAQUINA
ESMERALDA	JUANA/JUANITA

JULIETA	NELIA
JUSTINA	NEVA
LAUREANA	NIDIA
LAURENCIA/	NIEVES
LAURENTIA	NOEMI
LELIA	NUELA
LETICIA	OCTAVIA
LIA	ODELIA/ODILIA
LIANA	OLIMPIA
LIDIA	ONDINA
LILIA	PALMA
LILIOSA	PALOMA
LOLITA	PAOLA
LORENZA	PAULINA
LOURDES	PAZ
LUCELIA	PIA
LUCIA	PILAR
LUCINDA	RAFAELA
LUISA	RAMONA
LUPE	RAQUEL
LUZ	REYES
MAGDALENA	RÍA
MANUELA	SABANA
MARIBEL	SABINA
MARISOL	SAMARA
MERCEDES	SANCHA
MIGUELA	SARITA
MILAGROS	SERAFINA
MILENA	SOLANA
MIRANDA	SOLEDAD
MIREN	TAMAR
NADIA	TIA
NARDA	TIANA
NATALIA	VALERIA

VIOLETA	ZAIDA
VIVIANA	ZAIRA
YOLANDA	ZITA
YSABEL	

BOYS

ACACIO	CLEMENTE/
ADAN	CLEMENTO
AGUSTIN	CLETO
ALEJANDRO	CONRADO
ALEJO	CORNELIO
ALONZO	CRISPO
ÁLVARO	CRISTÓBAL
AMADEO	CRUZ
AMADO	DANILO
AMANDO	DEMETRIO
ANDRÉS	DIEGO
ANSELMO	DOMINGO
ANTÓNIO	DONATO
AQUILINO	EDMUNDO
ARCINIO/ARSENIO	EDUARDO
ARLO	ELIGIO
ARMANDO	ELIO
AUGUSTO/	ELVIO
AUGUSTINO	EMILIO
AURELIO	ENRIQUE
BARNABUS	ESTEBAN
BASÍLIO	ESTEVAO
CALIXTO	EUGENIO
CALVINO	FABIO
CARLOS	FEDERICO
CELESTINO	FELIPE
CELIO	FÉLIX
CLAUDIO	FERNANDO

FIDEL	JORGE
FILIPE	JOSÉ
FRANCISCO	JULIO
FREDERICO	JUSTO/JUSTINO
GABINO	LAUREANO
GALO	LÁZARO
GREGORIO	LEANDRO
GUILLERMO	LEONARDO
GUTIERRE	LIBORIO
HECTOR	LISANDRO
HELIO	LOPE
HUGAN	LORENZO
IBAN	LUCIO
ÍÑIGO	LUIS
ISIDORO	MANUEL
JACINTO	MARCOS
JACOBO	MARINO
JAIME	MATEO
JANDINO	MAXIMO
JAVIER	MIGUEL
JENARO	NARNO
JOAQUIN	NATALIO

Madonna & Child

*Lourdes, the shrine of miracles, fit this tiny wonder better,
Madonna decided, than Lola, who what she wants she
gets . . . it seems entirely appropriate to name this child for
a tiny French mountain village that no one would have ever
heard of if not for its association with that other Madonna,
the Immaculate Girl.*

—NEW YORK

NEREO	RICARDO
NICASIO	RODRIGO
NILO	RUBEN
NOÉ	SALVADOR
OCTAVIO	SANCHO
ORILIO	SANTIAGO
ORLANDO	SEVASTIÁN
ÓSCAR	SEVERINO
OTILIO	SILVANO
PABLO	TABO
PACO	TADEO
PASQUAL	TAJO
PATRICIO	TEODORO
PAULO	TITO
PAZ	TOMÁS
PEDRO	TULIO
PLÁCIDO	VALERIO
QUINTILIO/QUINTO	VASCO
RAFAEL	VENTURO
RAIMUNDO	VIDAL
RAMÓN	VIVIANO
RAUL	YAGO
REY/REYNALDO	ZENOBIO

Variazioni on a Theme

Sometimes a good way to find a slightly unusual and exotic name is to consider foreign variations on what otherwise might be considered a fairly prosaic English name.
Some of those we particularly like—with their English
cognates—are:

GIRLS

ADETTE (*French*)	*for*	ADELINE
ADRIANA (*Italian*)		ADRIENNE
AINE (*Irish*)		ANNA
ALEJANDRA (*Spanish*)		ALEXANDRA
ALEKA (*Hawaiian*)		ALICE
ALESSANDRA (*Italian*)		ALEXANDRA
ALESSIA (*Italian*)		ALEXA
ALEXANDRINE (*French*)		ALEXANDRA
ALIDA (*Hungarian*)		ADELAIDE
ALIZ (*Hungarian*)		ALICE
AMALIE (*German*)		EMILY
AMANDINE (*French*)		AMANDA
ANAÏS (*Hebrew*)		ANN
ANIELA (*Polish*)		ANGELA
ANIKA (*Czech*)		ANNA
ANNELLA (*Scottish*)		ANNE
ANNIK/ANNIKA (*Slavic*)		ANN
AVRIL (*French*)		APRIL
BARBRO (*Swedish*)		BARBARA
BERTILLE (*French*)		BERTHA
BLANCHETTE (*French*)		BLANCHE
CAITRIONA (*Irish*)		KATHERINE
CARO (*Spanish*)		CAROL
CATIA (*Portuguese*)		CATHERINE
CHIARA (*Italian*)		CLAIRE
DAEL (*Dutch*)		DALE
DASHA (*Russian*)		DOROTHY
EDDA (*Polish*)		EDITH
ELSBETH (*German, Scottish*)		ELIZABETH
EMILIA (*Italian*)		EMILY
ENRICA (*Spanish*)		HENRIETTA
EVVA (*Russian*)		EVE
FEODORA (*Russian*)		THEODORA

FIONNULA (*Irish*)	FLORA
FLANN (*Irish*)	FLORENCE
GINEVRA (*Italian*)	GENEVIEVE
GRANIA (*Irish*)	GRACE
ISABEAU (*French*)	ISABEL
JANICA (*Czech*)	JANE
JENICA (*Romanian*)	JANE
JENSINE (*Scandinavian*)	JANE
KASIA (*Polish*)	KATHERINE
LILIA (*Spanish*)	LILLIAN
LILIJANA (*Slavic*)	LILLIAN
LISETTE (*French*)	ELIZABETH
LORENZA (*Italian*)	LAURA
LUCIENNE (*French*)	LUCY
MAIRE (*Irish*)	MARY
MAIREAD (*Irish*)	MARGARET
MALIA (*Hawaiian*)	MARY
MANON (*French*)	MARY
MARGIT (*Hungarian*)	MARGARET
MARIT (*Scandinavian*)	MARGARET
MARITZA (*German*)	MARISA
MARZIA (*Italian*)	MARCIA
MÉLISANDE (*French*)	MELISSA
MIGUELA (*Spanish*)	MICHAELA
MOIRA (*Irish*)	MARY
NICOLA (*Italian*)	NICOLE
NOEMI (*Italian*)	NAOMI
OONA (*Irish*)	AGNES
PAOLA (*Italian*)	PAULA
PAVIA (*Russian*)	PAULA
ROZA (*Slavic*)	ROSE
SINEAD (*Irish*)	JANE
SIOBHAN (*Irish*)	JOAN
SORCHA (*Irish*)	SARAH
VARVARA (*Russian*)	BARBARA

VERONIQUE (*French*)		VERONICA
VITTORIA (*Italian*)		VICTORIA
XUXA (*Portuguese*)		SUSANNAH
YNEZ (*Spanish*)		AGNES
ZARITA (*Spanish*)		SARAH
ZOIA (*Slavic*)		ZOE
ZUSA (*Czech/Polish*)		SUSAN
ZUZI (*Swiss*)		SUSAN

BOYS

ABRAN (*Spanish*)	for	ABRAHAM
ADRIANO (*Italian*)		ADRIAN
ALASTAIR/ALASDAIR (*Scottish*)		ALEXANDER
ALEJANDRO/JANDO (*Spanish*)		ALEXANDER
ALESSANDRO/SANDRO (*Italian*)		ALEXANDER
ALEXANDRU (*Romanian*)		ALEXANDER
ALEXIOS (*Greek*)		ALEXANDER
ALLESIO (*Italian*)		ALEXANDER
ALUN (*Welsh*)		ALAN
ANDERS (*Swedish, Danish*)		ANDREW
ANDREAS (*German, Greek*)		ANDREW
ARAM (*Armenian*)		ABRAHAM
ARNO (*Italian*)		ARNOLD
ARRIGO (*Italian*)		HENRY
BARDO (*Danish*)		BARTHOLOMEW
BARTO (*Spanish*)		BARTHOLOMEW
BAZIL (*Czech*)		BASIL
BENOÎT (*French*)		BENEDICT
BJØRN (*Scandinavian*)		BERNARD
CHARLOT (*French*)		CHARLES
CLAUDIO (*Spanish/Italian*)		CLAUDE

CLOVIS (*French*)	LOUIS
COLIN (*Irish*)	NICHOLAS
DANO (*Czech*)	DANIEL
DEWI (*Welsh*)	DAVID
DUARTE (*Portuguese*)	EDWARD
EAMON (*Irish*)	EDMUND
EDO (*Czech*)	EDWARD
EERO (*Finnish*)	ERIC
ELIA (*Italian*)	ELIJAH
ESTEBAN (*Spanish*)	STEPHEN
ETIENNE (*French*)	STEPHEN
EWAN (*Scottish*)	EVAN
FRANCHOT (*French*)	FRANCIS
GERRIT (*Dutch*)	GERALD
GRAEME (*Scottish*)	GRAHAM
GWILYM (*Welsh*)	WILLIAM
HEW (*Welsh*)	HUGH
ILIE (*Romanian*)	ELIAS
JAAN (*Estonian*)	JOHN
JACO (*Portuguese*)	JACOB
JENO (*Hungarian*)	EUGENE
JENS (*Danish*)	JOHN
JORGEN, JOREN (*Danish*)	GEORGE
LARS (*Swedish*)	LAWRENCE
LEV (*Russian*)	LEO
LIAM (*Irish*)	WILLIAM
LORCAN (*Irish*)	LAURENCE
LUC (*French*)	LUKE
LUCIANO (*Italian*)	LUCIAN
MARCOS (*Spanish*)	MARCUS
MATTEO (*Italian*)	MATTHEW
MIGUEL (*Spanish*)	MICHAEL
MOZES (*Dutch*)	MOSES
NIALL (*Scottish, Irish*)	NEIL
NICOLO (*Italian*)	NICHOLAS

NIELS (*Danish*)	NEIL
NILO (*Finnish*)	NEIL
OLIVIER (*French*)	OLIVER
ONDRO (*Czech*)	ANDREW
ORLANDO (*Italian/Spanish*)	ROLAND
PABLO (*Spanish*)	PAUL
PADRAIC/PADRAIG (*Irish*)	PATRICK
PAOLO (*Italian*)	PAUL
PHILIPPE (*French*)	PHILIP
PIERO/PIETRO (*Italian*)	PETER
PIET (*Dutch*)	PETER
RAOUL (*French*)	RUDOLPH
REDMOND (*Irish*)	RAYMOND
ROBINET (*French*)	ROBERT
SAMO (*Czech*)	SAMUEL
SAMU (*Hungarian*)	SAMUEL
SEAMUS (*Irish*)	JAMES
SIMEON (*French*)	SIMON
TADEO (*Spanish*)	THADDEUS
TAVISH (*Scottish*)	THOMAS
TOMAZ (*Portuguese*)	THOMAS
UILLIAM (*Irish*)	WILLIAM
VASILIS (*Greek*)	BASIL
VITTORIO (*Italian*)	VICTOR
WILLEM (*Dutch*)	WILLIAM
YOËL (*Hebrew*)	JOEL
ZAKO (*Hungarian*)	ZACHARIAH
ZAMIEL (*German*)	SAMUEL

Only a few short years ago, we felt perfectly comfortable saying that there was no such thing as a "Jewish" first name anymore; now we're not so sure. For although large numbers of Jewish parents continue to follow national trends, and there are as many Kyle Cohens as there are Kyle Culhanes, a growing percentage are now, like members of other ethnic and religious groups, looking back into their own heritage, at less common Old Testament names, at Hebrew names, and at names that have become popularized in Israel.

From the early biblical period on, first names have held a powerful, often symbolic significance for Jews. In the beginning, names were given that reflected some momentous event—either public or within the family—which had taken place around the time of the baby's birth. Later, with the taking of the Jews into Babylonian captivity, Palestinian Jews appropriated the Egyptian practice of naming children after deceased family members.

A dichotomy in this matter developed between the Ashkenazi Jews from Central and Eastern Europe and the Sephardim from Spain and the Balkan countries, North Africa, and the Middle East. The former believed in honoring deceased parents and grandparents in order to preserve their name and memory, also holding the superstition that naming a baby after an older living relative might confuse the Angel of Death, while the latter had no such strictures. In fact, Sephardic Jews evolved a fixed convention for baby naming: the oldest grandson was named for his paternal grandfather, the oldest granddaughter for her father's mother, whether the grandparents were living or not. Subsequent offspring would be named for their maternal grandparents, followed by uncles and aunts.

Contrary to widespread belief, there are no Jewish laws pertaining to the subject of naming a baby after a deceased relative, and no reference to it in the Bible. Actually, names borrowed from the Bible did not come into use until the sixteenth century—prior to that each Old Testament personage, from Adam and Eve on, was thought to have exclusive title to his or her name.

When masses of Jewish immigrants arrived at Ellis Island at the end of the nineteenth century, most of them held on to a somewhat transliterated version of their own names. It was with their children, the first American-born generation, that the nomenclature suddenly changed. Following the old tradition of using the same initial letter for the English name as for the Hebrew one, and in an effort at instant assimilation, these newcomers were determined to bestow on their sons and daughters the most elegant-sounding, nonethnic Anglo names they could find. Thus, the descendant of Moishe might be called Murray (a Scottish surname), Morton or Milton (British surnames), Myron (a classical Greek name), or Marvin (Old Welsh). The strategy backfired, however, when these names were adopted in such prodigious numbers that Milton, Marvin, and so forth began to be thought of as "Jewish" names.

The names Milton and Marvin and their generational

357

peers, such as Seymour, Stanley, and Sheldon, are rarely given to babies now, and the reason for this can be explained by the theory we call the Kosher Curve. As we said, first-generation immigrants typically try to renounce any hint of their ethnicity by choosing the most mainstream names of their new country. It isn't until the third or fourth generation that there is a resurgence of ethnic identity and pride, plus sufficient psychological distance, for the original names to sound fresh and youthful enough to be bestowed on a baby. By the 1970s, for instance, the world was ready for a new era of Maxes, Sams, Bens, Jakes, Mollys, and Annies, while the eighties and nineties saw a rebirth of Annas, Hannahs, Henrys, Harrys, Jacks, Sarahs, Rachels, and Rebeccas. The big question: Are we ready to bring back Shirley and Sherman? Not quite yet.

The Kosher Curve

The following chart tracks some representative American-Jewish given names and their permutations from the turn of the last century to the present.

ABE	ARTHUR	ALAN	ADAM	AUSTIN
ANNIE	ANN	ANITA	ANNIE	ANNA
BEN	BERNARD	BARRY	BEN	BENJAMIN
CLARA	CLAIRE	CAROL	CARLY	CALEIGH
DORA	DOROTHY	DIANE	DEBBIE	DYLAN
FANNY	FRANCES	FRANCINE	FERN	FRANCESCA
HANNAH	HELEN	HELENE	HEATHER	HANNAH
HARRY	HENRY	HARRIS	HARRISON	HENRY
ISAAC	IRVING	IRWIN	IRA	ISAIAH
JAKE	JACK	JAY	JASON	JACOB
JENNY	JEAN	JEANETTE	JENNIFER	JENNA
LILY	LILIAN	LINDA	LORI	LILY

MAX	MARVIN	MITCHELL	MICHAEL	MILO
MOLLY	MARIAN	MARSHA	MARCY	MADISON
NELLIE	NORMA	NANCY	NICOLE	NELL
RACHEL	RUTH	RENEE	RANDI	RACHEL
ROSE	ROSALIE	RHODA	RHONDA	ROSIE
SADIE	SYLVIA	SUSAN	STACY	SADIE
SAM	SHELDON	STEVEN	SAM	SAWYER
SARAH	SALLY	SHEILA	SHELLY	SARAH
SOPHIE	SHIRLEY	SHARON	SHERRY	SOPHIE
TESSIE	THELMA	TERRY	TIFFANY	TESSA

Hebrew & Israeli Names

According to an Israeli friend, only the most Orthodox Jewish families in Israel use the kind of traditional Old Testament names—Rebecca, Noah—favored by American Jews. Instead, they turn to choices like these:

GIRLS

ABIAH	ARIZA
ABIRA	ASHRA
ADAH	ATARA
ADAYA	AVIVAH
ADIAH	AZUBAH
ADINA	BAARA
AHLAI	BAT-SHEVA/
ALIMA	BATHSHEBA
ALIYAH	BETHE
ALIZA	BINA
AMALYA	BITHIA
AMMA	BLUMA
ANINA	CARMA
ARIELA	CARNIA

CHANIA	HADASSAH
CHARNA	IDRA
CHAYA	ILANA
CHIBA	INBAR
DALYA	JETRA
DEVORAH	JORDANA
DORIT	JOSEFA
DOVEVA	KANARA
ELIANA	KELILA
ELIEZRA	KETURAH
ELIORA	KETZIAH
ELISHEBA	KHANNAH
ELULA	KIRIAH
GALIA	LEEONA
GAVRIELA	LEVIAH
GITEL	LILIT
GOLDA	LINIT

Jewish Naming Ceremonies

For several generations, it has been traditional to name a male child at the time of his circumcision, the eighth day after his birth. At that time the mohel (circumciser) recites a Hebrew prayer for the child, incorporating his name ("Let his name be called in Israel as _____, the son of _____.").

The naming ceremony for girls is of much more recent origin. Called brit bat, brit banot Yisrael, *or* simchat bat, *it became prevalent in the 1960s and 1970s, with the advent of feminism. Because the ceremony is so new, there are no precise rituals and the celebration is open to the creativity of the family, but there is usually a ceremonial pronouncement of the child's name, as well as stories and reflections on the relative whose memory the baby honors.*

LIORA	SANSANA
LIVYA	SAPHIRA
MAHALIA/MAHALAH	SARAI/SHARAI
MARAH	SHAI
MENORAH	SHIFRA
MIKA/MICAH	SHOSHANNAH
MIRYAM	SHUA
NAAMAH	SHULAMIT/SHULA
NAARAH	TALMA
NATANIAH	TALYA
NEDIVA	TAMAR
NEILA	TAVORA
NEVONAH	TIRZAH
NIMA	TOVAH
NISSA	TZAHALA
NOAH	TZILA
NOOMI/NAOMI	TZINA
OFFIR	TZOFI/TZOFIA
OPHIRA	VARDA
ORPAH	YAEL/JAEL
PAZIAH/PAZ	YAFA
PENINA	YASMIN
RAANANA	YEMIMA
RAISA	ZAAVA
RAKHEL	ZAHARA
RAYNA	ZARA
RAZIELA/RAZ	ZAVIDA
RENANA	ZEMORAH
RIVKA	ZILLAH
SAHAR	ZIRAH
SAMIRA	

BOYS

ABBA	BARUCH
ABIEL	BENAIAH
ADAEL	BENONI
ADIN	BENZION
ADIR	BINYAMIN
ADLAI	BOAZ
ADON	CHAGAI
ADRIEL	CHAI
AHAB	CHAIM
AHARON	CHALIL
ALON	CHAZON
AMAL	DEVIR
AMIDOR	DIVON
AMIEL	DORAN
AMIR	DOV
AMIT	DOVEV
AMOZ	EFRON
ARIAV	EITAN
ARIEL	ELAN
ARLES	ELAZAR
ARON	ELIAM
ASA	ELIAZ
ASAEL	ELIHU
ASHER	ELISHA
ASSAF	EPHRAIM
AVIAH	ETAN
AVIEL	EZRI
AVIV	GAAL
AVRAHAM	GAHAM
AZ	GALIL
AZAI	GAMALIEL
AZIEL	GAVRIEL
BARAQ	GEDALIAH

GERSHOM	NOAZ
GERSON	OMAN
GILEAD	ORAN
GURIEL	OREN
HILLEL	OZ
HODIAH	RAPHAEL
HOSEA	RAVIV
IDAN	RAZ
IDO	RENON
ILAN	REUEL
ISHMAEL	SAMAL
ITAI	SELIG
ITHRO	SETH
ITZAK	SHALLUM
KALIL	SHAMIR
KEMUEL	SHAVIV
KENAN	SHILOH
KOLAIAH	SHIMON
LABAN	SION
LAEL	TABEEL
LAVI	TALMAI
LEV	TEVYE
LEVI	TOBIYAH
MACABEE	TOVIEL
MALACHI	TZEVI
MALKAM	URI
MALUCH	URIEL
MAON	UZIAH
MAOZ	YAAKOV
MEIR	YAAL
MENAHEM	YABAL
MICHA	YABIN
NAOR	YAMIN
NEHEMIAH	YAOSH
NOAM	YARED

YASHIV	ZAKAI
YEDIDIYAH	ZALMAN
YEHUDAH/JUDAH	ZAMIR
YITZCHAK	ZAN
YOAB/JOAB	ZARED
YOAV	ZAVACHIAH
YOEL/JOEL	ZAVID
YONAH/JONAH	ZEBEDEE
YOSHA	ZIV
YOSSI	ZVI

Conan, Patron Saint of Late-Night TV

And Other Unusual,
Lively, and Surprising Saints' Names

If because of tradition or religion you want to give your child a saint's name, you don't have to settle for obvious choices like Anne, Cecelia, Anthony, or Joseph. Yes, there really is a Saint Fabian, as well as Saints Chad, Benno, Phoebe, Susanna, and Colette. What follows is a selective list of unexpected saints' names:

FEMALE

ADELA	AVA
ADELAIDE	BEATRICE
AGATHA	BEATRIX
ALBINA	BIBIANA
ANASTASIA	BRIDGET/BRIGID
ANGELA	CANDIDA
ANGELINA	CHARITY
ANTONIA	CHRISTINA
APOLLONIA	CLARE
AQUILINA	CLAUDIA
ARIADNE	CLEOPATRA
AUDREY	CLOTILDA
AURIA	COLETTE

COLUMBA	LUCY
CRISPINA	LYDIA
DARIA	MADELEINE
DELPHINA	MARCELLA
DIANA	MARINA
DOROTHY	MARTINA
EBBA	MATILDA
EDITH	MAURA
EMILY	MELANIA
EMMA	MICHELINA
EUGENIA	NATALIA
EULALIA	ODILIA
EVA	OLIVE
FABIOLA	PAULA
FAITH	PETRONILLA
FELICITY	PHOEBE
FLORA	PRISCILLA
FRANCA	REGINA
GEMMA	RITA
GENEVIEVE	ROSALIA
HEDDA	SABINA
HYACINTH	SALOME
IDA	SANCHIA
ISABEL	SERAPHINA
JANE	SILVA
JOANNA	SUSANNA
JOAQUINA	TATIANA
JULIA	THEA
JULIANA	THEODORA
JUSTINA	THEODOSIA
LELIA	VERENA
LEWINA	WINIFRED
LOUISA	ZENOBIA
LUCRETIA	ZITA

MALE

AARON	CLEMENT
ABEL	CLETUS
ABRAHAM	CLOUD
ADAM	COLMAN
ADOLF	CONAN
ADRIAN	CONRAD
AIDAN	CORNELIUS
ALBERT	CRISPIN
ALEXANDER	CYPRIAN
ALEXIS	CYRIL
AMBROSE	DAMIAN
AMIAS	DANIEL
ANSELM	DECLAN
ARNOLD	DIEGO
ARTEMAS	DONALD
AUBREY	DUNSTAN
AUSTIN	EDMUND
BARDO	EDWIN
BARNABAS	ELIAS
BARTHOLOMEW	EPHRAEM
BASIL	ERASMUS
BENEDICT	ERIC
BENJAMIN	ERNEST
BENNO	FABIAN
BERTRAND	FELIX
BLANE	FERDINAND
BORIS	FERGUS
BRENDAN	FINNIAN
BRICE	FLAVIAN
BRUNO	FLORIAN
CASSIAN	GERARD
CHAD	GILBERT

GILES	MAXIMILIAN
GODFREY	MEL
GREGORY	MILO
GUNTHER	MOSES
GUY	MUNGO
HENRY	NARCISSUS
HERBERT	NOEL
HILARY	NORBERT
HUBERT	OLIVER
HUGH	OSWALD
HUMBERT	OTTO
ISAAC	OWEN
ISIDORE	PIRAN
ISRAEL	QUENTIN
JASON	RALPH
JOACHIM	RAYMOND
JONAH	REMI
JORDAN	ROCCO (*Italian*
JULIAN	*version of Saint*
JULIUS	*Roch*)
JUSTIN	ROCK
KEVIN	RODERIC
KIERAN	RUFUS
KILIAN	RUPERT
LAMBERT	SAMSON
LEANDER	SEBASTIAN
LEO	SILAS
LEONARD	SIMEON
LINUS	SIMON
LLOYD	SYLVESTER
LUCIAN	THEODORE
LUCIUS	TITUS
MALACHY	VIRGIL
MARIUS	WILFRED

WOLFGANG	ZACHARY
YVES	ZENO

Some Celtic Saints

FEMALE

AIDEEN	GWENN
AINE	INA
ALMA	JENIFRY
BERYAN	MARGARET
BREACA	MORGANA
BRIGID	MORWENNA
CEARA	ORNA
CIAR	RIONA
COLUMBA	RIVANON
CONNA	TALULLA
DOMINICA	TARA
EITHNE	

MALE

AENGUS	BROGAN
AIDAN	CADOC
ALAR	CASS
ALOR	CELLACH
AUSTELL	CIARAN
BARRI	COLM
BECAN	CONALL
BLANE	CONAN
BRAN	CONLEY
BRAZIL	CONRAN
BRECCAN	CORCAN
BRENDAN	CORMAC

DAVID	KADO
DECLAN	KILIAN
DENIEL	LORCAN
DEWI	MALACHY
DONAN	MALCOLM
EOAN	MEALLAN
EWEN	ORAN
FALLON	PADRAIG
FAOLAN	RIAN
FERGUS	RONAN
FINNAN	RUADAN
FINNIAN	SAMZUN
GARMON	TIARNAN
IVAR	TOLA
JARLATH	TUDI

Every time somebody calls me a saint, I repeat my name and tell them no saint was ever named Roxy.

—REYNOLDS PRICE,
ROXANNA SLADE

FAMILY

Family is a central consideration when choosing names, from wrestling over individual choices to finding names from the family tree to keeping everyone in the family from trying to dominate your name decision.

In this section, we offer advice on how to reconcile your name tastes with your mate's, how to deal with your family's name advice and opinions, and what to do if your sister wants to give her baby the same name you want to give yours.

Also, here are thoughts on how to construct a family of names for siblings, what to do about naming twins, and whether or not you should make your son a junior.

And what to do if you can't decide on a name, or if two months later you still can't quite get used to the one you picked? Hint: Don't panic unless truly desperate.

You Say Maria, I Say Mariah

When Couples Disagree About Names

Most couples agree on whether they want kids. They often reach an easy accord on *when* they want them. Many even are like-minded on such sticky issues as where they'd prefer to raise their children, how they'd like to educate them, and what style of discipline they believe in.

Choosing a name can prove more problematic than any of the above.

Names are one of those subjects that summon up all kinds of hopes and fears, desires and secrets that you might otherwise never have guessed about your mate. How else, but on the hunt for the perfect name, would you discover that your husband once got his nose bloodied on the playground by a red-haired she-bully named Kelly, and ever since cannot abide the name? When might you have occasion to confess that you dated not one but, um, *three* guys named Michael, so he might not want to push that one for your firstborn son?

Such individual associations are par for the baby-naming course. Conceiving your child may have made you feel, more than any other step you've taken together, as if you had finally and truly become one. Choosing its name can remind you that, nope, you're still actually two.

There are all those people with all those names that each of you knew and loved or hated before you met each other. Those ancient experiences and emotions are key determinants of whether you like a name or loathe it. If you and your spouse retreat to separate corners and draw up individual lists of your favorite names, then exchange your lists, chances are you'll cross off half of each other's picks because you went to third grade with an Elizabeth whose nose was always running, or had a college roommate named Daniel who told terrible jokes.

Then there are your individual families and backgrounds to consider. Couples who successfully negotiate religious differences and complicated family holidays sometimes find themselves stymied by conflicting name ideas and requirements. One couple we know, for instance, compromise his Jewish and her Catholic backgrounds by attending a Unitarian church, but when naming their baby hit a deep divide when he wanted to follow religious tradition and give their child a name that started with the same letter as that of his recently deceased grandmother, and she bucked against being pinned down to only names beginning with *s*.

Another factor that can make for difficult name negotiations between prospective parents is that, in most cases, one of you is a man and the other is a woman. A study by Charles Joubert of the University of Northern Alabama demonstrated that men and women often have very different tastes in and ideas about names.

Joubert asked his male and female subjects to choose a name for a hypothetical child from a list he provided. Men, he found, were more likely to choose common or old-dated names for children of either sex, but less likely to propose recently popular names. Women were more likely to propose a common name for a boy than for a girl, less likely to select unusual names for boys than for girls.

Another issue: men and women often have very mixed ideas on the child's gender identity and on the signals a name sends out. Many moms, for example, like boys' names that sound creative and nontraditional, but some dads are fearful of giving their son a name that might label the boy as a wimp.

"There are two kinds of boys' names," one father told us, "the kind that makes you sound like you can hit a baseball and the kind that makes you sound like you'd sit in the outfield looking at the clouds. I was the type of kid who looked at the clouds, but I want my son to be a ball-hitter." A Bob, in other words, or a Dave, a Steve, or a Charlie. Not a Miles or a Jasper.

On the other hand, moms tend to be more comfortable with girls' names that are androgynous or even decidedly masculine, while dads seem to like frillier, more traditional girls' names. Mom campaigns for Alix, for example, while Dad favors Alicia; Mom likes Sydney, Dad opts for Samantha.

Why the gender gap? Some mothers may be more sensitive than their spouses to sexism and stereotyping. And for girls, moms tend to think about names they would have liked to have had themselves, while dads are looking at the issue from the outside in. Of course, when it comes to naming boys, the situation is reversed, and it's the father who can imagine firsthand what it might be like to be a Cyril when teams are being picked.

What of gay couples? There, the associations to names might be more similar, but the gender issues may get more complicated. A gay male couple we know who were adopting a baby daughter, for instance, wanted to give her the family name Carson. But, they worried (as did we), was it unfair to give a girl who was sure to face complex gender issues in her upbringing a name that further muddied the gender waters? Maybe, and yet this was probably the only child they would have and they dearly wanted to use a name that had been in the family for generations. The solution: They named her Carson, and call her the more conventional (and feminine) Carrie.

How to resolve any naming problems you and your spouse might be having? Here are some tips:

Talk about issues like image and gender before you talk about names. What do you each hope for in a child? Is your fantasy child energetic or studious, "all-boy" or gentle, feminine or tomboy? Coming to agreement on these matters, or at least getting them out in the open, can help when you're choosing a name, not to mention raising your child.

Rule out all names of ex-girlfriends and ex-boyfriends. No matter how much you like the name Emily, do not proceed with it if your husband had a long, torrid affair with

---

The Art of Compromise

Niki, the name we finally gave to my younger daughter, is not an abbreviation; it was a compromise I reached with her father. For paradoxically it was he who wanted to give her a Japanese name, and I—perhaps out of some selfish desire not to be reminded of the past—insisted on an English one. He finally agreed to Niki, thinking it had some vague echo of the East about it.

—KAZUO ISHIGURO, *A PALE VIEW OF THE HILLS*

an Emily way back when. Do not tell yourself you'll forget: You won't, and neither will he.

Make a "no" list as well as a "yes" list. Most couples only make lists of the names they like; it can help to make lists, too, of the names that are absolutely out for each of you. Include those you'd rule out for personal reasons (the roommate who stole all your clothes) as well as names you simply hate. Agree that neither of you will bring up the names on each other's "absolutely not" lists, no matter how much you like them or how neutral they may be for you.

Avoid using the name-selection process as an opportunity to criticize each other's loved ones. When he campaigns for naming your son Morton after his father, this is not an excuse to tell him how much you dislike his father, no matter how much you detest the name Morton.

Investigate the reasons for each other's choices. Let's say you love a name your spouse hates. Instead of fighting over the name itself, explore what it is about the name that appeals to you. Figuring out whether you like a name because it's classic, or feminine, or stylish can lead you to other names with the same characteristics that both of you like.

Remember that parenthood is a joint venture. Just as your child will be a unique blend of characteristics from both of you, so should you endeavor to arrive at a name that combines each of your sensibilities and tastes. If you absolutely can't find a name you both love, agree that one of you will choose the first name, the other one the middle. Or one will name this child, the other will name the next. Such enlightened negotiation and compromise is what marriage is all about.

Family Names

Parents today are shaking the family tree in an energetic attempt to come up with names that are personally significant as well as stylish. One satisfying benefit of a family name is that it conveys the essence of a loved one, bestowing his or her best qualities on your child. Even if you never knew the forebear for whom you name a child, family stories about the person—his heroism during the Civil War, her solo flight over the mountains of Peru—come alive again through the name, granting your child an instant and noble legacy.

Of course, the power of names is not to be taken lightly. While you may love the melody of Grandpa Malachy's name, will you be able to hear it without thinking of his sour disposition? Or maybe it's the name itself that hits a wrong note: Great-aunt Mildred may be a saint and a millionaire, but could you really burden your adorable baby with her unfashionable moniker?

In colonial America, most children were named after relatives. In one extended Southern clan whose naming patterns were analyzed, 90 percent of the families used the father's name, 79 percent used the paternal grandfather's name, and 40 percent used the maternal grand-

Call Me Calvin

Among European Jews it's traditional to name a child in memory of someone. People like my parents tended to fulfill that obligation loosely by giving the child the same Hebrew name as the person being memorialized and an English name that had the same first sound. Like my cousin Keith and my cousin Kenneth, I was named in memory of my father's father—whose own name eventually acquired a consistent spelling of Kusel . . . Honoring some other departed relative, my father came up with the rather tony middle name of Marshall. ("It's an old family name," I've sometimes explained. "Not our family, but still an old family name.")

—CALVIN TRILLIN, *MESSAGES FROM MY FATHER*

father's name for a son. Girls were named for kin less often than boys, but family names were still widely used: 72 percent of families named a daughter for her mother, 44 percent for paternal grandmothers, and 52 percent for maternal grandmothers.

Many Latin countries have strict family-naming protocols that are followed even today. The first son is named after the father's father, the first daughter after the father's mother, the second son and daughter after the mother's parents, and subsequent children after aunts and uncles, first on the paternal and then on the maternal side of the family. In some traditions, this pattern deviates so that boys are more often named after the father's side of the family, and girls after the mother's side.

Historically, family names were important because they helped consolidate kinship ties and family wealth. Today, the motivation for choosing a family name may be more generally to strengthen family ties and imbue the child with a sense of history. Who you name your child after, and how you do it, is less rigid, more creative.

There are, in fact, several ways to honor terrific family members with less-than-terrific names or to mollify a difficult yet prominent relative without clouding the everyday existence of your child. Mildred might make a fine middle name, which can always be shorted to the letter *M*. Or you might choose a variation such as Millie or Millicent, which both have an old-fashioned sweetness that Mildred lacks. And if you have two grandpas battling for name superiority, why not use both as middle names, as the royals do? Prince William's full name, for instance, is William Arthur Philip Louis Windsor.

There may also be some great names hiding deeper in the family vault. Look to ancestors' middle names, which may be maiden names or the names of their ancestors. Collecting family records and birth certificates is a valuable exercise that can yield family names that might otherwise be forgotten.

Transforming last names into first names is another way to resurrect family names. Politicos James Carville and Mary Matalin pulled an innovative switch when they named their daughter Matalin Mary Carville.

Be open-minded about the names you unearth. Many choices may not seem consistent with today's fashions, but if you give names time—or focus on the people you love who held them first—they may start to sound better to you. A friend who gave her daughter her mother's name of Margaret, rather than the faddier version Megan, finds that she loves the authentic version more and more over time.

If you don't find a name you like in your family tree, consider a new name with the same meaning as a family original: Grandma Gloria, for instance, might be honored

Putting the Name
Before the Baby

In this age of amniocentesis and ultrasound, many parents have the option of knowing their baby's sex—thus making a firm decision on a name—long before his or her arrival.

While these medical advances have been a boon for mothers and babies alike, and knowing your child's sex can cut the work of choosing a name in half, we nevertheless caution against telling the world your child's gender and name months before his or her actual arrival.

Announcing in mid-pregnancy that a boy named Dawson is waiting to be born can have a dampening effect on his entrance into the world. For one thing, other people tend to draw a more or less complete picture of little Dawson's looks and personality, based on his name and their knowledge of his parents, long before they get a chance to meet him! For another, you may find that other people are actually less eager to meet him. Instead of waiting by the phone for news of your baby's sex and name, they may receive your announcement with a bored, "Oh, Dawson's finally here."

The only real advantage we can cite for sharing your child's name before his birth is not really that much of a plus: People can give you shower gifts of little T-shirts with Dawson spelled out on the back.

Bad Advice?

What are you going to name the baby?

That's the question of the hour, or rather, the question of the entire nine months leading up to your baby's birth. Everyone from your family and friends to the woman selling newspapers at the corner will want to know. The problem is that all those people will have opinions, too—contradictory, confusing, often debilitating.

Let's say you and your mate have agreed that, if the baby is a boy, you will name him Ned. You tell your mother-in-law.

"I had a great-uncle Ned," she says. Pause. "He drank."

You tell your best friend.

"Have you noticed," she says, "how so many nerdy movie characters are called Ned?"

You tell your brother.

"Sounds like a seventy-year-old," he says.

You tell your ten-year-old, who makes gagging noises. "All the kids will hate him!" she cries.

Your four-year-old agrees with his sister. "I hate him," he says.

Before all these outside opinions, you thought Ned was a fine name; now you're not so sure. And even if you still like the name Ned, you don't want your child's grandmother to associate him with the family alcoholic, your friends to gossip about how bad your taste is, or your children to reject the baby because of his name.

So you and your husband come up with a new idea. Let's say it's Jack. This time, your mother-in-law approves, your best friend thinks it's too groovy, your brother thinks it's bland, and your kids still hate it.

All right: How about Omar? Your mother-in-law, brother, and best friend all think it's too bizarre; the ten-year-old thinks it's cool; the four-year-old stands fast in his dislike.

At this point, you may be catching on to the fact that the four-year-old might be having problems with the idea of the baby, beyond choosing its name. And it also might be dawning on you that, no matter what name you set forth, there's going to be someone who doesn't like it. How do you decide which naming advice you take to heart, which you disregard?

The first step might be to consider your sources. People who've never had kids may be ignorant of swings in style and may also be out of touch with how names affect kids. Other children in your family may have a very good idea of how a name will be perceived by fifth graders, but no long-range take on a name's viability. A friend or relative who's had children in the past five years, however, may be able to give you an educated opinion on a name's popularity, as well as advise you on how the choice of a name feels to a parent over time.

The next step may be to review the general taste of those offering their opinions. Would you let these people choose what color you paint your house? Would you let them pick out your clothes? Their tastes in other matters are a good indication of the validity of their taste in names.

The final step—which often proves to be very enlightening—is to ask those who offer their opinions for name suggestions of their own. You may well find that your mother-in-law loves the name John, too basic for your tastes. Your best friend suggests Homer and Jethro, which you find too offbeat. Your brother likes Darryl and Curtis, too déclassé. The ten-year-old offers Max and Sam, the names of the most popular boys in her class, but too popular for you. And the four-year-old's idea of a good name? Rainbow Boy.

Despite all those negative opinions, you may find Ned sounds better by the minute.

Baby Jr.

The easiest solution to the question of what to name a baby boy is simply to repeat the father's name, appending to it the letters *Jr.* Although this practice is fading out of fashion, it does have certain advantages: a direct link with a progenitor, the pride that goes with carrying on a family name.

But the disadvantages can outweigh the benefits. The child may well feel he's inheriting an identity along with a name, that he's merely a paler shadow of his father, that he will always be number two.

In addition, if a boy is actually addressed by the same name as his father, countless confusions will arise, from the most obvious, such as "Which Donald do you want, Big Donald or Little Donald?" on the phone, and fathers and sons opening (and reading) each other's mail, to subtler ones, like mother having to call the two most important males in her life, husband and son, by the same name.

On the other hand, if the child is actually called Junior, he is somewhat dehumanized, almost like being referred to as a number, and a lesser number than his father at that. More common is for the child to be known by the familiar, childish form of the name, a practice that spawns its own perils. Dad is Don and junior is Donny, forever locked by his name into an adolescent (or younger) image of himself that persists long after he leaves home. Or, even worse, he might be known to the world as Bud, Buster, Butch, Sonny, Skip, or Chip.

Giving a boy the same name as his father and grandfather—making him a III—is a somewhat different issue. On the positive side, it could be argued that you're carrying on a family tradition rather than purely indulging in egotism. And honorable WASP nicknames for IIIs—

Big Trouble with Junior

In a study ominously titled "The Trouble with Junior," researcher Catherine Cameron comes to the conclusion that boys named after their fathers do tend to run into more trouble down the line than those with individual names—they encounter more child abuse and later are more delinquent. The reason? Cameron says that although all sons carry their father's surnames through life and thus add luster or tarnish to that name, since juniors replicate their fathers' entire names, they may therefore be more susceptible to parental expectations, becoming a focus for pride or a target for abuse.

Among the results cited were: a higher rate of juniors was found in a hospital psychiatric ward than in the general population, and there was a higher percentage of parental abuse in the histories of those boys. Statistically, 21 percent of the institutionalized boys were juniors, while only 10 percent were found in a regular high school; and 37 percent of the juniors had been abused as children, as opposed to 15 percent of those not father-named.

Tripp, Tre, or Trey—are not quite as humiliating as the ones many juniors are saddled with. On the down side, little Frederick or Albert the third has the image of not one but two grown-up men to live up to, with a fairly strong (and potentially overwhelming) mandate to carry on the family tradition.

Only one president in the history of the United States has been a junior—James Earl Carter Jr., who, as we all know, insisted on being known by his childhood nickname of Jimmy. Gerald Ford was born Leslie Lynch King Jr., but his name was changed when he was adopted by his stepfather. Former Vice President Al Gore is a junior, the man we know as Bill Clinton was born William Jefferson Blythe IV, and George Walker Bush differs from his father George Herbert Walker Bush only by the subtraction of one middle name. Relatively few juniors are to be found among high achievers in sports or the fine arts. However, there are lots of military men, junior grade.

How to avoid the pitfalls of juniordom and still name your son after his father? You could go the royal route and name him Donald Dalton Duckworth II. Or the child could be given a different middle name, say Donald Duncan Duckworth, be called Duncan by the family, and later sign his memos D. Duncan Duckworth. But before taking this approach, remember the old saying, "Don't trust anyone who parts his name on the side."

Some Juniors Who Made Names for Themselves

KAREEM ABDUL-JABBAR *(Ferdinand Lewis Alcindor Jr.)*
MUHUMMAD ALI *(Cassius Marcellus Clay Jr.)*
ED BEGLEY JR.

ROY BLOUNT JR.

MARLON BRANDO JR.

WILLIAM F. BUCKLEY JR.

JOSÉ CANSECO JR.

JIMMY CARTER *(James Earl Carter Jr.)*

TOM CLANCY *(Thomas L. Clancy Jr.)*

JOHNNIE L. COCHRAN JR.

HARRY CONNICK JR.

BILL COSBY *(William H. Cosby Jr.)*

WALTER CRONKITE *(Walter Leland Cronkite Jr.)*

ROBERT DE NIRO JR.

JOHN DENVER *(Henry John Deutschendorf Jr.)*

JOHNNY DEPP *(John Christopher Depp Jr.)*

ROBERT DOWNEY JR.

CLINT EASTWOOD *(Clinton Eastwood Jr.)*

GERALD FORD *(Leslie Lynch King Jr.)*

CUBA GOODING JR.

AL GORE *(Albert Arnold Gore Jr.)*

LOUIS GOSSETT JR.

KEN GRIFFEY JR.

JULIO IGLESIAS JR.

DON IMUS *(John Donald Imus Jr.)*

RICK JAMES *(James A. Johnson Jr.)*

MAGIC JOHNSON *(Earvin Johnson Jr.)*

QUINCY JONES JR.

ELMORE LEONARD *(Elmore John Leonard Jr.)*

BILL MAHER *(William Maher Jr.)*

ED MCMAHON *(Edward Leo Peter McMahon Jr.)*

NELLY *(Cornel Haynes Jr.)*

RONALD REAGAN JR.

ROBERT REDFORD *(Charles Robert Redford Jr.)*

JUDGE REINHOLD *(Edward Ernest Reinhold Jr.)*

BURT REYNOLDS *(Burton Leon Reynolds Jr.)*

MICKEY ROONEY *(Joe Yule Jr.)*

MICKEY ROURKE *(Philip André Rourke Jr.)*

NOLAN RYAN *(Lynn Nolan Ryan Jr.)*

ANTONIO SABATO JR.

WILLARD SCOTT *(Willard Herman Scott Jr.)*

RIP TORN *(Elmore Torn Jr.)*

GORE VIDAL *(Eugene Luther Vidal Jr.)*

KURT VONNEGUT JR.

DENZEL WASHINGTON JR.

FRANK ZAPPA *(Francis Vincent Zappa Jr.)*

EDWARD ALBEE *(Edward Franklin Albee III)*

ALEC BALDWIN *(Alexander Rae Baldwin III)*

BEAU BRIDGES *(Lloyd Vernet Bridges III)*

WILLIAM BURROUGHS III

BILL CLINTON *(William Jefferson Blythe IV)*

TOM CRUISE *(Thomas Cruise Mapother IV)*

TED DANSON *(Edward Bridge Danson III)*

MILES DAVIS *(Miles Dewey Davis III)*

EMINEM *(Marshall Bruce Mathers III)*

LAURENCE FISHBURNE III

BILL GATES *(William Henry Gates III)*

JACK LEMMON *(John Uhler Lemmon III)*

TRINI LOPEZ *(Trinidad Lopez III)*

LUKE PERRY *(Coy Luther Perry III)*

RICHARD PRYOR *(Richard Franklin Lennox Thomas Pryor III)*

TED TURNER *(Robert Edward Turner III)*

Sibling Names

(For First-Time Parents Also)

If you're having your second, third, fourth child, or beyond, you have probably already experienced the inherent difficulties and dilemmas involving sibling names. Ideally, the names you choose for later children should "go with" the name you picked for your first child: They should be harmonious in rhythm and style. At the same time, names of later children should be different enough from the first child's name to avoid confusion. Yes, there are families with a Jane and a Jean, a Larry and a Harry, an Ellen and an Eleanor, but the resulting mix-ups do not seem worth the cuteness.

The real problem with sibling names arises because most parents don't consider later names when they choose the first. But the first choice sets the pattern, narrowing future options. Here's how it works:

Because we have personal experience with this one, let's say you decided to name your first child, a girl, Rory. Good enough, but now you're about to have your second. Names that rhyme are out: Good-bye, Laurie, Corey, Glory, Maury, Tory, and so on. So too with similar-sounding names: everything in the Rose family, the Mary family, the Doria group, the Lauras, Coras, Noras, and

Floras, not to mention Larry, Gerry, Terry; Rowen, Rourke, Rollo. You get the idea.

Also, because Rory is such a distinctively Celtic name, it would sound odd with a name from a different ethnic background. Rory and Francesca won't do, for example. In terms of image, Rory is clearly a high-energy name. Would it be fair to pair her name with one from the No-Nonsense group? Would a little sister named Ruth, for example, always feel bookwormish by contrast; would Rory, conversely, feel flighty in comparison? Another consideration is the name's ambisexuality. Choosing a sister's name from the Feminine or Feminissima group—Angelica, for instance, or Melissa—might not only sound discordant but could make the two girls feel differently about their sexuality. And if the sibling is a boy, giving him a unisex name could make matters even more confusing. A girl named Rory with a brother named Ashley? It just wouldn't work. Finally, Rory is a somewhat unusual name, and a more classic choice for a brother or sister could also strike the wrong chord. Rory and Jane? Rory and John? Somehow they just don't belong together.

Further complications set in if you have changed your ideas about names after living with your real live first choice for a few years. You may regret choosing a unisex name like Rory because of all the confusion over whether the child is a boy or a girl, and may also wish you had chosen a more common name that was easier for the child to pronounce and for others to understand. You may really want to name your second child Jane or John, yet not feel comfortable with those choices.

The point of all this is to encourage you to consider future possibilities when you're choosing the name of your first child. If your two favorite names are Anna and Hannah, for example, realize that picking one now rules out the other forever. When you're deciding among several names, consider the future implications of each. Imagining which names might follow for other children may help you narrow the field.

What, in particular, works and what doesn't? Without taste or value judgments on the specific names, we can tell you some instances of sibling names we're familiar with that do work. Jane and William, for instance, or Sam and Lily. Both pairings are good because, for one, the girls' names are clearly feminine and the boys' names are clearly masculine. The style is consistent: fashionable, but not to the point of cliché. And the names sound harmonious but not confusingly alike. Another good brother-and-sister combo is Elizabeth and Charles, called Libby and Charley. Both are classic names that happen to be in style now, and both nicknames are gently old-fashioned, more compatible than, say, Liza and Chuck would be.

Two brothers whose names catch the right rhythm are Felix and Leo. Both are traditional names—saints' names in fact—that, because they haven't been widely used for some years, have an appealingly offbeat quality. The x and the o endings provide different but equally unusual sounds for the two names, and they are further related by both being feline.

We know a family of three girls named Melissa, Danielle, and Lauren. Their mother wanted to name the third daughter Patricia. But the classic Patricia—or Pat or Patti—simply did not sound like the sister of the more modern Melissa and Danielle, so Lauren she became.

When the name of a fictional character breaks rank with those of his or her siblings, there's usually some symbolism involved. The classic case is *Little Women*'s Meg, Jo, Beth, and Amy. Even if you haven't read the book, guess which one was the tomboy with ambitions greater than her sisters?

So too in real life, where the child with a name that is

"different" from those of his brothers and sisters may also feel different in spirit. We know of a family with four children named Mary, Christopher, Nicole, and Alexandra. It's clear here too which one considers herself the odd child out.

If you already have your first child and are choosing a name for a sibling, keep the following guidelines in mind:

Don't be cute: No rhymes, sound plays, precious pairings. Resist the temptation, for example, to name Daisy's sister Maisie, Darcy, or Hyacinth.

Don't fall into the same-initial trap: A trend of the fifties and sixties was to choose sibling names all starting with the same letter. Sometimes, parents didn't consider the consequences if they had chosen to start with the letter *E* and happened to have, say, five boys. Edward was fine for the first, Eliot okay for the second, but by the birth of their fifth son they were stuck with choices like Earl, Elmer, and Egbert. While few parents have five children today, the same-initial trend should be avoided as dated and overly precious.

Do maintain consistency of style, image, sex, and tradition: This rule is to be interpreted loosely, but, as detailed in the example of Rory, sibling names should ideally stay in the same, well, family.

Be careful about sexual distinctions: If you choose a boyish name for your daughter, and later have a son, go with a boy's name that is clearly masculine. So too if you give your boy a unisex name; both he and his little sister will fare better if her name is distinctly feminine. The names of same-sex children should not have widely divergent sexual images: Bruno's brother shouldn't be named Blair, for instance; nor should Belinda's sister.

Avoid using two names with the same nickname: This problem usually crops up when parents, hoping for a junior, despair at the third girl and name her Roberta or Christina or Geraldine. She then becomes Bobbie or Chris or Gerry. When her long-awaited little brother is born five years later, he is named Robert or Christopher or Gerald. Try as the parents might to prevent it, they may end up with a Bobbie and a Bobby, Chris and Chris, or Gerry and Gerry, in addition, of course, to Bobby, Chris, or Gerry Sr. The trend toward smaller families has headed off most occurrences of this problem in recent years, but it still happens. If you're entirely positive that if you ever have a boy you'll name him Christopher, don't name a girl Christina when you give up hope on having a son, or vice versa. Accidents do happen.

Double Trouble

Twins offer a rare opportunity for parents to choose two related names at the same time, but also multiply the difficulties inherent in sibling names. With twins, it can be more tempting to use rhyme, sound play, and same-initial names, but in our opinion pairings like Eddie and Teddy, Faith and Charity, or Charles and Charlotte should be relegated to a time capsule. While same-initial names that are clearly distinct from each other—George and Grace, say, or Nora and Natalie—are okay, different-initial names that are consistent in style and tone are preferable.

Some celebrity examples that work: Tilda Swinton's Honor and Xavier, Joan Lunden's Kate and Max, Robert De Niro's Julian and Aaron, and Jason Kidd's Miah and Jazelle. Although each of these sets of names is very different in style and feel, they all embody the qualities that matter most in twin names. Each name in the set is distinct from the other, yet they make a harmonious pair—exactly what most parents would want from the twins themselves.

Gender identity is an especially sticky issue when it comes to naming twins. With two children of the same sex, you want to pick a pair of names in the same gender league. That means two distinctly feminine ones (Carolina and Susannah, for instance), two straightforwardly masculine ones (Henry and William), or two equally androgynous choices (such as Jordan and Morgan). Whether your twins are of the same gender or a girl and a boy, you want to avoid names with a discordant gender image, such as Dakota and David or Alex and Allegra. Way too confusing, in too many ways.

Twin names should be compatible stylistically too. As detailed in the section on sibling names, pairings like Posy and Walter or Candida and Jennifer are too discordant. You want names that have a similar image and style standing—not a Top-10 name and an unusual one, or a trendy name with a traditional one. Posy's twin would better be named, perhaps, Barnaby; Walter's sister might be Margaret; Candida's twin could conceivably be called Gabriella; and Jennifer's obvious other half is—who else?—Jason.

Twin Starbabies

ANTON & OLIVIA ..... *Al Pacino & Beverly D'Angelo*
AVA & STELLA .... *Peri Gilpin*
CHRISTIAN &
   EDWARD .... *Mel Gibson*
CRISTINA &
   VICTORIA .... *Julio Iglesias*

DAKOTA ALAN & ...... *Chuck Norris*
   DANILEE KELLY
ELIZA & KATYA........ *Earl Spencer*
EVA RUTH & .... *Martie Maguire*
   KATHLEEN EMILIE
GRACE & ISABELLE .. *Lance Armstrong*
HENRY DAVID & .... *James Taylor*
   RUFUS LOGAN
HONOR & XAVIER ..... *Tilda Swinton*
HUDSON & .... *Marcia Gay Hardin*
   JULITTA DEE
JAKE & HUNTER .... *Niki Taylor*
JORDAN & THEO .... *Cheryl Tiegs*
JULIAN & AARON ..... *Robert De Niro & Toukie Smith*
KATE .... *Joan Lunden*
   ELIZABETH & MAX AARON
KRISTOPHER .... *Jane Seymour*
   STEVEN & JOHN STACY
MALCOLM ....*Denzel Washington*
  & OLIVIA
MIAH & JAZELLE .... *Jason Kidd*
NICOLO & ISABEL ..... *Stanley Tucci*
RODNEY .... *Holly Robinson Peete*
   JACKSON & RYAN ELIZABETH
SCHUYLER .... *Michael J. Fox & Tracy Pollan*
   FRANCES & AQUILLAH KATHLEEN
SHAINA & SAM .... *Jason Hervey*
STELLA .... *Dave Matthews*
   BUSINA & GRACE ANNE
WALKER ....*Adrienne Barbeau*
   STEVEN & WILLIAM DALTON

It is Thanksgiving. You and your sister-in-law, both newly pregnant, are sitting with the rest of the family around the table. The conversation turns to names.

"If we have a boy, of course he will be Richard the Third," says your sister-in-law, smiling sweetly at your father. Your brother, Richard Jr., beams.

You, on the other hand, choke on your cranberry sauce. Ever since you were a little girl, you've wanted to name your first son Richard. Besides being your father's name, it's also your husband's father's name, your brother's name, and your favorite name for a boy in all the world.

"We were planning on Richard, too," you manage to sputter.

"You can't have it," booms your brother. "Clearly it's our name."

"There's room for two Richards in the family," you reason. "We'll just use different nicknames."

"That's stupid," your brother says. "Ricky and Richie?"

"Now, now," soothes your mother. "What if you both have girls?"

"Amanda," you and your brother say in unison.

If you and your spouse have proliferating siblings, the issue of who gets to use which names is one you may have to face. And a difficult issue it is. Does a son have absolute dibs on the father's name? Is there room in a family for two cousins with the same name? Is there a pecking order for who gets traditional family names? Is getting there first a good enough reason to usurp somebody else's name? Can you set claims on a name to begin with?

How you answered these questions depends a lot on your individual family. In some families, the oldest son has eternal right to his father's name, even if he never has a son of his own. In others, it's first-come, first-served, with the understanding that there will be no later duplications. And some families just play catch-as-catch-can, and worry later about how they'll deal with three cousins named, say, Eric.

If you anticipate some name-wrestling within your own family, keep the following tips in mind:

Announce your choices early on: If you have an absolute favorite name you're sure you will use, don't make a secret of it. Planting it in everyone's mind as "your" name can help avoid problems later.

Don't steal someone else's name: We're not talking about naming your baby Letitia, unaware that, on the same day in a different state, your sister is naming her baby Letitia. We're talking about naming your baby Letitia when your sister has been saying since she was fifteen that her fondest wish in life was to have a little girl named Letitia. And your sister is eight months' pregnant. And knows she's having a girl.

Avoid carbon copies: Two little Caroline Townsend Smiths in a close-knit family is one too many. If you want to use the same first and middle names that a sibling uses, can you live with a different nickname—Carrie, for instance? Or can you vary the middle name, so that, at least within the family, one cousin is called Caroline Townsend and the other, say, Caroline Louise? The only case in which two cousins named Caroline Townsend and called Caroline can work is if they have different last names.

Honor family traditions: If the oldest child of the oldest child in your family is always named Taylor, don't break rank, unless your oldest sibling is a nun, priest, or gay rights organizer who has formally renounced rights to the name.

Take unintentional, unimportant duplications in stride: We know two sisters-in-law, living across the country from each other, who were pregnant at the same time: Jane due in January, and Anne in April. During their annual Christmas Eve phone conversation, Jane said she was sure she'd have a boy, and that they were planning to name him Edward. "That's our name," gasped Anne. "Too bad," Jane said blithely. After a few minutes of intense anxiety, Anne decided Jane was right. Neither had officially "claimed" Edward, nor was it a name with any family significance. It would be as ridiculous to insist that Jane change her choice at the eleventh hour as it would be to deny her own son the name just so it wouldn't duplicate that of a cousin he'd see, at best, once a year. Besides, Jane favored the nickname Eddie, while Anne preferred Ted. PS: Due to mitigating circumstances, neither baby was named Edward. They ended up Juliet and Josephine.

The Name Becomes the Child

Finally comes the day when you hold your live child in your arms and make a final decision on a real live name. At that point, all the lists you've made, the considerations you've weighed, and the options you've juggled fall by the wayside, and you and your child are left with your ultimate choice.

What happens then?

Well, on the one hand, the struggle over Miranda versus Molly seems less crucial in the face of 3:00 A.M. feedings, colic, and the high cost of diapers. And it doesn't take long for your baby's persona to dominate the name, for your baby to become his or her name. For the first two weeks, you may find yourself still calling little Miranda "It"; for the next few, you may feel self-conscious each time you pronounce the name; but a month later you'll find that when you say "Miranda," you don't hear the sound of the name but see instead your child's curved lips and dark curls.

On the other hand, once you've settled on a name, you deal with its myriad implications, often for the first time. You may discover, for instance, that your Aunt Elizabeth is not satisfied to be honored by a mere middle name, that people on the street do not necessarily assume Jordan is a girl, and that friends have to suppress a snicker when you tell them you've named your son Henry.

This may not be fun. This may cause you to retrieve your original lists of possibilities and say to your spouse in the middle of the night, "Maybe we should have named him Michael." And of course, it is possible to change a child's name two days or two months or even two years after you've given it, but it's not easy for many reasons, and it's not what we're considering here.

Better than contemplating a name change would be to mull over the fact that choosing one option—in names as in everything else—always means forgoing all others. That the name you've selected inevitably becomes influenced by reality, while the ones you've rejected remain fantasies, entirely pleasant because you alone control them. That in fact if you had chosen Michael, say, you might then be worrying about its ordinariness, and wishing in the middle of the night that you had gone with something more distinctive, like . . . Henry.

Obviously, much of the value of this book is that it helps you anticipate the real-world repercussions of a name. And much of the impetus for writing it came from our own experiences and those of our friends in choosing names for children and living with those choices.

One of our friends, for instance, has two children: Emily and Jeremy. "When Emily was born we were living in the country and it seemed like a really special, unusual name," she says. "Then when she was a few months old we moved to the city and I discovered that there were little Emilys everywhere. I felt terrible. I would listen in the playground for other kids named Emily, I would pore over nursery school class lists for other Emilys, and if she was the only Emily I'd feel so relieved. On one hand I feel badly because it seems as if the name is a cliché, but there also aren't so many Emilys as I'd originally feared."

Our friend pinpoints another reason why she was unaware of how widely used the name Emily was (and another reason we wrote this book): "Having a first child, I didn't really know any other young parents. I had no idea what people were talking about when they named their kids or what the new style was. My idea of a trendy name was still Barbara or Sue."

What then of Jeremy's name? "That one I haven't had so many problems with," she says, "except that some people keep trying to call him Jerry."

Parents who've chosen less usual names talk of unanticipated problems with pronunciation and comprehension. A little girl named Leigh is sometimes called "Lay"; a child named Hannah is called Anna by some people. One of us has some regrets about calling her daughter Rory because the name is more often understood as Laurie, Corey, Tory, Dory, or even Gloria or Marie, than its rightful self.

Then there's the issue of the child's name vis-à-vis his or her looks or personality. Many parents wait to make a name choice until they see which of their finalists best fits the child. This makes some sense, but you should be aware that a newborn is not necessarily representative of the five- or twelve-year-old he or she will become. The chubby, noisy infant daughter you name Casey may grow into a dainty, ultrafeminine ballet dancer, while the delicate baby who seems to be the quintessential Arabella may become, ten years later, goalie on the neighborhood boys' hockey team.

This brings us to the flip side of this issue: Children can irrevocably color our perceptions of their names. You undoubtedly have unique feelings about certain names based on the children you know who bear them, and so do we. When we disagreed about whether to include a particular name on a list here, it was usually because we each knew people who brought different things to it: a handsome and irreverent Ralph, for example, versus a boorish one; an adorable kid named Kermit versus the frog on TV.

Reading this book can help prepare you for some of a name's eventualities, then, but not for others. You wouldn't be surprised, as our friend was, that Emily is a fashionable name or that some people are bent on using undesirable nicknames. Neither will you be unaware of both the advantages and the complications of giving your child a popular or an unusual name, or that Cameron can also be a girl's name, or that Henry has an intellectual image, and so can be perceived by some people as a bit nerdy.

But no one, including you, has ultimate control over the person your child turns out to be. A name can remind you of your hopes and fears way back when childbirth was a point on the horizon, but your child—the one who's laughing or crawling or walking across the room in his own special way—can remind you that Henry by any other name, be it Michael or Melchizedek, would still be your own sweet boy.

Index